Palgrave Macmillan Asian Business Series

Series Editor

Yingqi Wei, Business School, University of Leeds, Leeds, UK

The Palgrave Macmillan Asian Business Series publishes theoretical and empirical studies that contribute forward-looking social perspectives on the study of management issues not just in Asia, but by implication elsewhere. The series specifically aims at the development of new frontiers in the scope, themes and methods of business and management studies in Asia, a region which is seen as key to studies of modern management, organization, strategies, human resources and technologies. The series invites practitioners, policy-makers and academic researchers to join us at the cutting edge of constructive perspectives on Asian management, seeking to contribute towards the development of civil societies in Asia and further a field.

Each submission is submitted for single blind peer review. For further information please see our website: https://www.palgrave.com/gp/book-authors/your-career/early-career-researcher-hub/peer-review-process.

To submit a book proposal for inclusion in this series please email Liz Barlow at: liz.barlow@palgrave.com. Details of how to download a proposal form can be found here: https://www.palgrave.com/gp/book-authors/publishing-guidelines/submit-a-proposal.

This series is indexed in Scopus

Maria Altamira

Chinese Firms in the Global Market

Understanding the Development of Capabilities of Chinese Multinationals

palgrave macmillan

Maria Altamira
UBI Business School
Brussels, Belgium

ISSN 2661-8435 ISSN 2661-8443 (electronic)
Palgrave Macmillan Asian Business Series
ISBN 978-3-031-59226-3 ISBN 978-3-031-59227-0 (eBook)
https://doi.org/10.1007/978-3-031-59227-0

This Palgrave Macmillan imprint is published by the registered company Springer Nature Switzerland AG
The registered company address is: Gewerbestrasse 11, 6330 Cham, Switzerland

Paper in this product is recyclable.

To my life partner, for his endless support, guidance, and faith on me.
To my parents, for their love, dedication and beyond.

Contents

Abbreviations

AT	Agency Theory
BRI	Belt and Road Initiative
CCP	Chinese Communist Party
CSA	Country-Specific Advantages
EM	Emerging Markets
EU	European Union
FDI	Foreign Direct Investment
FSA	Firm-Specific Advantages
GDP	Gross Domestic Product
GSA	Government Specific Advantages
IMF	International Monetary Fund
IT	Information Technology
IT	Institutional Theory
MENA	Middle East North Africa
MNEs	Multinational Enterprises
NC	National Champions
OFDI	Outbound Foreign Direct Investment
OPFs	Other Private Firms
R&D	Research and Development
RBV	Resource-Based View

SAR	Special Administrative Regions
SEO	State-Owned Enterprises
SEZ	Special Economic Zones
SMEs	Small and Medium Enterprises
SO NCs	State-Owned National Champions
TCT	Transactions Cost Theory
TFP	Total Factor Productivity
TVE	Townships and Village Enterprises
UK	United Kingdom
US	United States
WTO	World Trade Organization

List of Figures

List of Tables

1
Introduction

1.1 Context and Motivation

How do institutional elements (formal and informal) influence the development of capabilities of Chinese companies at home? Do these capabilities help Chinese companies enhance sustainable competitive advantage abroad? The answers to these questions are relevant to deepen the understanding of how Chinese firms expanding abroad develop their capabilities, including marketing, as well as how and to what extent these capabilities are transferrable to their overseas operations.

This is an important and timely topic. After the reforms adopted by Deng Xiaoping in 1978 and especially since the Open-Door Policy was established in 1979, China became the largest recipient of Foreign Direct Investment (FDI). Twenty years later, thanks to the Go Global Strategy launched in 1999, the country started to become an important outbound investor. Chinese firms began to cross borders, investing first in resource-seeking (mainly state-owned enterprises) and later in market-seeking (mainly private and public firms) ventures overseas. The latter became the area with the highest rate of increase during the 2000s. In this context, the country not only became the world's second-largest economy in 2010 (Deng, 2012), but also the third-largest foreign

M. Altamira, *Chinese Firms in the Global Market*, Palgrave Macmillan Asian Business Series, https://doi.org/10.1007/978-3-031-59227-0_1

investor in 2013 (second, if China and Hong Kong are considered together) (UNCTAD, 2019). Since then, and especially until 2020, Chinese firms had been investing abroad, especially in Western markets, at an unprecedented pace; a report showed that China's global stock of outbound foreign direct investment (OFDI) grew at an annual average rate of 20% from 2010 to 2017 (CEIC, 2020). In terms of destination markets, the European Union (EU) and the United States (US) were the two preferred destinations, especially the EU, where FDI stocks grew 77 times from 2002 to 2012 (Amendolagine et al., 2017). This international expansion has been driven partly by firm-level strategic considerations to access international markets and diversify risks and partly by strong government initiatives promoting the international expansion of specific Chinese firms and sectors. However, since 2017, Chinese OFDI has been experiencing a decline due to more restrictive policies from the Chinese government affecting capital controls and a reduction of liquidity, especially for state-owned enterprises (SOEs) operating in international markets (Hanemann et al., 2019), in addition to stronger and more restrictive regulatory programmes established in host countries, especially in the US and the EU and increasing geopolitical rivalries. Chinese FDI in Europe reached the lowest level in ten years with just EUR 7.9 billion in 2022, 22% less compared to 2021 (Kratz et al., 2023). This, along with the slowdown of the economy, is creating a new challenging scenario for Chinese firms and the Chinese government; initiatives such as "Made in China 2025", the "Belt and Road Initiative" (BRI) or more recently the "Dual Circulation" strategy have been defined not only to address the need to return to sustained domestic economic growth, especially after the COVID-19 outbreak and the country leaving its zero-Covid policy in early 2023, but also to continue to increase China's influence and role in the international context (Chen, 2023; Huang, 2016; Ma et al., 2018; Yao, 2020). This current scenario is expected to provide unique opportunities to study the future role of China on the international scene, while understanding how Chinese firms will continue to develop and compete with incumbent firms in developed markets.

Moreover, in the context of growth and expansion, the relevant role that marketing plays in determining firms' performance has been widely recognised (Hult et al., 2005; Katsikeas et al., 2006; Morgan, 2012; Morgan et al., 2018; Wu, 2013b). To successfully deploy resources to support differentiation strategies, firms need marketing capabilities to enable and drive a sustained delivery of the planned benefits to customers (Day, 2013; Noble et al., 2002). Numerous studies have been carried out to understand the development of marketing capabilities as well as their importance for the performance of firms (Darroch et al., 2004; Day, 1994, 2013; Morgan et al., 2009, 2018; Vorhies et al., 2009). However, most of them have focused on Western and/or incumbent firms with very few studies available for emerging markets (EM) firms in general and from China in particular (see Deng, 2012; Kaufmann and Roesch, 2012; Mellahi et al., 2010; Mutlu et al., 2015; Sun, 2017; Williamson et al., 2013; Wu, 2013a, b; Yan et al., 2017; Zheng Zhou, 2006). In addition, the limited studies have mostly approached the capability development of Chinese firms using mostly quantitative methods of analysis, in which the author usually follows a deductive rather than an inductive approach as in the present study, in which the author is part of what is being observed, interacts with participants, interprets and makes sense of data and develops theory after its analysis (Birkinshaw et al., 2011; Dong et al., 2013; Easterby-Smith et al., 2002; Fang & Zou, 2009; Wu, 2013b). This is an important opportunity for further studies in the field as the home institutional environment for Chinese firms is unique and highly dynamic and complex, and the understanding from an inductive approach, of how managers from Chinese firms navigate, negotiate, adapt, and make sense of the institutional environment, define their marketing strategies and therefore their capabilities, and justify their expansion path going abroad is likely to provide novel insights for management theory and practice. Thus, the main aim of this book is to analyse how home institutional elements influence the design and development of Chinese firms' capabilities at home, and whether and how these capabilities are applicable in a different business environment. Within this, the book aims: (i) to provide an in-depth understanding of Chinese firms' business strategies, objectives, and competitive advantages at home and abroad in different environments, (ii) to develop useful insights about the Chinese business and institutional environment and how it influences the development of relevant capabilities at home and abroad and (iii) to help practitioners, academics and policy-makers to understand the rapid rise of Chinese multinationals in and outside China. All in all, this book contributes to the understanding of how Chinese firms are developing their strategies at home, how they have created competitive advantages at home and abroad and, more importantly, how and why Chinese firms are becoming global competitors.

1.2 Structure

After this introduction, Chapter 2 "China's transition to a market economy. Past, present and future trends" presents the macro framework of the study, which aims to frame the context of the study while providing a background for the analysis. It focuses on the past (mainly the forty years of reforms in China since 1978), on the present situation of China and the challenges the country is facing in the international context, and on future trends for the country and its business environment. The chapter also analyses the present business relationships between China and international relevant markets as well as the challenges in the near future.

Chapter 3 "China's institutional framework, capabilities and internationalisation strategies of Chinese multinationals" introduces the literature review of the book. The section begins with a review of China's OFDI trends found in the literature. The main theoretical lenses used in the analysis are then introduced: Institutional Theory and Institutional Theory in China, and The Resource-Based View and The Resource-Based View in China; the latter is operationalised using marketing capabilities. The link between institutions and capabilities in China is then introduced, with a focus on government support and informal relations (the two most relevant institutional elements in China identified in the literature). Finally, a review of the literature about the internationalisation of Chinese multinationals and the influence of Chinese domestic institutions (with a special focus on the main internationalisation policies and the use of personal relations abroad) in the development of capabilities abroad is also included. Finally, a review of the literature

about the internationalisation of Chinese multinationals and the influence of Chinese domestic institutions in the development of marketing capabilities abroad is also included.

Chapter 4 "A narrative inquiry strategy to analyse capabilities of Chinese multinationals" explains how the analysis was carried out. First, it defines the research philosophy. Second, it explains the research design adopted and the strategy (Narrative Inquiry), following the objectives of the study. Third, the chapter continues with the sample selection process and data collection methods, with a focus on how narrative interviews were developed. Fourth, it explains the challenges addressed during the data analysis process. It ends with a detailed explanation of the data analysis process.

Chapter 5 "A narrative analysis of Chinese managers′ personal experiences" is one of the most important ones as it reports and analyses the experiences shared by the interviewed managers. The chapter is divided into two main parts, following the structure of the narratives. On the one hand, the first part focuses on the managers′ insights and experiences working in the Chinese business environment and doing business in China. It identifies the most salient characteristics of the Chinese business environment and how they impact the development of these capabilities: (i) the discriminatory government support (positive and negative), (ii) an intensive use of personal relations (with government officials and business partners) and (iii) a unique strategic mindset embedded in the Chinese culture and philosophy. On the other hand, the second part addresses the international environment and focuses on the Chinese managers′ opinions and experiences designing, implementing, and leading the international strategy of the company in overseas markets. This chapter makes tangible the impact of the Government policies supporting firms′ expansion, the challenges faced by the different types of firms, and the capabilities developed by these firms.

Chapter 6 "A framework to understand the development of capabilities of Chinese multinationals" presents the most important part of this work, in which the results of the analysis and the development of the framework are introduced. Firstly, the framework presents the elements influencing the development of capabilities in the domestic market as well as the capabilities defined and developed by each of the different types of Chinese multinationals analysed. Secondly, the framework shows the capabilities applied in a first stage of the internationalisation expansion of the firms (i.e., during the first years of activity in international markets) followed by those developed in a second stage (i.e., after three years of experience abroad). In sum, the results show how different types of firms are applying and developing abroad the capabilities defined at home, and how these capabilities have become the source of competitive advantage in international markets. It is expected that this framework can be used by practitioners and policy makers to analyse the development and competitiveness of companies.

Chapter 7 "Contributions" presents the main academic and theoretical contributions of the study:

Academic and theoretical contributions:

- Institutional Theory (IT). It enriches the understanding of the influence of the domestic environment in the development of strategic options, mainly the definition and development of capabilities by three different types of Chinese firms, and of how this domestic environment influences the development of capabilities in the international context.
- The Resource-Based View (RBV) of the firm and capability-building. The study provides a comprehensive understanding of the definition and development of capabilities that are relevant to the Chinese business environment, and how these capabilities are the source of competitive advantage of these firms in overseas markets.

Finally, Chapter 8 "Practical implications in today´s business context and concluding remarks" presents the practical implications of the study:

- First, the framework is expected to be useful to deeply understand the rapid rise of Chinese multinationals while becoming more familiar with the Chinese business and institutional environment and practices. This will also assist firms to adapt better their business strategies and minimise cross-cultural misunderstandings and/or conflict.
- Second, the study focuses on why and how Chinese multinationals have been able to develop sustained competitive advantages abroad.

Policy makers, academics, firms, and managers will therefore gain more in-depth understanding of Chinese firms' business strategies, objectives, and the capabilities they have developed in this market based on their home environment. In this sense, the study will provide useful tools to identify and benefit from the advantages of cooperating with Chinese firms.

- Third, the study includes in the sample state-owned firms and National Champions. In this context, findings show that beyond some other relevant capabilities (adaptive capability in the case of Private NCs), the resource-bridging capability with Chinese government officials is key to secure long-term presence in international markets. This contributes to the existing debate among international firms about the strong support of the Chinese government for these firms and to what extent the government is responsible for its success. Indeed, the findings shed some light on the current business scenario of tensions between Western economies and China.

In addition, a critical perspective on the current business and geopolitical scenario in the short and medium term and on the potential directions that the results of the present study may take is provided. This chapter ends with the limitations of the study, directions for future research, and concluding remarks.

References

Amendolagine, V., Amighini, A., & Rabelloti, R. (2017). Chinese multinationals in Europe. In *Understanding China Today*. Springer International Publishing.

Birkinshaw, J., Brannen, M., & Tung, R. (2011). From a distance and generalizable to upclose and grounded: Reclaiming a place for qualitative methods in international business research. *Journal of International Business Studies, 42*, 573–581. https://doi.org/10.1057/jibs.2011.19

CEIC. (2020). https://www.ceicdata.com/datapage/en/country/china

Chen, Z. (2023). *Review of economic impact of COVID-19 on China's economy: Positive and negative.* Paper presented at the Proceedings of the 6th International Conference on Economic Management and Green Development, Singapore.

Darroch, J., Miles, M. P., Jardine, A., & Cook, E. (2004). The 2004 AMA definition of marketing and its relationship to a market orientation: An extension of Cook, Rayburn, & Abercrombie (1992). *Journal of Marketing Theory and Practice, 12*(4), 29–38.

Day, G. (1994). The capabilities of market-driven organizations. *Journal of Marketing, 58*, 37–51. https://doi.org/10.1177/002224299405800404

Day, G. (2013). Closing the marketing capability gap. *Journal of Marketing, 75*(4), 183–195.

Deng, P. (2012). The internationalization of Chinese firms: A critical review and future research. *International Journal of Management Reviews, 14*(4). https://doi.org/10.1111/j.1468-2370.2011.00323.x

Dong, C., Bingxin Li, C., & Tse, D. K. (2013). Do business and political ties differ in cultivating marketing channels for foreign and local firms in China? *Journal of International Marketing, 21*(1), 39–56.

Easterby-Smith, M., Thorpe, R., & Lowe, A. (2002). *Management research: An introduction* (2nd ed.). Sage.

Fang, E., & Zou, S. (2009). Antecedents and consequences of marketing dynamic capabilities in international joint ventures. *Journal of International Business Studies, 40*(5), 742–761.

Hanemann, T., Huotari, M., & Kratz, A. (2019). *Chinese FDI in Europe: 2018 trends and impact of new screening policies.* https://rhg.com/wp-content/uploads/2019/03/RHG-MERICS-COFDI-Update-2019.pdf

Huang, Y. (2016). Understanding China's Belt & Road Initiative: Motivation, framework and assessment. *China Economic Review, 40*(C), 314–321.

Hult, G., Ketchen, D., & Slater, S. (2005). Market orientation and performance: An integration of disparate approaches. *Strategic Management Journal, 26*(12), 1173–1181.

Katsikeas, C., Samiee, S., & Theodosiou, M. (2006). Strategy fit and performance consequences of international marketing standardization. *Strategic Management Journal, 27*(9), 867–890.

Kaufmann, L., & Roesch, J.-F. (2012). Constraints to building and deploying marketing capabilities by emerging market firms in advanced markets. *Journal of International Marketing, 20*(4), 1–24.

Kratz, A., Zenglein, M., Sebastian, G., & Witzke, M. (2023). *Chinese FDI in Europe: 2022 update*. https://rhg.com/research/chinese-fdi-in-europe-2022-update/

Ma, H., Wu, X., Yan, L., Huang, H., Wu, H., Xiong, J., & Zhang, J. (2018). Strategic plan of "Made in China 2025" and its implementation. In *Analysing the impacts of industry 4.0 in modern business environments*. IGI Global.

Mellahi, K., Demirbag, M., Tamer Cavusgil, S., & Danis, W. (2010). Marketing strategies of MNCs for emerging markets: Internationalisation and market entry mode. *International Marketing Review, 27*(2), 267–271.

Morgan, N. (2012). Marketing and business performance. *Journal of the Academy of Marketing Science, 40*(1), 102–119.

Morgan, N., Douglas, W., & Mason, C. (2009). Market orientation, marketing capabilities and firm performance. *Strategic Management Journal, 30*, 909–920. https://doi.org/10.1002/smj.764

Morgan, N., Feng, H., & Whitler, K. (2018). Marketing capabilities in international marketing. *Journal of International Marketing, 26*(1), 61–95.

Mutlu, C., Zhan, W., Peng, M., & Lin, Z. (2015). Competing in (and out of) transition economies. *Asia Pacific Journal of Management, 32*(3), 571–596.

Noble, C., Rajiv, K., & Kumar, A. (2002). Market orientation and alternative strategic orientations: A longitudinal assessment of performance implications. *Journal of Marketing, 66*(4), 25–39.

Sun, F. (2017). Relationship versus transaction marketing in China: An institutional approach. *Business and Management Studies, 3*(2), 47–60.

UNCTAD. (2019). *World investment report*. United Nations Conference on Trade and Development.

Vorhies, D., Morgan, R., & Autry, C. W. (2009). Product-market strategy and the marketing capabilities of the firm: Impact on market effectiveness and cash flow performance. *Strategic Management Journal, 30*(12), 1310–1334.

Williamson, P., Ramamurti, R., Fleury, A., & Leme Fleury, M. (2013). *The competitive advantage of emerging market multinationals*. Cambridge University Press.

Wu, J. (2013a). Diverse institutional environments and product innovation of emerging market firms. *Management International Review, 53*(1), 39–59.

Wu, J. (2013b). Marketing capabilities, institutional development, and the performance of emerging market firms: A multinational study. *International Journal of Research in Marketing, 30*(1), 36–45.

Yan, H., He, X., & Cheng, B. (2017). Managerial ties, market orientation, and export performance: Chinese firms experience. *Management and Organization Review, 13*(3), 611–638.
Yao, K. (2020). *What we know about China's 'dual circulation' economic strategy*. https://www.reuters.com/article/china-economy-transformation-explainer-idUSKBN2600B5
Zheng Zhou, K. (2006). Innovation, imitation, and new product performance: The case of China. *Industrial Marketing Management, 35*(3), 394–402.

2

China's Transition to a Market Economy. Past, Present and Future Trends

2.1 Introduction

This chapter introduces the framework of this book, and it presents a review of the past, present, and future trends of the Chinese business environment. The chapter is structured as follows. First, it briefly introduces a general overview of China with a focus on the milestones of its evolution and development. Second, it offers an analysis of the more than 40 years of reforms since 1978, a key period to understand the history and the country's domestic and international development in the context of this study. Third, the chapter analyses the present situation of the country with a focus on Chinese investments. Finally, it ends with a discussion on the current challenges and geopolitical rivalries as well as on future trends.

M. Altamira, *Chinese Firms in the Global Market*, Palgrave Macmillan Asian Business Series, https://doi.org/10.1007/978-3-031-59227-0_2

2.2 Overview of China

The People's Republic of China is the second most populous country worldwide (recently surpassed by India in 2023) with more than 1.3 billion inhabitants and a single-party state led by the Chinese Communist Party (CCP). The country is divided into 22 provinces, five autonomous regions (Xinjiang, Inner Mongolia, Tibet, Ningxia, and Guangxi), four municipalities directly administered by the government (Beijing, Shanghai, Tianjin, and Chongqing), and two Special Administrative Regions (SARs) (Hong Kong and Macao) (Fornes & Mendez, 2018). Since China began to open its economy after Deng Xiaoping's reforms in 1978, the country's Gross Domestic Product (GDP) has experienced an average growth rate of 10% per year while around 850 million people have been lifted out of poverty (World Bank, 2020), transforming the country into an upper-middle-income state. Income inequality has decreased over the past years; however, around 370 million Chinese are still living below the middle-income poverty line.

In 2010, China became the second-largest economy, surpassing Japan and behind the United States (IMF, 2011). But being a superpower economy was not new for the Chinese, as during 18 out of 20 centuries, China had the largest economy worldwide, being, for example, one of the major global innovators contributing to the progress of mankind, introducing the so-called "four great inventions of Ancient China": papermaking, gunpowder, printing, and the compass. But after the Ming dynasty, the country's economic development began to slow while Europe's rapid development enabled it to surpass China in the latter part of the Qing dynasty (Fornes & Mendez, 2018).

China's growth since 1978, mainly based on resource- and labour-intensive manufacturing, capital investments, and exports, has positioned China as the world's fastest-growing economy, the largest exporter and second-largest importer of goods worldwide (World Bank, 2020). However, in recent years, this growth seems to have slowed down, leading to some social, economic, and environmental challenges. Some structural constraints, such as the decline in labour force growth, a slowing productivity, and more recently, the COVID-19 health emergency, seem to explain this slowdown; Chinese GDP grew 3% in 2022, expecting to expand 5.2% in 2023, as a result of the country leaving zero-COVID-19, but slowing again in 2024 after the reopening boost (Cerdeiro & Jain-Chandra, 2023).

In this context, the challenge today is finding new drivers of growth to ensure China's high-quality, sustainable, and sound development path in the long term, while completing the transition to a market-based economic system. The role of the government is being tested in ensuring stable market expectations and a fair and trustworthy business environment, not only in China but also in the world. The latest policies of President Xi Jinping, such as the BRI (also known as One Belt, One Road, or The New Silk Road) aimed at empowering the role of China in the world business environment, the "Made in China 2025" or more recently, the "Dual Circulation" policy, both focused on the development of the domestic market with an emphasis on Chinese innovation, is expected to address these challenges. However, these initiatives have met with mixed responses internationally. The US in particular views these initiatives as a sign of China′s mercantilist approach.

2.3 China's Evolution Since 1978. More Than 40 Years of Reforms

To analyse China's reforms since 1978 is important to understand the country's evolution, especially since the opening up of the economy in 1979. A deep knowledge about the path followed by the country, circumstances, and government decisions and their effects on China's domestic and international development is crucial to understand China's current and future situation as well as the different reforms and policies defined by the Chinese government.

Between 1949 and 1976, the Chinese Communist Party (CCP), under the leadership of Mao Zedong, implemented socialist economic policies. During this period, central planning of industry was introduced, and agriculture collectivised (Huenemann, 2017). However, following the collapse of the Great Leap Forward (the five-year plan from 1958 to 1961 promoted by the CCP leader to boost the Chinese economy and industry) and the political split with Moscow, China's economic policies started to be questioned by a more conventional wave in the party, led by Deng Xiaoping. After Mao's death in 1976, new reforms started to be promoted and developed and in 1977 Deng Xiaoping became the new leader.

Between 18th and 22nd December 1978, the eleventh Central Committee of the CCP was held. This event was the first milestone of the new phase of reforms; the committee, under Deng Xiaoping's leadership, decided to focus on economic development based on market-based reforms. The country started to move from a centrally planned economy to market exchange with an opening of the country to international trade and investments (Fang et al., 2018). During the 40 years of reforms, three main phases can be identified: (i) market-seeking reforms, from 1978 to 1993, (ii) market building reforms, from 1993 to 2003, and (iii) market enhancing reforms, from 2003 onwards (Hofman, 2018).

From 1978 to 1993, the period with the most important reforms, the main goal of the Chinese authorities was the search for new and more effective economic institutions. The first reform was focused on the countryside. For the first time, Deng Xiaoping allowed peasants to produce on their own, eliminating the sales of surplus to the state, while prices for many agricultural products started to be set by the rules of the free market. In addition, from a demographic point of view, the Chinese president defined the one-child policy aimed at reducing food shortages. This controversial measure was adopted with scepticism, but a slow-down in population growth was achieved a few years after the policy was established, accomplishing another important goal of Deng's government (Spar & Oi, 2006).

In addition to these radical measures in the countryside, one of the major reforms affecting the opening of the Chinese economy was defined. In 1979, the Open-Door policy, the first relevant internationalisation policy defined by the Chinese government, was developed with the aim of changing the Chinese economic system with the opening of its borders for the first time to external international investment and exports. China developed four "Special Economic Zones" (SEZs) which welcomed international investment with tax incentives, new foreign exchange policies and positive regulations to attract international firms.

By the beginning of the 90s, in one decade, the benefits of these initiatives were clear: FDI reached $11.2 billion in 1992, against $4 billion in previous years (Spar & Oi, 2006).

Another new action towards market orientation was the development of the private sector. Until 1978, only State-Owned Enterprises (SOEs) and other firms responding to provincial or municipal authorities were allowed. In this context, until this date, profits and losses were not relevant, and enterprises, usually very large corporations in which workers could expect guaranteed lifetime employment and a firm-based welfare system, only focused on producing the allocated quota at government-established prices. Corporations were inefficient, with outdated skills and technology. By the mid-80s, for the first time, managers could set wages, make investment decisions, and retain profits. However, even privately owned new firms were still responding to local or central government, even selling at regulated rather than at market prices. The influence and control of the government was still evident and most private firms continued to suffer from government restrictions (such as limited bank loans at high rates). In any case, they were more market-oriented than ever (Spar & Oi, 2006). In this line, another market-oriented initiative was the establishment of Townships and Village enterprises (TVEs), small, specialised manufacturers usually led by local officers, but with a strong capitalist orientation. Each village or town raised money from different sources such as loans from local banks or agricultural profits and developed different types of products benefiting from the gaps left by SOEs. TVEs grew at around 30% a year during the 80s, and their exports increased at an average of 60%. Finally, this phase of reform ended with new initiatives in terms of price settings. Prior to this period, prices in China had been unchanged. After 1984, the state developed a version of the dual-price system established in agriculture and applied it to other industries. Firms were still required to sell their production quota to the State at established prices, but they could now sell their surplus at market-based prices. This dual system, however, promoted the rise of corruption.

The 90s, the second phase of reforms, was a period of building upon what was already developed while at the same time consolidating government efforts. An important milestone, in 1992, was the tour of President

Deng to the south of China and the opening of the Shanghai and Shenzhen stock exchanges. One major decision was the establishment of the "divided tax system", which eliminated extra-budgetary revenues, along with the progressive adjustment of dual exchange rates, which ended in 1994 with these merging into only one exchange rate defined by the market. During this period, privatisations continued to develop, but only a few firms were allowed to be totally private while the majority of them remained in state hands (Spar & Oi, 2006).

Finally, the 2000s represented the phase of market enhancing reforms. Under prime minister Zhu Rongji's leadership, industrial development continued to be market-oriented, characterised, for example, by the closure of under-performing SOEs and by another step towards the opening of the economy, the "Go Global" policy, which included the country's accession to the World Trade Organization (WTO) in 2001. However, in the domestic scenario, the Chinese government decided to focus on innovation and technology policies, moving from market-oriented policies towards a strong intervention of the government in these sectors (Ling & Naughton, 2016). In 2003, China's innovation policies shifted drastically, experiencing a return to an interventionist industrial policy. Between 2003 and 2013, the Chinese government moved towards a more traditional and institutionalised concept of technology development and specified technology and industrial objectives (Ling & Naughton, 2016), conceptualised by the publication of the Medium-Term Strategy for Science and Technology and the development of the 16 Megaprojects in innovation and technology (Hofman, 2018). Policies and government interventions continued in this direction with the new measures adopted at the 14th Party Congress on productivity and innovation, the 13th Five-Year Plan, and finally the most recent Made in China 2025 Strategy defined in 2015 by President Xi Jinping. During the 18th Party Congress in 2014, market-oriented initiatives were still considered key for the country's development, however, the government also confirmed that an economic system with predominantly state ownership should have a key role in the future development of the country.

All in all, in the past 44 years, China's transformation has been evident, moving from a planned to a market-oriented economy, and from a dual economy to neoclassical growth (Fang et al., 2018). Economic reforms and especially the opening of the economy to the world have created a business and institutional environment of extraordinary economic growth with a GDP per capita rising from $156.39 in 1978 to $12,720.20 in 2022 (World Bank, 2023). More than four decades of reforms involving price determination, new resource allocation systems, privatisation of firms, the development of foreign trade and investment, and a stronger government-led environment in the past few years, have contributed to the impressive development of the country (Fang et al., 2018); a development that was drastically impacted by the pandemic, China being the first country to address the uncertainties of a new business environment (Chen, 2023; World Bank, 2023).

2.4 China's Present Situation and Main Government Policies

As introduced above, China has experienced more than 40 years of impressive growth, mainly since 1979, when the first reforms leading to a market-oriented economy were defined. In this context of growth, poverty has been drastically reduced while China has rapidly become an upper-middle-income country. Since 2010, when China became the second-largest economy worldwide, companies have continued growing thanks to an endlessly growing domestic market full of new consumers hungry for new products and services and to the continuous support from the Chinese government. As a result, China has become the largest consumption market in purchasing power parity (PPP) (Zipser et al., 2021).

However, the country has been experiencing several challenges in recent years that are drastically changing the domestic market, such as an ageing population, a rural–urban divide, insufficient innovation, and a continuing reliance on carbon-based energy sources (Dollar et al., 2021). This represents a difficult business scenario that has been aggravated by the COVID-19 emergency since 2020. Indeed, despite the impressive economic recovery during 2023, the year in which China finally opened the country after restrictions, the economy only grew 0.8%

in the second quarter, compared to 2.2% in the first one; a recovery that has been lower than expected by authorities and previous predictions. On the one hand, high interest has impacted the export-oriented Chinese economy with a weak demand for Chinese products, especially for electronics (The editorial board, 2023). On the other hand, consumer confidence (including among Chinese) about China's market development is becoming weaker. Consumers' debt has created an asset bubble, with urban housing prices increasing impressively in recent years (Huang, 2016), along with an increasingly and unprecedent level of unemployment in young people (mainly due to the consequences of the above; the contraction of the manufacturing sector and the slowdown of the property sector, which accounts for a quarter of activity) (Hale & Langley, 2023). Finally, investments have also slowed down, due to a more restrictive regulatory framework for tech firms and international investors and the geopolitical tensions with the United States (US) (The editorial board, 2023). Actually, it is in this context that the government has recently implemented some macroeconomic expansionary policies including tax relief measures for SMEs, spending on infrastructures or modest interest-rate-based easing measures (International Monetary Fund, 2023).

Aware of the need for economic reforms, Xi Jinping already started announcing major policies in 2013 with the definition and launch of Belt and Road Initiative, with the aim of not only addressing the need to return to sustained domestic economic growth, but also to increase China's influence in the international context in the medium and long term. The BRI was dubbed the most challenging government-led internationalisation policy ever defined by a government. The main objective of the initiative was to boost economic development through win–win international cooperation while following four main principles: "(1) openness and cooperation; (2) harmony and inclusiveness; (3) market-based operation; and (4) mutually beneficial and win–win for all countries" (Huang, 2016, p. 318). The BRI has reached more than 150 countries and more than 30% of global GDP and consists of one Silk Road Economic "Belt" and the Maritime Silk Road. The "Belt" itself is made of three main routes: a first from China through Central Asia to Europe, a second from China, through Central and West Asia, the Persian Gulf ending in the Mediterranean (in Europe), and a third from China, through the South China Sea to the Indian Ocean. The Maritime Silk Road links China's eastern ports to Western European ports, going through the South China Sea, the Indian Ocean, and Africa. However, the impact after 10 years has not reached expectations, mainly due to questioning of debt sustainability, the pandemic effects, and the domestic economic slowdown. Even if China is trying to boost confidence on the policy, the government would need to face the difficulties for Chinese firms of doing business overseas, mainly the international scrutiny of firms linked to the BRI and the challenges in global economic governance (Gong, 2023).

In 2015, President Xi Jinping launched the "Made in China 2025" policy, focused on the Chinese manufacturing industry with the aim of transforming the country from a low-cost giant manufacturing centre into a world-leading manufacturing one (Ma et al., 2018). To achieve this goal, the policy contemplated three main steps and goals covering the period 2015–2049: (i) to move the country from a manufacturing centre to a manufacturing power by 2025, (ii) to reach the medium level of the world manufacturing powers by 2035, and (iii) to consolidate China as a "manufacturing power and list China's comprehensive manufacturing strength into the world's top list by 2049" (Ma et al., 2018, p. 4). Although the term seems no longer to be used by Chinese authorities, especially after the trade war with the US started, the policy remains alive with the government providing large amounts of subsidies to large tech companies, electric vehicle manufacturers, and chipmakers, in an effort of the government to continue promoting innovation leadership (Kawase, 2022).

Finally, more recently, in 2021, China announced the new "Dual Circulation" strategy, an economic policy aimed at boosting economic growth by focusing on stimulating domestic demand as well as on promoting exports, creating the necessary conditions for the domestic and the international markets to support each other (Yao, 2020). As outlined in the 14th Five-Year Plan (2021–2025), the focus of the new policies is on reaching sustainability of growth and improving the quality of life (Asian Development Bank, 2021). It also includes measures to close the urban–rural divide, to reduce carbon dioxide emissions before

2030 and reach carbon neutrality before 2060 as well as to lay down the path for the country to become a global leader in innovation by 2035 (following the goals of the Made in China 2025). Under this situation, it seems evident that the country may be considering an increasingly inward-looking strategy while relying less on its international development and international partners (Chandler & McGregor, 2020), which on the other hand may contrast with the main objectives of the BRI. Indeed, state-owned firms, in order to follow the strategies of the Dual Circulation strategy and the 14th Five-year plan, have already been directed and incentivized to invest only in the domestic market.

2.5 China's Role in the International Business Context. Challenges and Future Trends

China's impressive growth in recent decades has been based on two main areas: manufacturing (mainly heavy machinery) and investments; being the basis of the so-called "China Miracle" (Huang, 2016). However, as previously discussed, current trends confirm that China can no longer continue to rely on this model but needs to find new ways to support strong economic development while trying to come back to a sustained growth model. In this sense, the country should continue to promote technological innovation and industrial upgrading while considering a restructuration of the financial system, along with a new role to be played by state-owned firms both at home and abroad. Indeed, several leading industries have emerged in recent years as the main source for this recovery, such as the household electronic industry or e-commerce, while several Chinese firms are already successfully competing in the international context, being globally competitive. Some sectors and industries in which China is leading the way internationally are internet services, telecommunication equipment, electronic batteries, or large machinery equipment (Huang, 2016; Kratz et al., 2023). But the increasingly active role of China in the international economic architecture along with the consequences of China's latest political and economic decisions have been creating tensions and challenges with the West. The current global economic governance is already having implications for China and its role in the international business context; implications that are expected to have major impacts in the near future on the most relevant international policies; the BRI and the Made in China 2025 (Fornes & Altamira, 2023; Gong, 2023; Hale & Langley, 2023).

The Covid-Zero policies and related lockdowns have severely impacted the global value chain, with a negative effect on foreign investors that are trying to reduce their dependency on the country, with the resulting globalisation retreats and an increased protectionism (Gong, 2023). New strategies such as the "China plus One" framework, in which companies try to reduce their dependency on the country, are predicted to change international business trade in the near future. In addition, the Russia-Ukraine war and the escalation of US-China tensions over Taiwan might also impact countries with a strong reliance on China's supply chain while they see their vulnerability to Chinese economic future increased (Gong, 2023). Although moving production from China seems difficult, the international business and trade scenario will be largely impacted by these new trends (Ho-Him, 2023).

Moreover, the US-China impact of the trade war on the global economy and on the relations of China with third-party countries is already evident. This situation between the two largest economies will accelerate their gradual decoupling and the probable division of the global economy and business environment into two blocks. Indeed, both countries have already undertaken a race to win the technological competition. On the one hand, the US is developing large investments in new technologies (mainly Artificial Intelligence (AI)) to slow China's plans to gain a technological advantage, in addition to further specific initiatives such as the United States Innovation and Competition Act of 2021 to compete with China (Financial Times Reporters, 2022; Fornes & Altamira, 2023). On the other hand, and within the Made in China 2025 framework, China has decided to continue pushing its tech industry to move towards the country's technological self-sufficiency, especially in the context of AI (Weinland, 2022). Meanwhile, US sanctions on Chinese SOEs (companies heavily involved in the BRI), in addition to the EU-China investment framework approved by the European parliament in 2019 encouraging countries to specifically review and control investments in the so-called "sensitive sectors", are making businesses reconsider the risks of doing business with Chinese counterparts while China is making efforts to strengthen business links with other countries, especially within the BRI framework (European Parliament, 2020).

In conclusion, in the above situation, it is clear that China has been facing the increasing challenge of Western partners' confusion and scepticism about the strong role played by the Chinese government and its SOEs in the international scene and about whether the country is really committed to continue to develop a market-oriented economy or, on the contrary, whether the Chinese government is reasserting its control of the economy. In particular, Chinese firms seem to be addressing the increasing negative perceptions related to a perceived lack of transparency affecting competition rules, policies, and incentives from the Chinese government that may discriminate against Western firms and an apparent stronger control of the Chinese government in the domestic economy as indicated by the latest policies and plans resulting in a potentially even stronger role of Chinese SOEs (European Commission, 2020; International Monetary Fund, 2023).

How Chinese authorities will face and respond to the above-mentioned challenges, the growing scrutiny and scepticism shown by the West in particular, as well as the direction that recent government initiatives would take will definitely define the country's future role in the international context and shape the future international economic and business scenario. Third parties that desire to work with Chinese SOEs would need to review the potential geopolitical impact on their operations, technology, and reputation.

However, international development will continue to be key for China. Catching up with advanced economies will still be dependent on the country′s involvement in global trade and investments. Also, because the alarming possible decoupling between China and the West would have major consequences for global productivity and growth (Dollar et al., 2021). In fact, despite the inward-looking focus recently adopted, it seems the country will continue to engage in international business, mainly within a renewed BRI as introduced by President Xi Jinping during the 10th anniversary of the policy in November 2023 (Banach & Gunter, 2023). The overview of China's outwards foreign investments in 2022 showed that it was generally stable with an increase of 0.9%, especially in some industries that grew relatively quickly in countries within the BRI (Chow, 2023). Another positive sign is the country's membership of recent economic agreements, such as the Regional Comprehensive Economic Partnership and the Comprehensive Agreement on Investment with the European Union, where it has demonstrated to be a key player in critical industries for the future of the region. For example, the European Union has become the principal market for Chinese global electric vehicles, being battery's investments the most important ones in the region as for 2022. Actually, China has confirmed further greenfield expansion plans in the electric vehicle (EV) value chains in Europe (Kratz et al., 2023).

All in all, despite the slowdown of the domestic Chinese economy, the country has demonstrated that Chinese firms are competitors abroad with many incumbent firms from developed countries. In this context, policies such as the BRI or the Made in China 2025 represent an opportunity for China to reconsider its role in the international context while exploring cooperation with new partners creating new markets for Chinese investments and strong opportunities for growth. Even though a rebound of foreign investments in 2023 is unlikely, the end of the zero-Covid policy is expected to boost a gradual recovery of Chinese international business developments adapted to the new trends and challenges in the global context (Chow, 2023).

2.6 Conclusion

This chapter introduced the macro framework of this study. In the past four decades, China has gone through different reforms, moving from a planned to a market-oriented economy. However, nowadays, the country is experiencing several challenges in the domestic market, resulting in a slowdown of the economy. To address this situation, the Chinese government has already developed and implemented major policies such as the

"Belt and Road Initiative" and the "Made in China 2025", and more recently, the new "Dual Circulation Strategy", aimed at boosting not only the decreasing domestic market, but at promoting a stronger role of the country in the international context. In this sense, and in the context of the book, the current international business scenario provides not only interesting future challenges for Chinese firms, but also unprecedented opportunities to analyse the present and future role of the country, and especially of its firms, both at home and abroad. It seems there is a need for authors, incumbent firms, and policy makers to understand how Chinese firms are developing their strategies at home while facing the current economic and business domestic scenario, how they have been creating competitive advantages at home and abroad and, more importantly, how and why Chinese firms have already become global competitors of Western leading firms, despite the above-mentioned challenges. As the largest trading block of China (beyond ASEAN counties) (Cash & Zhang, 2023), and also because one of the main objectives of the study is to understand how Chinese firms behave in business environments different from the Chinese, this book will focus on the internationalisation of Chinese firms into the EU.

References

Asian Development Bank. (2021). *The 14th five-year plan of the People's Republic of China: Fostering high-quality development*. https://www.adb.org/publications/14th-five-year-plan-high-quality-development-prc

Banach, C., & Gunter, J. (2023). *How the BRI is shaping global trade and what to expect from the initiative in its second decade*. https://merics.org/en/tracker/how-bri-shaping-global-trade-and-what-expect-initiative-its-second-decade

Cash, J., & Zhang, E. (2023, July 13). *China's exports fall most in three years as global economy falters*. https://www.reuters.com/markets/asia/chinas-june-exports-fall-124-imports-drop-68-2023-07-13/

Cerdeiro, D., & Jain-Chandra, S. (2023). *China's economy is rebounding, but reforms are still needed*. https://www.imf.org/en/News/Articles/2023/02/02/cf-chinas-economy-is-rebounding-but-reforms-are-still-needed

Chandler, C., & McGregor, G. (2020). Xi Jinping's new economic strategy for China: 'Dual circulation' or doublespeak? *Fortune.*

Chen, Z. (2023). *Review of economic impact of COVID-19 on China's economy: Positive and negative.* Paper presented at the Proceedings of the 6th International Conference on Economic Management and Green Development, Singapore.

Chow, L. (2023). *Overview of China outbound investment of 2022.* https://www.ey.com/en_cn/china-overseas-investment-network/overview-of-china-outbound-investment-of-2022#:~:text=China%20overall%20outward%20direct%20investment,to%20US%2421.0%20billion1

Dollar, D., Huang, Y., & Yao, Y. (2021). *China's long-term success will depend primarily on addressing its internal challenges* [Press release]. https://www.imf.org/external/pubs/ft/fandd/2021/06/the-future-of-china-dollar-huang-yao.htm

European Commission. (2020). *Countries and regions.* China. https://ec.europa.eu/trade/policy/countries-and-regions/countries/china/

European Parliament. (2020). *Legal analysis of international trade law and digital trade.* Policy Department for External Relations.

Fang, C., Garnaut, R., & Song, L. (2018). 40 years of China's reform and development: How reform captured China's demographic dividend. In S. S. A. Press (Ed.), *China's 40 years of reform and development* (pp. 1978–2018). Anu Press.

Financial Times Reporters. (2022, October 22). How the US chip export controls have turned the screws on China. *Financial Times.*

Fornes, G., & Altamira, M. (2023). *Digitalization, technology and global business: How technology is shaping value creation across borders.* Palgrave.

Fornes, G., & Mendez, A. (2018). *The China-Latin America axis: Emerging markets and their role in an increasingly globalised world* (2nd ed.). Palgrave Macmillan.

Gong, X. (2023). *The Belt and Road Initiative is still China's "Gala" but without as much luster* [Press release]. https://carnegieendowment.org/2023/03/03/belt-and-road-initiative-is-still-china-s-gala-but-without-as-much-luster-pub-89207

Hale, T., & Langley, W. (2023, September 30). Weak China manufacturing data adds to pressure on economy. *Financial Times.* https://www.ft.com/content/386580c9-88f2-4368-84ff-fbe2d962e062

Ho-Him, C. (2023, April 23). Shifting production from China is impossible, says shipping boss. *Financial Times.* https://www.ft.com/content/ed7357fa-1da5-485c-ae59-ed21ab1e6e9d

Hofman, B. (2018). *Reflections on forty years of China's reforms*. Fudan University's Fanhai School of International Finance.
Huang, Y. (2016). Understanding China's Belt & Road Initiative: Motivation, framework and assessment. *China Economic Review, 40*(C), 314–321.
Huenemann, R. (2017). *Economic reforms, 1978–present*. https://www.oxfordbibliographies.com/view/document/obo-9780199920082/obo-9780199920082-0008.xml
IMF. (2011). *World Economic Outlook database*. http://www.imf.org/external/pubs/ft/weo/2010/02/weodata/index.aspx
International Monetary Fund. (2023). *People's Republic of China 2022 Article IV Consultation—Press release; staff report; and statement by the executive director for the People's Republic of China* [Press release].
Kawase, K. (2022, August 2). Made in China 2025 plan thrives with subsidies for tech and EV makers. *Financial Times*. https://www.ft.com/content/f7df0f64-25b5-4526-82fa-ca1b554b541b
Kratz, A., Zenglein, M., Sebastian, G., & Witzke, M. (2023). *Chinese FDI in Europe: 2022 update*. https://rhg.com/research/chinese-fdi-in-europe-2022-update/
Ling, C., & Naughton, B. (2016). An institutionalized policy-making mechanism: China's return totechno-industrial policy. *Research Policy, 45*(10), 2138–2152.
Ma, H., Wu, X., Yan, L., Huang, H., Wu, H., Xiong, J., & Zhang, J. (2018). Strategic plan of "Made in China 2025" and its implementation. In *Analysing the impacts of industry 4.0 in modern business environments*. IGI Global.
Spar, D., & Oi, J. (2006). China: Building "capitalism with socialist characteristics". *Harvard Business School*.
The Editorial Board. (2023, July 17). China's sluggish economic recovery. *Financial Times*. https://www.ft.com/content/d7528b7f-d879-4b47-a45b-cbb58545e7be
Weinland, D. (2022, November 18). The tech war between America and China is just getting started. *The Economist*.
World Bank. (2020). *World Bank data*. https://data.worldbank.org/country/china
World Bank. (2023). *China's GDP (current thousands US$) per capita evolution 1978–2022*. https://data.worldbank.org/indicator/NY.GDP.PCAP.CD?locations=CN

Yao, K. (2020). *What we know about China's 'dual circulation' economic strategy*. https://www.reuters.com/article/china-economy-transformation-explainer-idUSKBN2600B5

Zipser, D., Seong, J., & Woetzel, J. (2021). *Five consumer trends shaping the next decade of growth in China*. https://www.mckinsey.com/cn/our-insights/our-insights/five-consumer-trends-shaping-the-next-decade-of-growth-in-china

3

China's Institutional Framework, Capabilities, and Internationalisation Strategies of Chinese Multinationals

3.1 Introduction

This chapter introduces the literature review of the book. The section begins with a review of China's Outward Foreign Direct Investment (OFDI) trends found in the literature. The main theoretical lenses framing the analysis are then introduced: Institutional Theory and Institutional Theory in China, and The Resource-Based View and The Resource-Based View in China. The link between institutions and capabilities in China is then discussed, with a focus on government support and informal relations (the two most relevant institutional elements in China identified in the literature). Finally, a review of the literature about the internationalisation of Chinese multinationals and the influence of Chinese domestic institutions (with a special focus on the main internationalisation policies and the use of personal relations abroad) in the development of capabilities abroad is also included.

M. Altamira, *Chinese Firms in the Global Market*, Palgrave Macmillan Asian Business Series, https://doi.org/10.1007/978-3-031-59227-0_3

3.2 China's Outward Foreign Direct Investment Trends

Since 1979, China's OFDI has experienced a strong evolution. Three different stages can be identified based on Government policies, scope of investment, characteristics as well as issues and objectives of the internationalisation process. The table below shows the analysis developed by (Table 3.1).

As identified in the table, the most relevant characteristic of Chinese firms' internationalisation process has been the influence of the government through different policies (Alon et al., 2018; Altamira et al., 2022; Angulo-Ruiz et al., 2019; Cardoza et al., 2015; Hong et al., 2015; Wang & Gao, 2019; Zou et al., 2022). A good example of this is the Open-Door policy launched in 1979, the Go Out or Go Global initiative in 2000 or more recently, as introduced in the previous section, the Belt and Road Initiative (BRI), also known as One Belt, One Road, or The New Silk Road), a strategy launched in 2013 by the Chinese government with the aim of promoting integration of China with the world business environment (Du & Zhang, 2018; PRC, 2017; Zou et al., 2022). Moreover, in the early years of Chinese OFDI, most of the focus was on the acquisition of strategic resources in Asia, Latin America, and Africa, initiatives led by a government in need of natural resources to feed the rapid growth of the economy. During the following decades, the focus has been shifting, arguably with support from the government (Hong et al., 2015), to the acquisition of advanced technology, brands, distribution channels and other strategic assets in developed countries mainly to enhance international competitiveness and also satisfy the changing consumption at home (He et al., 2019; Oliveira et al., 2017; Parmentola, 2017; Wang & Gao, 2019).

This, for most Chinese companies, has created a pattern of international expansion that is different from that captured by most mainstream theories (mostly based on Western-based firms). Due to this, Barney and Zhang (2009) started a debate in the literature that still continues today, whether a theory of Chinese management (i.e., applying received theories in a Chinese context) can explain what firms from China are doing, or a Chinese Theory of Management (i.e., creating new explanations for

Table 3.1 Stages of Chinese OFDI

Stage of OFDI	Stage 1: 1979–1990	Stage 2: 1991–1999	Stage 3: 2000–present
Government policy	"Open-Door" policy. OFDI included in National Development plan	Second stage of the "Open-Door policy" SOEs were permitted to invest in international markets	Accession to World Trade Organization in 2001 China "Go out" policy and support to particular industries More recently, the "Belt and Road Initiative" and "Made in China 2025"
Scope of investment	First investment in Japan and spread to 45 countries to a value of US$1.2 First investment in Japan and spread to 45 countries to a value of US$1.2 billion	Chinese companies had a presence in 140 countries worldwide	Chinese companies have a global presence
Characteristics and issues	Poorly managed and poor performing internationalisations	Mixed results with some firms having substantial losses	Chinese government cautious with this approach due to past experience where some firms had substantial losses and worries of the outflow of capital
Objective	Pursuit of government goals	Gain access to technology, management skills, and natural resources	Gain access to technology, management skills, natural resources and access to new markets

management phenomena unique to the Chinese) is needed. The debate started mainly because focusing on only one approach could risk much of what can be learned from Chinese organisations and their management. In this sense, some authors have defended that there are opportunities in the Chinese management context for an extension of mainstream theories (Child & Rodrigues, 2005; Deng, 2012; Narula, 2012). Others, like Boisot and Meyer (2008), Deng et al. (2017), and Mathews (2006) have argued that Chinese firms' behaviour does not respond to received internationalisation theories and therefore there exists the opportunity for the development of new ones. Following this idea, Buckley et al. (2007) stated that "Chinese outward investors clearly present marked contrasts from the conventional model in key aspects" (pp. 513–514), an idea reinforced in their retrospective (Buckley et al., 2018) based on the previous article in which they noted the need for a special theory for Chinese firms, especially due to their specific business and institutional context, although not "exceptional". Similarly, Haasis and Liefner (2019), Hernandez and Guillen (2018), and Lattemann and Alon (2015) showed that while it seems clear that EM multinationals, including those in China, do differ from Western multinationals in terms of their stage of development, their entry modes, strategic options or their capabilities, classic theories may still be valid but the inclusion of some boundary conditions and the adaptation of some assumptions are needed. In addition, they challenged scholars to consider extant theory as evolving.

In the meantime, and until the debate is settled, most research works have found the need to combine different mainstream concepts to understand and explain the international expansion of Chinese companies (Alon et al., 2018; Hoskisson et al., 2000). Following this pattern, the present study is framed by combining two well-established theoretical frameworks: Institutional Theory (IT) (North, 1990) and the Resource-Based View (RBV) of the firm (Barney, 1991).

3.3 Theoretical Framework

3.3.1 Institutional Theory

The institutional environment, defined as the "set of fundamental political, social and legal ground rules that establishes the basis for production, exchange and distribution" (Davis & North, 1971) is formed by formal institutions like regulatory frameworks, laws, or standards, and informal institutions like norms, values, or practices (North, 1990). The international business literature has shown that the institutional environment impacts companies' performance due to cultural distance (Hofstede, 1981), unfamiliarity with business conditions (or liability of foreignness) (Johanson & Vahlne, 1977), different public policies, legal institutions, and regulatory structures (North, 1990; Peng et al., 2005), among others. In this context, research has proven that institutions matter, but what is relevant is *how* institutions matter (Peng et al., 2008) to get useful insights for companies' and managers' decision-making processes as well as for their evaluation of available strategic options at home and abroad (Khanna & Palepu, 2010).

This appears more relevant when studying the performance of companies in EMs. In this context, most of the literature on strategy and internationalisation in these markets is based on adaptations of mainstream theories developed in Western economies. Hoskisson et al. (2000), one of the first works to analyse this, examined strategy implementation in EMs through four received mainstream theories: institutional theory (IT), transaction costs theory (TCT), agency theory (AT), and resource-based theory (RBV). They argued that important institutional changes are taking place in emerging economies and these might affect the response of firms operating in those markets (Hoskisson et al., 2000). Wright et al. (2005) complemented these findings and, by highlighting the unique social, political, and economic contexts as well as firm characteristics of emerging economies, concluded that IT is definitely gaining "more and substantial prominence" (Wright et al., 2005, p. 22) on strategy research in emerging economies (Surdu et al., 2018). Meyer and Peng (2016) have added that IT is the most appropriate theory to understand companies' "micro-behavioural differences across emerging economies and around the world" (p. 16). Finally, a more recent review on internationalisation of Chinese firms (Haasis & Liefner, 2019) also showed that IT is still the most prominent theoretical perspective to study the behaviour of these firms.

In fact, one of the main characteristics of these markets is their relatively weaker institutional environment compared to that found in Western or developed contexts (Cardoza et al., 2015; Hoskisson et al., 2000; Ramamurti, 2012; Rottig, 2016). Weaknesses are tangible in three main areas: (i) information problems: comprehensive, reliable, and objective information to make decisions is not always widely available;

(ii) misguided regulations: political goals are sometimes prioritised over economic efficiency reducing, therefore, the chances to take full advantage of business opportunities; and (iii) inefficient judicial systems: independent judicial systems enforcing contracts in a reliable and predictable way are not always present in emerging economies (Khanna & Palepu, 1997). These institutional voids, usually taken for granted in developed economies where they play a role in providing a stable business environment, are elements frequently missing in most EMs (Meyer, 2004; Meyer & Peng, 2016; Meyer et al., 2009). In this context, two main questions arise: How can EM firms grow in these weak institutional environments? How can institutional voids be filled to offer firms an enabling environment to grow? (Boisot & Meyer, 2008; Peng et al., 2008).

A growing number of works have attempted to answer these questions by showing that EM firms are exploiting the low levels of institutionalisation in their home markets to support the companies' development and expansion (see for example Cardoza and Fornes, 2011; Elango and Pattnaik, 2007; Estrin and Prevezer, 2011; Fornes et al., 2021; Hong et al., 2015; Peng et al., 2008; Tracey and Phillips, 2011; Williamson et al., 2013). A partial answer to these questions seems to lie in informal institutions that link the micro and macro levels creating thus inter-organisational strategies that are based on alliances and networks (Estrin & Prevezer, 2011; Fornes & Cardoza, 2018; Fornes et al., 2016, 2021; Meyer & Peng, 2016; Nee & Opper, 2012; Peng & Luo, 2000; Shou et al., 2012). More specifically, informal institutions help companies to face the challenges of weaker institutional environments in two main areas: (i) overcoming market failures, and (ii) reducing transaction costs. They help to overcome market failures by, for example, getting access to capital, sometimes at below market rates or subsidised/soft loans (Buckley et al., 2007), by accessing state-supported research and/or capital (Williamson et al., 2013), or by protecting operations from domestic and international competitors (Hoskisson et al., 2000). Informal institutions also assist in reducing transaction costs by creating mechanisms for improving access to market information, firms matching, and referral (Rauch & Trindale, 2002), by expanding the market and deepening competitive positioning (Park & Luo, 2001), or by strengthening the corporate governance (Estrin & Prevezer, 2011).

Institutional Theory and China

Peng (2002) argued that institutions evolve from informal to formal and North (1990) that they do it in a slow incremental fashion. This idea is supported by Estrin and Prevezer (2011) who analysed the importance of the weak and unstable formal institutional framework and the role of informal institutions in EMs like China. In fact, in the country, interpersonal networks have created "multiplex relationships that provide the sinews of enforceable trust and the conduits of information flow" which enables robust firm action (Nee & Opper, 2012, p. 259), a unique institutional environment that seems to have its origin in the country's economic development since the reforms started at the end of the 70s and the resulting institutional changes.

In 1978, the Chinese economy was dominated by SOEs and the economic policies of the state (Nee & Opper, 2012). As a response to low economic performance, the Chinese government defined economic reforms with the aim of stimulating productivity. Consequently, a shift to a more market-oriented economy was initialised opening new opportunities for profit making and the development of new types of companies; a new development that was based mainly on entrepreneurship initiatives. However, during the first decade of economic changes, when the first new companies in the form of small and medium enterprises (SMEs) developed by entrepreneurs started to arise in China, the government did not yet offer strong support to new forms of firms such as property rights, transparent rules, or a registration process. Instead, entrepreneurs were able to develop their business thanks to innovative informal arrangements within networks of economic actors that provided the necessary funding and business norms and helped to overcome the barriers to enter the market, overcoming, thus, the absence of defined formal rules supporting the development of this type of new company structure while suffering at the same time from competitive exclusion from SOEs. But this situation did not prevent firms from growing. On the contrary, it was as a result of this situation that a dynamic enterprise economy based on bottom-up entrepreneurial actions and social norms (also known as informal institutions) emerged in China. In this sense, bottom-up institutional innovation played a key role in enabling economic development, allowing the private sector to respond effectively to changing market opportunities resulting in a new private enterprise economy.

In other words, in China, companies have flourished and grown in an informal institutional context, and in this process, they have acted as institutional innovators for setting standards, norms, behaviours, and relations. This bottom-up institutional drive initially enabled the establishment of a free market economy, which was then followed by the creation of formal institutions to guide its development. This happened as "political actors maintained a wait-and-see position" and acted once the economy had shifted so profoundly that "institutional adaptations could no longer be postponed"; a dynamic that contrasts with state-centred theory (Nee & Opper, 2012, p. 262). In fact, it was only after the private economy became a powerful emergent force that the government (central and local) started to develop the legal and regulatory structure to legitimise private companies. Bottom-up institutional innovations followed by top-down accommodating change of formal rules by the state had become the common pattern, social norms and networks being the source of endogenous institutional change.

However, despite the market-oriented reforms and the scenario described above, the Chinese government is still the main economic actor dictating actions, rules, and policies in China (Altamira et al., 2022; Chenyan et al., 2022; Fornes et al., 2018). Chinese firms operate in a highly regulated business environment characterised by strong government influence and a high level of government presence in companies, in the form of ownership or participation of members of the party (Angulo-Ruiz et al., 2019; Chenyan et al., 2022; Estrin & Prevezer, 2011; Hong et al., 2015; Yi et al., 2017). According to a recent report (Peterson Institute for International Economics, 2023), Chinese state-owned firms still account for 40–60% of the economy. In addition, the government presence can also be identified in private or public companies where managers are sometimes former government officials and where *lishu* relationships (informal connections between companies and members of the party) are still one of the most important business connections (Buckley, 2018).

Summing up, the institutional environment in China has been through radical transformation during the past several decades and as a consequence firms' strategic options are conditioned by their industry environment as well as by the formal and informal institutional frameworks (Cardoza et al., 2014, 2015; Fornes et al., 2021; Hoskisson et al., 2000; Peng, 2002; Wright et al., 2005). Domestic institutions in China, such as the legal and regulatory frameworks, ownership patterns, social norms, and other informal institutions have been proven to have an important effect on the firms' decision-making process and as a result in the definition and development of their capabilities (Altamira et al., 2022; Buckley et al., 2007, 2018; Cardoza et al., 2014, 2015; Cui & Jiang, 2012; Hong et al., 2015; Yi et al., 2017).

3.3.2 The Resource-Based View of the Firm

As shown in previous sections, IT has been one of the most commonly theoretical frameworks adopted by scholars when it comes to studying management in Chinese firms (Li & Li, 2000; Peng, 2002; Peng et al., 2008; Wu, 2013a; Yi et al., 2017) followed by a combination with other theories, especially the RBV (Alon et al., 2018; Hoskisson et al., 2000) mainly because the institutional environment affects the development of firm capabilities (Altamira et al., 2022; Chen & Wu, 2011; Child & Rodrigues, 2005; Shou et al., 2012; Wu, 2013b; Yan et al., 2017; Yi et al., 2017; Zhang et al., 2015). Indeed, drawing from research on Asian organisations, Peng (2002) and Meyer and Peng (2016) showed the need to adopt an institution-based view, in addition to other mainstream theories, to account for differences present in business strategy, especially in China. As established in the previous section, institutional environments in EMs present different and unique characteristics and it is in this environment that Chinese firms design, manufacture, distribute, and sell their products/services; an institutional context that creates particular challenges when defining their strategies and, therefore, when developing their capabilities.

The Resource-Based View of the firm (RBV) (Barney, 1991) states that in order to achieve sustained competitive advantage, a firm should accumulate unique tangible and intangible resources or capabilities that are heterogenous and immobile as well as valuable, rare, and costly to imitate. In addition, and probably more importantly, the firm should be organised to capture the resulting value (Barney, 1991; Ju et al., 2013; Wernerfelt, 1984). In fact, a firm's ability to deploy resources through organisational capabilities may be more important than the absolute resource level in driving performance (D'Oria et al., 2021; DeSarbo et al., 2006). This is based on theoretical explanations on how firms overcome resource deficiencies by deploying their available resources in ways that outperform similar deployments by competitors. Recently, D'Oria et al. (2021) combined the RBV and the resource orchestration framework to emphasise on the combination of capabilities and managerial actions to realise the performance goals, giving clarity on why some firms outperform others, having the same capabilities. That is, focusing on the use in addition to resource accumulation. In this line, the RBV recognises the constraining nature of the context in which the organisation operates, its history, and its strategic goals (Teece et al., 1997). Therefore, taking a dynamic perspective, a firm is constrained by the path it has travelled and, as a consequence, a firm's sustained competitive advantage would depend on the environment, the stability of market demand, as well on the ease of replicability and imitation by competitors. This creates a strong positive relationship between firm capabilities, sustained competitive advantage, institutional environment, and firm performance (Ju et al., 2013).

The Resource-Based View of the Firm and China

Several researchers have questioned the suitability of the RBV in Chinese firms as they apparently lack strong Firm-Specific Advantages (FSA) that are the pillars of the unique tangible and intangible capabilities (Lattemann et al., 2017; Peng, 2012; Ramamurti & Hillemann, 2018). They claim that firms from EMs, including China, possess mainly basic and ordinary resources that make it difficult to create strong core competences (Peng et al., 2018).

To overcome this organisational void, Luo and Child (2015) found that Chinese firms do have unique compositional capabilities; firms from this country possess the ability to "cater to local market requirements by creatively and speedily combining available resources, which, considered separately, are not advantageous per se" (Peng et al., 2018, p. 834); this combination is mainly the result of having strategic capabilities related to Research and Development (R&D), and firm-strategic assets such as proprietary technology or global brands, which are still young and relatively weak in comparison to firms from developed markets (Williamson et al., 2013). The ability of Chinese firms to recombine assets and available resources, in addition to their opportunity-seeking ambitions (Peng et al., 2018), is helping them to leverage their internal weaknesses and capitalise on market needs. These compositional capabilities can explain the firm's ability to respond quickly to market needs; for example, by developing low cost or "good enough" products or services with the right quality-price balance (Lattemann et al., 2017; Oliveira et al., 2017), or by creating novel and innovative products similar to those from Western firms but at a lower price.

In addition, Chinese firms have demonstrated other capabilities, such as flexibility and adaptability, the ability to unlock latent demand in low-end segments, the skills to deal with weak institutions, and assets defined by and embedded in their domestic business environment (Altamira et al., 2022; He et al., 2019; Lattemann et al., 2017). Chen and Wu (2011) identified two types of corporate capabilities from the management and marketing literature that would be particularly relevant in the Chinese business context: (i) adaptive capability, a firm's ability to respond and adapt to market changes and maintain its competitive advantage over time; China is characterised by a high level of uncertainty with rapid economic changes, and the ability to make good predictions of market needs, plan the need of resources and effectively respond to environmental changes, among others, are becoming imperative for survival and growth, and (ii) resource-bridging capability: a firm's ability to access and obtain relevant resources such as bank loans, government approvals, access to financial capital or relevant information about the market; China presents an underdeveloped infrastructure and insufficient institutional support, so the ability to secure access to critical resources becomes crucial.

Marketing Capabilities in China

Marketing literature shows that a company that has adopted the marketing concept or considers marketing as "the activity, set of institutions, and processes for creating, communicating, delivering, and exchanging offerings that have value for customers, clients, partners, and society at large" (Gundlach & Wilkie, 2009, p. 260) will place their customers at the top of the organisation's list of priorities and will focus on capturing and satisfying them in order to create a sustainable and profitable relationship (Darroch et al., 2004; Day, 1994). A firm implementing this marketing concept is said to be market-oriented or to have adopted market orientation as an asset/capability. Day (1994) and Guenzi and Troilo (2006) showed that market-oriented companies are better equipped and positioned to generate superior customer value and, as a consequence, to develop a sustainable competitive advantage. In fact, several studies have demonstrated that market orientation is positively related to firm performance (Adams et al., 2019; Day, 1994; Ge & Ding, 2005; Guenzi & Troilo, 2006; Morgan et al., 2009a; Tajeddini & Ratten, 2020). Related to this, the ability to generate superior customer value is dependent on the availability of creating and developing distinctive marketing capabilities (Day, 1994; Guenzi & Troilo, 2006).

In this context, marketing capabilities are defined in the literature as complex bundles of skills and accumulated knowledge, exercised through organisational processes, that enable firms to coordinate activities and make use of their market-based knowledge and assets (Day, 1994). In addition, the role marketing plays in determining firm performance has been widely recognised, (see for example Alqahtani and Uslay, 2020; Hult et al., 2005; Katsikeas et al., 2006; Otto et al., 2020). To successfully deploy resources in support of differentiation, firms need marketing capabilities that enable them to repeatedly deliver desired benefit bundles to customers (Noble et al., 2002). Different types of marketing capabilities have been explored in previous studies.

Morgan et al. (2009a) identified seven marketing capabilities required for a market-driven company: pricing, product management, distribution management, marketing communications, selling, marketing planning, and market implementation. The author grouped them into two distinct sets: (i) specialised marketing capabilities, and (ii) architectural marketing capabilities. Specialised marketing capabilities are the functionally focused capabilities built around the integration of the specialised knowledge held by the firm's marketing employees and the communication of benefits to current and potential customers (Day, 1994; Slater & Narver, 1993; Tripsas, 1997). On the other hand, architectural marketing capabilities are those that give strategic focus to the specialised marketing capabilities and drive the deployment of resources to achieve strategic goals. Both types of marketing capabilities are necessary enablers of product differentiation and precursors of the firm's competitive advantage (Pasa & Shugan, 1996).

Day (1994) classified marketing capabilities into market sensing, which defines to what extent the company is well equipped and organised to monitor and assess the changes in the market in order to anticipate marketing actions, and customer linking capabilities; which considers the skills, abilities, and processes needed to "achieve collaborative customer relationships so individual customer needs are quickly apparent to all functions and well-defined procedures are in place for responding to them" (p. 49). Some years later and with the purpose of closing the marketing capabilities gap while including new trends in the market such as the Internet (Day, 2011), the same author challenged the market-driven approach to marketing capabilities, and by emphasising on the need to consider the market learning process and the dynamic characteristic of the environment, he defined three complementary key marketing capabilities: (i) static capabilities, which are stable and based on process activities that are routinized, (ii) dynamic capabilities, which can be augmented and reconfigured or are newly developed in order to look for new opportunities in a changing dynamic environment, and (iii) adaptive capabilities, which enable anticipation and are based on flexible processes so they can be reconfigured and redefined if needed according to market volatility. Although the three capabilities are needed to achieve sustainable competitive advantage, firms should focus on the development of adaptive capabilities that would enhance the existing dynamic ones. Moreover, for the successful development of the adaptive capabilities, the author defined three other necessary marketing capabilities: (i) a vigilant market capability to be aware of the latest changes in the market, (ii) an adaptive market experimentation capability for continuous learning and (iii) an open marketing capability to develop relations with stakeholders by using new media technologies.

Indeed, aware of the need to consider the continuous changes in the market, several authors extended the research on dynamic marketing capabilities, combining the RBV and the dynamic capability view (Teece et al., 1997). For example, Barrales-Molina et al. (2013) developed a review on Dynamic Marketing Capabilities (DMCs) and by conceptualising DMCs as capabilities that use market knowledge to adapt organisational recourses, and analysing the differences with marketing capabilities, concluded that new product development (NPD) and proactive market orientation are the most "rigorously grounded DMCs" (p. 13). Following this area of research, Morgan et al. (2009b) linked dynamic marketing capabilities and profit growth and performance. They extended the knowledge about dynamic marketing capabilities by analysing the positive direct effect of three dynamic marketing capabilities, namely CRM capability, brand management capability and market-sensing capability on profit growth rates in terms of revenues and margins.

Numerous studies have been carried out concerning the development of marketing capabilities as well as their importance for the performance of Western firms (Adams et al., 2019; Alqahtani & Uslay, 2020; Darroch et al., 2004; Day, 1994, 2013; Morgan et al., 2009a, b), however, very few studies have been carried out to date on EM firms in general and China in particular. This was highlighted in a review a few years ago on the marketing of multinationals from EMs (Kamboj & Rhaman, 2015) which found that, compared with Western multinationals, research on EMs-based firms is noticeably absent from writing in international business strategy and as a consequence, the knowledge of their international marketing strategies is incomplete. The authors also demonstrated the increasing interest among researchers in the study of the relationship between firm capabilities, marketing capabilities in particular, and firms' performance tendency towards EM.

This is an interesting opportunity in the fields of international business and marketing in China, as the institutional environment has profound influence on the type of marketing capabilities developed to gain competitive advantage in the marketplace. Changes in the economy due to the transition from a planned economy to a market economy have been providing a suitable scenario for testing market orientation and therefore the influence of the institutional environment on the development of marketing capabilities as the increased competition in the market has forced Chinese firms to become increasingly market-oriented (Ge & Ding, 2005; Nee & Opper, 2012; Sun, 2017). In this context, Ge and Ding (2005) have shown that market orientation and firm performance are positively related in Chinese multinationals and He and Wei (2011) indicated that a market-oriented corporate culture facilitates innovation, a key factor in delivering superior corporate performance (see also Ge & Ding, 2005; Yan et al., 2017; Liu & Su, 2013; and Yang et al., 2012). Also, Ju et al. (2013) and Wu (2013b) have shown the moderating effect of elements of the institutional environment, such as the level of market development or the legal effectiveness in the link between firm capabilities and firm performance in China. Shou et al. (2012), one of the few works combining IT and RBV to study marketing capabilities in China, incorporated informal institutions (i.e., Guanxi, see below) to the analysis and found that the performance of technology capabilities is less important when informal institutions are relevant and the legal system inefficient, while informal institutions strengthen the marketing capabilities of Chinese firms, weakening those from foreign firms. He et al. (2012, p. 27) also combined the two theoretical frameworks to analyse how Chinese firms can "enhance export performance by aligning its export channels with its level of market orientation capabilities, contingent on the institutional distance between the home and export market" (p. 27). Finally, Chen and Wu (2011), focusing only on informal institutions, studied the link between two different types of personal relationships or networks (with the government and with business partners), and the adaptive capability and the resource-bridging capability. They demonstrated that both types of personal relationships have a positive impact on both capabilities; while relationships with government officials have a greater impact on resource-bridging capability, relationships with business partners have a similar positive effect on both capabilities.

Following this analysis, it can be appreciated that few works have introduced both formal and informal institutions in the analysis. This has recently been highlighted by Haasis and Liefner (2019) who found that despite the increasing interest in the influence on institutions as drivers and antecedents of Chinese OFDI, no recent articles include both formal and informal elements. In addition, scarce attention has been devoted to investigating how particular marketing capabilities are defined in China and how relevant Chinese institutional elements are in this definition, combining, thus, IT and RBV.

3.3.3 Institutions and the Development of Marketing Capabilities in China

Institutions, especially the political, social, cultural, and economic systems surrounding firms, have an impact and play a fundamental role in firms' behaviour and in the social environment in which those firms operate (Hoskisson et al., 2000; North, 1990) and as a consequence shape the social and organisational behaviour (Scott, 1995). Within this context, capabilities are the pillars where companies' performance is based both in domestic and international markets. Peng et al. (2008) stated that strategic decisions are driven by both industry conditions and firm capabilities and also that they are influenced by the formal and informal conditions of the institutional framework that managers confront. The point is that the constant and rapid changes in social, economic, and political institutions in China, especially since the economic reforms promoted by the Chinese government at the end of the 1970s, make institutional factors important drivers of Chinese managers' decision-making process, strategic formulation and implementation (Hoskisson et al., 2000). Drawing from previous studies about the Chinese institutional environment (Cardoza et al., 2011; Cui & Jiang, 2012; Estrin & Prevezer, 2011; Fornes et al., 2021; Yang & Stoltenberg, 2014; Yi et al., 2017; Zhang et al., 2015) and based on the analysis of the Chinese business scenario developed in the first section, the following two institutional forces seem to have the greatest impact on the development of business activities in China: (i) the political influence of the

Chinese government, and (ii) the relevance of informal relations. In addition, there are two additional complementary elements, Chinese culture, and Chinese philosophy, that strongly influence Chinese managers' decision-making processes and strategy implementation (Deng, 2012; Haasis & Liefner, 2019; Liu, 2015; Yau, 1988; Yau et al., 2009).

The Political Influence of the Chinese Government

In China, despite the market-oriented reforms, most business activities are still under the control of the government (Angulo-Ruiz et al., 2019; Buckley, 2018; Nee & Opper, 2012; Peterson Institute for International Economics, 2023; Yi et al., 2017). State-owned companies, in which managers are usually selected by the CPC or are former CPC members, are still the main players in the Chinese business environment. This can be extended to private or public firms (non-state-owned companies), where *lishu* relationships (meaning informal connections between companies and members of the party) are still among the most important business connections (Buckley, 2018). China's government (at central, provincial, city, or prefecture level) plays a fundamental role in Chinese firms' strategic options as it influences and determines "the structure of the firm, directorial and senior management appointments, business plans, projects and operational decisions" defined by Chinese managers (Buckley et al., 2018, p. 14). Also, in the international context, Child and Rodrigues (2005) and Cardoza et al. (2015) found, for example, that Chinese companies have received preferential support from the government mainly through assistance and access to international joint ventures, state ownership and/or funding, or access to technological knowledge. Managers' decision-making processes and therefore firms' capabilities definition and international expansion are influenced by a very particular Chinese domestic institutional environment, highly regulated with a strong government presence (Chenyan et al., 2022), characterised by "weak legal and regulatory frameworks, ownership patterns, public funding access, or government participation in firms" (Cardoza et al., 2015, p. 4).

Lin (2010) was one of the first studies to analyse the impact of institutions in the development of capabilities differentiating between different types of Chinese companies. He found that state-owned and private multinationals are subject to different environmental effects and, as a consequence, they faced different strategic options and developed different capabilities, suggesting that SOEs would be stronger than private firms in terms of dynamic capabilities. In this sense, private Chinese firms seem to face formal institutional constraints, such as inefficient legal frameworks and weak intellectual property rights that might discourage the pursuit of innovations, making it relatively difficult for businesses to invest in R&D or to build global brands. In fact, Yi et al. (2017) showed that the higher the state-participation in ownership, the higher the effect of R&D intensity on innovation performance, an influence that is higher in regions where innovation is a strategic activity of the government. Also in this context, Williamson et al. (2013) considered government-specific advantages (GSAs) to capture the quality of government-created assets that influence the development of companies' (SOEs and private firms) capabilities, which will be determinant in, for example, the motivation for and process of internationalisation of the firms, in combination with additional Chinese unique country-specific and firm-strategic assets.

The Relevance of Informal Relations

Informal relations in China are known as guanxi, which refers to the set of connexions or ties to secure favours in personal and organisational relations that have "significant effects on business operations, survival, and growth" (Park & Luo, 2001, p. 473). It is one of the most relevant informal institutions in China (Chen et al., 2013; Estrin & Prevezer, 2011), and one of the three most important Chinese cultural values and characteristics together with Face—*mianzi*—and Reciprocity—*renqing* (Yau et al., 2009).

Several authors have recognised the importance of this informal institution and its influence in the development of capabilities. For example, Peng and Luo (2000) showed that the capacity for building relations to overcome institutional voids is pursued to develop firms' capabilities. The authors demonstrated that guanxi leads to higher firm performance and benefits market expansion and competitive positioning of firms. This is mainly because the capabilities of firms operating in EMs are still relatively low in comparison with, for example, their Western counterparts (Chen & Wu, 2011; Kaufmann & Roesch, 2012; Lattemann et al., 2017; Rugman & Li, 2007); in fact, in such a context, firms with inferior resources and capabilities would have a higher level of external dependence. However, Peng and Luo (2000) also demonstrated that despite guanxi being important, it is not sufficient and therefore strong firm capabilities are also needed for good and sustainable performance.

Several authors have studied the role of informal institutions as efficient and culturally viable mechanisms to minimise and/or offset this external dependence. For example, as already mentioned above, Chen and Wu (2011) studied the common practice of guanxi in Chinese organisations by analysing the relationship between guanxi and corporate and marketing capabilities, a relation that proved to be positive as the informal connections helped to secure "deals with suppliers, orders from buyers, and approval from the government" (Park & Luo, 2001, p. 463). Shou et al. (2012) showed that in comparison with Western firms, Chinese firms are better able to leverage their guanxi to enhance their marketing capabilities, in particular market sensing, customer linking, and channel bonding, in the domestic market. The most important thing is that these informal relations moderate and facilitate business by building trust and leverage in both domestic and international markets, having an impact on business performance.

In this context, two types of guanxi can be identified (Chen & Wu, 2011; Park & Luo, 2001): (i) political guanxi, which refers to personal networks with government officials and regulatory agencies, and (ii) business guanxi, which refers to personal ties with business partners, including suppliers, customers, competitors, and other collaborators. While the first type of guanxi functions vertically or hierarchically and has a greater impact on resource-bridging capability, the second type operates horizontally and has a similar positive effect on both resource-bridging and adaptive capabilities.

Informal institutions, in the form of guanxi, were crucial in the development of private industry in China from the end of the 70s and in the resulting new managerial capabilities. As introduced above, bottom-up institutional innovation played a key role in enabling economic development, allowing the private sector to respond effectively to changing market opportunities resulting in a new private enterprise economy and therefore new capabilities (Nee & Opper, 2012).

In the Chinese state-controlled economic environment at the beginning of the 80s, the lack of consumer orientation and the lack of market pressure defined the managerial capabilities needed at that time by Chinese companies. Efforts in SOEs, the dominant firm structure at that time, were focused on the fulfilment of production quotas, the development of relations with the government, and the negotiation of resources (Nee & Opper, 2012). With the support of the government and without the risk of firms' closure, efficient use of resources and the development of capabilities were not evident. In this context, challenges for new private firms emerged; with no formal rules and laws defined to develop a company, how could firms develop their business strategy and grow in the long term in a market still dominated by SOEs? The answer was the gradual learning process based on bottom-up actions resulting in informal institutional mechanisms (Nee & Opper, 2012). Through personalised exchange, multiplex relationships, information sharing, and joint market development and short-term financing, private firms and other SMEs found ways to reduce uncertainty while enhancing sustainable capability development. In other words, business guanxi with business partners helped Chinese firms to secure access to relevant market resources.

In addition, the emergence of new private firms and SMEs resulted in an increasingly competitive environment. The more intense the competition in the market, the more pressure assumed by private firms; this resulted in a greater flexibility and adaptability, which as a consequence enhanced the development of new internal marketing capabilities (Nee & Opper, 2012). Firms were systematically analysing other firms' market signals and adapting their products, accordingly, differentiating and specialising with respect mainly to price. In this sense, newly developed marketing capabilities, such as new product and service development, being close to competitors, and having a well-known brand seemed to play a determinant role in successful long-term competitive advantage. Also, as a result of a market with a lot of competitors, innovative activities seemed to become a survival imperative.

In this environment, not only were relations between firms relevant to secure their successful development, but relations with the government as well (Buckley, 2018; Nee & Opper, 2012; Yi et al., 2017). Political guanxi, especially in the Chinese institutional context previous to the economic reforms, was based on personal ties linked to the positional power of the politician, meaning that for other economic actors, personal connections with politicians were the basis for mutual trust leading to successful business relations. With the gradual development of the new economic scenario, more focus had been given to the importance of developing firm capabilities as opposed to investing in positional advantage through political capital. However, private firms and SMEs found that cultivating good ties with the local government was still a valuable asset as a consequence of the challenges found during the first years of the economic reforms. This was evident in, for example, the need to reduce the risk of unfavourable treatment by politicians and regulatory agents or to secure timely and relevant information from regulators, or officials (Nee & Opper, 2012).

This situation can still be appreciated today. Political guanxi helps firms to gain political legitimacy and avoid uncertainty in economic transition (Fornes et al., 2021; Park & Luo, 2001) and provides shortcuts to government-related resources such as bank loans, tax payments, government support plans (Buckley, 2018; Fornes et al., 2021; Park & Luo, 2001) and industry trends (Chen & Wu, 2011). Also, many keep their *lishu* relationships which provides evidence of how Chinese firms are still state-influenced (Buckley et al., 2018). Due to this, the development of personal ties with government officials has become a common practice among private firms and represents a valued asset for the success of business operations. However, it has been shown that the positive impact of personal ties with the government differs depending on the characteristics of the markets and industries; political connections are valued by firms looking to secure an advantage to access resources controlled by the

State or when doing business in strategic industries directly controlled by the government,

In sum, in recent years and as the market reforms have been settling in, Chinese private firms have strengthened their capability development combined with a management ability to detect and react to market opportunities to succeed in the Chinese marketplace. In addition to this, informal institutions (including guanxi as the most relevant in China), in the form of interfirm connections, customer and supplier networks, or personal ties with the government, as described above, still play a crucial role in the development of firm marketing capabilities. In this context, Chen and Wu (2011) demonstrated that while political guanxi has a strong positive influence on the development of a resource-bridging capability, business guanxi enhances the development of an adaptive capability.

Chinese Culture and Chinese Philosophy

Chinese companies, especially SMEs and private firms, have been facing many challenges and have perceived several constraints for their successful development, starting with no prior business knowledge and limited resources. So, how have Chinese firms been able to develop and grow in such a challenging institutional environment? A possible answer to this may lie in the business strategies followed by Chinese managers working in Chinese firms based on their culture and philosophy (Haasis & Liefner 2019; Liu, 2015). Different from Western management practices, Chinese business strategies are based on codes, attitudes, and experiences that are embedded in the Chinese philosophy and culture, represented, for example, in Sun Tzu's *Art of War* or Confucianism (Zhang et al., 2015) which have been used to define the strategic mindset of Chinese managers and therefore the competitive advantages of Chinese firms. In this context, Yau (1988) investigated and showed how Chinese traditional cultural values such as *man to nature orientation*, *man to himself orientation*, *relational orientation*, *time orientation*, and *personal activity orientation* and their underlying principles have influenced the development of marketing capabilities, and suggested that further strong relationships exist between these values and other marketing concepts, such as consumer behaviour or market segmentation.

Liu (2015) defined the six elements underlying Chinese strategic thinking and the mindset of Chinese managers based on Chinese tradition and philosophy. To highlight the uniqueness of these elements, he showed how Chinese would contrast with Western thinking and how Western managers should consider and understand these elements when doing business with their Chinese counterparts. Below is the summary and description of these six elements and their strategic implications:

1. Tao. This is a Chinese concept and unique category of thinking. At the core of Tao is the notion that all the things consist of contradictions or opposites. Tao is also associated with "greatness". In strategy, Tao means to have a vision of the furthest horizon; a great vision is a prerequisite to achieve greatness. In practice, it means that when Western managers try to understand a mission, vision, or strategy statements they should go beyond the literal meaning of the words, because of the different ways in which Chinese may express their ideas.
2. Stratagem. This concept is at the core of the Chinese competitive approach. Chinese companies usually do not define long-term strategies but rather use stratagems. By definition, stratagems have military, diplomatic, and strategic connotations. In China, an effective stratagem takes a panoramic and holistic view of the situation and prioritises the utilisation of this stratagem to neutralise the competitor. This differs from Western strategic planning, where an assessment of the business environment is developed followed by the definition of objectives and goals for the short, medium, and long term. In addition, at the core of the stratagem is the achievement of a strategic objective through the unorthodox in battles. Deception, by giving the opponent a misguided impression, or taking the competitor by surprise, are ways of understanding the unorthodox and are tactics usually developed by Chinese firms. The stratagem is part of the "Chinese-ness" of doing business and Western managers should deal with it when competing with their Chinese counterparts.

3. Shi. This is a unique Chinese strategic factor having a significant effect on business, politics, and military decisions. It is a situation, trend, configuration, potential, or momentum that is key for an organisation in the context of business, but may be "ridden, borrowed, created, leading to the competitive advantage of the decision maker" (p. 99). *Shi* does not have a Western comparison or definition and is the "net outcome of an integral and holistic assessment of all pertinent factors, a trend, potential or momentum" (p. 100). In practice, Western managers should stand in the Chinese counterparts' shoes to examine the *shi* surrounding their strategic intentions, to avoid future misunderstandings.
4. Dialectic thinking. To understand the strategic mind of Chinese managers and decision makers, knowledge of the yin-yang is crucial. This concept incorporates contradictions and opposites. The three principles of dialectic thinking are: (i) the principle of change, meaning that change is expected, and flux of events can happen at any time, (ii) the principle of contradiction, suggesting that the reality is not precise, and that change is constant, and (iii) the principle of Holism which involves an orientation to the context of the field as a whole, understanding the relationship between the objects and different elements with the whole context of the situation. It might also be important to see the stratagem and dialectic thinking together in terms of business relations. Just as positive stratagems can be identified, negative stratagems also exist, which are the actions of cheating, corrupting, or conspiracy. So, by analysing the stratagem, Western managers can be in a better position to prevent stratagems and identify positive ones. It is important to understand this as in China legal systems and the court have been very recently developed following the principles of Chinese Confucianism and Chinese philosophy.
5. Competitor orientation. In Chinese culture, focusing on competition is based on the Chinese philosophy, competitors being the main target and the one guiding and defining the main organisational decisions. With this orientation, the competitor's strategy shapes the organisation's one. The goal is to beat the competitor. Having a competitor orientation in China tends to result in company behaviour that is unlikely to produce a newly developed technology

while being the world market leader. Chinese companies usually tend to define a follower strategy.

6. Agility. This element is also embedded in the Chinese culture and is part of the yin-yang idea. Chinese agility has two dimensions: (i) it implies that even smaller or weaker companies are still in the position of competing with the strong ones, and (ii) agility means the ability to adapt quickly to an emerging situation before the competitors. In addition, an important element of Chinese agility is "strategic detour" or achieving the strategic objectives through an indirect approach. This results not only in agility but also in adaptability.

These six elements, embedded in Chinese culture and philosophy, have a relevant impact on strategy formulation, and might help, especially Western counterparts, to understand the unique strategic Chinese mind behind the decision-making process of Chinese managers and therefore behind the competitive advantages of their Chinese firms. In a similar way, Zhang et al. (2015) analysed the moderating effect of Sun Tzu's three significant strategies on performance and their relationship with government influence (formal institution) and guanxi (informal institution). They applied the three strategies to the business context and explained how each of them defines unique competitive advantages and marketing capabilities of Chinese firms. First, "*Know your enemy, know yourself, your victory will never be endangered*" helps Chinese managers to understand environmental forces while knowing the competitors to successfully adopt a customer orientation. Second, "*Defeat one's opponent by a surprise move*" is related to differentiation and uniqueness in the offer enhancing the superiority of the firm. And third, "*he will win whose army is animated by the same spirit through all his ranks*" defines the unity and teamwork expected in the firm as well as within its networks. By adopting these strategies, Chinese private firms and SME successfully deal with the challenging institutional environment while achieving their goals. The research showed the moderating effects of the three strategies on the influence of the government and guanxi on firm performance; this reinforces the argument that both formal and informal institutions have an effect on firms' performance, especially when operating outside China (Zhang et al., 2015).

All in all, both formal and informal institutions play a determinant role in the definition of strategic choices by Chinese managers and, as a consequence, in the development of the required marketing capabilities of Chinese firms. The influence of institutions in Chinese companies becomes more evident due to the significant role of the government, the relevance of informal relations, as well as of Chinese culture and philosophy influencing Chinese strategic thinking. It has been shown that these elements strongly influence the decision-making process and the strategy implementation of Chinese managers and thereby the definition and development of Chinese marketing capabilities. Moreover, considering the institutional framework analysed above, it seems that this influence might be different depending on the type of company. Different types of companies (i.e., state-owned, collectively owned, private, or foreign invested) may face different institutional environments and underlying elements, influencing their operations and access to resources, and therefore Chinese managers might adopt different strategic positions (Lin, 2010). It is in this context that it seems interesting to analyse and understand how different types of Chinese firms incorporate the influence of relevant Chinese institutional elements (formal and informal) in the development of marketing capabilities in the Chinese context in order to further analyse whether they understand the need to adapt or define new capabilities when they operate in different institutional environments as a result of the international expansion of the firm.

3.3.4 The Internationalisation of Chinese Multinationals, the Influence of Domestic Institutions and the Development of Marketing Capabilities.

Chinese Institutions and the Internationalisation of Chinese Firms

Institutional Theory proposes that a firm's internationalisation strategy is shaped by the institutional framework of the home country of the firm and that it is facilitated or constrained by institutional forces that promote or obstruct the upgrading of existing resources and capabilities (Child & Rodrigues, 2005; Wang et al., 2012). It is in this context that the rise of Chinese MNCs and the particularities of their institutional framework have gained interest among scholars on the role of domestic institutions in the internationalisation process (Angulo-Ruiz et al., 2019; Buckley et al., 2007; Kim et al., 2019; Paul & Benito, 2018; Peng, 2012). Buckley et al. (2007), one of the first studies that focused on Chinese OFDI, identified three China-specific characteristics that affect the internationalisation of Chinese companies: (i) capital imperfections, (ii) special ownership advantages, and (iii) institutional factors. They found that home institutions, especially state ownership, play a fundamental role in the flow and direction of Chinese OFDI. In fact, the government plays both a direct and indirect influence in the internationalisation of Chinese companies. Policies such as the "Go Out" strategy or the "Belt and Road" initiative, are examples of the efforts of the Chinese government to enhance the internationalisation of Chinese companies, not only of SOEs but also of private or public ones (Angulo-Ruiz et al., 2019; Lattemann et al., 2017) developing their activities in strategic sectors or industries; non-state firms are especially active in responding to the internationalisation policies of the government in order to benefit from special conditions being "an important or very important factor in their OFDI decision-making process" (Du & Zhang, 2018, p. 193). In this context, the table below provides an overview of the main internationalisation policies developed by the Chinese government since 1979, its main characteristics and specific actions, as well as incentives defined at different stages (Bellabona & Spigarelli, 2007; Oliveira et al., 2017). The table also considers the actions that have been defined and developed since 2015 by the Chinese government to support the specific objectives of the BRI (OECD, 2018; Zou et al., 2022) (Table 3.2).

The above actions and the specific incentives and support from official institutions have strongly helped Chinese firms to successfully develop OFDI. Moreover, in addition to the government support, political stability, and economic growth have also been considered home-country-specific advantages, or Government Specific Advantages (GSA) (Ramamurti & Hillemann, 2018), complementing China's natural endowment, being one of the most important factors enhancing international

Table 3.2 Actions and incentives within the main internationalisation policies defined by the Chinese government since 1979

1979–1990: first stage of the Open-Door policy	1991–1999: second stage of the Open-Door policy	2000–2005: first stage of the Go Out policy	2006 to present: second stage of the Go Out policy including actions that are still active today (no BRI)	2015 to present: actions within the BRI including initiatives from Made in China 2025 adopted within the BRI
• No specific regulations or directions • Limited to SOEs and controlled case by case • Firms pushed to acquire technology and market shares • Standardisation of approval procedures	• Strong support of SOEs in strategic sectors (mining, energy, automotive, electronics, chemical, construction, and transport) • Guarantee of incentives and special rights for autonomy in decision-making and management • Stricter controls to avoid speculation and losses for SOEs	• Promotion of internationalisation of projects in light industries (textiles, machinery, and electronics) • Reductions on custom duties • Help with currency purchase • Financial aid to firms using Chinese raw materials or components in order to enhance exports	• Foreign expansion as central theme for the Chinese government • Definition of more concrete actions and incentives • Reduction of tax quotas and facilitation of rates of investments and access to information • Foreign market access report released by the Ministry of Commerce	• Funding of connectivity and construction projects through Chinese development banks • Policies to accelerate indigenous innovation and large-scale investment in human resources: training professionals overseas, and programmes attracting foreign professionals, scientists, and researchers

1979–1990: first stage of the Open-Door policy	1991–1999: second stage of the Open-Door policy	2000–2005: first stage of the Go Out policy	2006 to present: second stage of the Go Out policy including actions that are still active today (no BRI)	2015 to present: actions within the BRI including initiatives from Made in China 2025 adopted within the BRI
		• Supply of information and assistance services, promotion of incentives, simplification of administrative tasks, and reduction of investment risks • Specific guidelines to go abroad published for 67 countries • Facilitation of loans for the retrieval of natural resources, export of technology, goods, and equipment, opening of R&D centres and new M&A	• Elimination of foreign currency restrictions • Opening of the Overseas Business Service Center, to help in the internationalisation process of any Chinese firms willing to go abroad • Signature of reciprocal investment promotions with Western countries	• Promotion of global national champions: favourable access to capital for acquisitions in technology, investments in joint ventures, and/or acquisitions of companies in advanced economies • Preferential treatment for high-technology imports • Promotion of Chinese technology standards within the BRI to help open up markets for Chinese products

(continued)

Table 3.2 (continued)

1979–1990: first stage of the Open-Door policy	1991–1999: second stage of the Open-Door policy	2000–2005: first stage of the Go Out policy	2006 to present: second stage of the Go Out policy including actions that are still active today (no BRI)	2015 to present: actions within the BRI including initiatives from Made in China 2025 adopted within the BRI
				• The breakthrough industries for 2025 include: "next-generation IT, high-end digital control machine tools and robots; aerospace; oceanographic, engineering equipment and high-technology shipping; advanced rail transportation; energy efficient and new-energy automobiles; electrical power equipment with a focus on renewables; agricultural machinery; high-performance structural metals and materials; biopharmaceuticals; high-performance medical equipment; and high-end equipment" (OECD, 2018, p. 24)

competitiveness of Chinese firms (Angulo-Ruiz et al., 2019). Lattemann et al. (2017) and Oliveira et al. (2017) supported this idea and added that in the specific case of China, in addition to other specific advantages such as a large population or natural resources, GSA should even be considered as a Country Specific Advantage (CSA).

Moreover, the business and institutional context of the host country would also play an important role in the internationalisation process of Chinese firms, an element that should be considered and analysed by Chinese managers and senior managers in their decision-making process (Lattemann et al., 2017). In this context, Meyer and Peng (2016) previously showed how SOEs in particular need to adapt their entry strategies to reduce possible conflicts in the host country due to higher institutional pressures in the home market. Furthermore, Child and Marinova (2014), based on a combination of IT and RBV, studied the link between home and host market contexts and analysed how this link influences the development of firm-level elements (capabilities) involved in the internationalisation of Chinese firms. The authors analysed the context for business based on two dimensions: (i) political stability and (ii) institutional maturity; while China would be considered a country with a high political stability but immature institutions, Western markets, and the EU in particular, would be considered environments with political stability too, but with mature institutions. In this situation, they suggested that Chinese firms find the highest challenges when operating in these environments and that some Chinese institutional and firm-level characteristics, considered advantages in China, may turn into firm disadvantages when they operate in the EU, mainly due to the differences in terms of the maturity of institutions. More specifically, Chinese firms find in the EU sophisticated and mature markets which contrast with the rapidly changing and uncertain home environment, transparent legal and regulatory frameworks that challenge the perceived lack of transparency and high state manipulation of Chinese firms (both state-owned and private), and different management styles that find the most important challenges in terms of business practices, knowledge and expertise, weaknesses found in Chinese firms due to their short international business experience, that become even more evident when they enter into a different local context. Finally, Chinese firms should be more conscious of and sensitive to the different expected cultural behaviours, especially on how to behave in mature business contexts and the different importance given to certain institutional elements that are relevant in China such as, for example, personal relationships or guanxi. In this sense, it seems that Chinese managers need to rely on local managers and staff to overcome these disadvantages and adapt to the new local environment.

In fact, informal institutions in the form of personal relations or guanxi also play an important role in the international development of Chinese firms. For example Lin et al. (2016) analysed this influence and concluded that social networks not only facilitate business operations domestically but that guanxi between the manager and the management team, that is, internal connections or business guanxi, help to achieve firms' internationalisation goals in a more efficient manner and they observed that the market choices were also influenced by the business networks in the host market. Similarly, and based on the RBV and the market orientation literature, Yan et al. (2017) showed that managerial ties enhance the export performance of Chinese firms as they help to access to valuable resources, this performance being even better when firms demonstrate market orientation. Also, Oliveira et al. (2017) found that the domestic institutional framework affects firms' OFDI but that it differs depending on the ownership structure: whereas Chinese SOEs would be more dependent on government support (or political guanxi), private or listed firms would be more reliant on informal business relations (or business guanxi). This influence would also affect the access to resources and would, therefore, have an impact on the type of capabilities developed by the different types of firms.

From this analysis, it seems clear that, similar to what happens in the domestic environment, the Chinese institutional framework and the capabilities developed in China play a determinant role in the internationalisation decisions of Chinese firms, especially in the first steps of the process. In other words, GSAs, and CSAs, which could also include informal institutions such as guanxi, are important elements influencing the international development of Chinese firms, but which should also be considered within the host-country institutional context.

Firm Capabilities and the Internationalisation of Chinese Firms

According to the RBV (Barney, 1991) a firm's international development is influenced by the superior firm's specific assets or capabilities. As discussed above, some strategic and marketing capabilities from Chinese firms or firm-strategic assets such as global brands, are still young and may seem weak when compared to Western firms (Peng et al., 2018; Williamson et al., 2013). However, Chinese firms have been shown to have developed other capabilities, such as flexibility and adaptability, the ability to unlock latent demand in low-end segments, or capabilities in dealing with weak institutions that may be unique due to the particular characteristics of the domestic business environment they are framed in (Chen & Wu, 2011; He et al., 2019; Lattemann et al., 2017; Yang & Stoltenberg, 2014).

In this sense, the challenge faced by Chinese multinationals is whether these capabilities developed at home are applicable to the international scene in the long term in terms of transferability and the existence of a suitable market for their propositions (He et al., 2019). In other words, how will these firms compete and deploy their strategic options and marketing capabilities in markets with different institutional frameworks? This is relevant as during most of the first years of the opening of the Chinese economy, Chinese firms have been basing their competitiveness (mainly) on cost advantage and scale for medium technology products targeting low/medium income markets at home and abroad. For this, mainstream theories suggest that to upgrade and gain differentiation and brand advantage abroad, Chinese firms should develop a new set of capabilities to operate in diverse institutional environments and as a consequence strengthen their performance abroad (Cardoza & Fornes, 2013; Child & Rodrigues, 2005; Fornes et al., 2016).

In this context, Mathews (2006), one of the authors who challenged Western-developed theories, in his analysis of Dragon Multinationals, explained that those firms which lack substantial prior resource in their home market, based their strategies on the Linkage, Leverage, and Learning (LLL) framework. The author emphasised the idea that traditional theories do not necessarily apply and that there might be the opportunity to adapt existing ones or even develop new ones. According to the author, Chinese companies have distinctive characteristics compared to incumbent firms, namely: (i) accelerated internationalisation, (ii) organisational innovation, and (iii) strategic innovation. In fact, Chinese firms have been creating competitive advantage in international markets through three different sources: (i) innovation: they have been adopting new innovation models to be competitive in global markets such as cost innovation, application innovation, business model innovation, Shanzai innovation and technological innovation, (ii) value-chain configuration: an increasing number of Chinese multinationals have been succeeding by pursuing international production, and (iii) Merger and Acquisitions: this internationalisation route has provided an opportunity for Chinese firms to fill the gaps in their capabilities to succeed abroad and as such it appears to be the main route for internationalisation, especially nowadays in the context of the BRI (Du & Zhang, 2018; Peng et al., 2018; Williamson et al., 2013; Zou et al., 2022).

These three sources of competitive advantage have been interacting to facilitate the process of learning and to transform it into new capabilities that could be exploited at home and abroad. However, as mentioned by Deng (2009), the key would be to integrate the knowledge and capabilities acquired in the host market to develop a successful competitive advantage in the long run, especially to enhance performance in the post-M&A phase. Although Chinese capabilities are still young, Chinese firms learn not only "through experience but also through knowledge transfers" (Lattemann et al., 2017, p. 155). Chinese firms do possess dynamism and speed to absorb knowledge and practices, and the integration of new capabilities, if needed, would depend on their visionary leadership, their creative learning abilities, but also on a stronger international human resource management and a more global perspective, challenges faced by Chinese firms operating in the international scene, especially in Western institutional environments.

All in all, despite the recognition that the institutional environment varies greatly between countries, particularly between Western and emerging economies, and that the Chinese business environment offers an important context and opportunity to study the influence of domestic institutions on the development of marketing capabilities, little research has been conducted to understand how Chinese firms incorporate the influence of the domestic institutional environment (formal and informal) on the development of marketing capabilities abroad and how they understand the need to adapt or to define new firm capabilities, marketing capabilities in particular, when they enter new environments.

3.3.5 Streams of Literature and Major Findings

The table below summarises the most relevant streams of literature discussed in the present chapter. It presents the major findings relevant to the present study of each of the streams, leading to the main question the present book intends to address (Table 3.3).

3.4 Conclusion

The present study addresses an important and timely issue as Chinese firms, both SOEs and private, have been investing abroad at an unprecedented pace. This international expansion of Chinese companies is driven by strategic considerations to access international markets and diversify risks enhanced by the government's new initiatives "Made in China 2025", "The Belt and Road Initiative" and the "Dual Circulation" strategy (Du & Zhang, 2018; European Union Chamber of Commerce in China, 2020; Huang, 2016; Ma et al., 2018; Yao, 2020; Zou et al., 2022), initiatives that are expected to change the international business scenario in the coming years. In this kind of growth and expansion, the role that marketing plays in determining firms' performance has been widely recognised (Hult et al., 2005; Katsikeas et al., 2006; Morgan, 2012; Wu, 2013b); to successfully deploy resources to support differentiation strategies, firms need marketing capabilities to enable and drive a sustained delivery of the planned benefits to customers (Day, 2013; Noble et al., 2002).

Numerous studies have been carried out to understand the development of capabilities, however, most of them have focused on Western

Table 3.3 Streams of literature and major findings

Streams of literature	Major findings relevant to the research
Institutional Theory and Emerging Markets	One of the main characteristics of EMs is their relatively weaker institutional environment compared to that found in Western or developed contexts (Cardoza et al., 2015; Hoskisson et al., 2000; Ramamurti, 2012; Rottig, 2016). EM firms are exploiting the low levels of institutionalisation in their home markets to support the companies' development and expansion (see for example Cardoza & Fornes (2011); Elango & Pattnaik (2007); Estrin & Prevezer (2011); Hong et al. (2015); Peng et al. (2008); Tracey & Phillips (2011); Williamson et al. (2013)) by relying on informal institutions that link the micro and macro levels creating thus inter-organisational strategies that are based on alliances and networks (Estrin & Prevezer, 2011; Fornes & Cardoza, 2018; Fornes et al., 2016; Meyer & Peng, 2016; Nee & Opper, 2012; Peng & Luo, 2000; Shou et al., 2012)
Institutional Theory and China	The institutional environment in China has been through radical transformation during the past decades and as a consequence firms' strategic options are conditioned by their industry environment as well as by the formal and informal institutional frameworks (Cardoza et al., 2014, 2015; Hoskisson et al., 2000; Peng, 2002; Wright et al., 2005). The combination of domestic formal institutions in China, such as the legal and regulatory frameworks, ownership patterns, and informal institutions such as social norms or personal relationships have been proven to have an important effect on the firms' decision-making process and as a result in the definition and development of their capabilities (Buckley et al., 2007, 2018; Cardoza et al., 2014, 2015; Cui & Jiang, 2012; Hong et al., 2015; Yi et al., 2017)

(continued)

Table 3.3 (continued)

Streams of literature	Major findings relevant to the research
The Resource-Based View (operationalised using marketing capabilities) and China	Several researchers have questioned the suitability of the RBV in Chinese firms as they apparently lack strong Firm-Specific Advantages (FSA) that are the pillars of the unique tangible and intangible capabilities (Lattemann et al., 2017; Peng, 2012; Ramamurti & Hillemann, 2018). They claim that firms from EMs, including China, possess mainly basic and ordinary resources that make it difficult to create strong core competences (Peng et al., 2018). However, Chinese firms have demonstrated capabilities such as flexibility and adaptability, the ability to unlock latent demand in low-end segments, the skills to deal with weak institutions, and assets defined by and embedded in their domestic business environment (He et al., 2019; Lattemann et al., 2017)
Institutional Theory and the Resource-Based View (operationalised using marketing capabilities) in China	Both formal and informal institutions play a determinant role in the definition of strategic choices by Chinese managers and, as a consequence, in the development of the required marketing capabilities of Chinese firms. In this context, The RBV recognises the constraining nature of the context in which the organisation operates, its history, and its strategic goals (Teece et al., 1997). Therefore, taking a dynamic perspective, a firm is constrained by the path it has travelled and, as a consequence, a firm's sustained competitive advantage would depend on the environment, the stability of market demand, as well on the ease of replicability and imitation by competitors. This creates a strong positive relationship between firm capabilities, sustained competitive advantage, institutional environment, and firm performance (Ju et al., 2013), linking, this, the RBV and IT

(continued)

Table 3.3 (continued)

Streams of literature	Major findings relevant to the research
	The influence of institutions in Chinese companies becomes more evident due to the significant role of the government, the relevance of informal relations, as well as of Chinese culture and philosophy influencing Chinese strategic thinking. It has been shown that these elements strongly influence the decision-making process and the strategy implementation of Chinese managers and thereby the definition and development of Chinese marketing capabilities. It is in this context that it seems interesting to analyse and understand how different types of Chinese firms incorporate the influence of relevant Chinese institutional elements (formal and informal) in the development of marketing capabilities in the Chinese context in order to further analyse whether they understand the need to adapt or define new capabilities when they operate in different institutional environments as a result of the international expansion of the firm
Internationalisation of Chinese firms and the influence of domestic institutions (IT)	Similar to what happens in the domestic environment, the Chinese institutional framework and the capabilities developed in China play a determinant role in the internationalisation decisions of Chinese firms, especially in the first steps of the process. GSAs, and CSAs, which could also include informal institutions such as guanxi, are important elements influencing the international development of Chinese firms, but which should also be considered within the host-country institutional context (Lattemann et al., 2017; Oliveira et al., 2017)

(continued)

Table 3.3 (continued)

Streams of literature	Major findings relevant to the research
Internationalisation of Chinese firms and the RBV (operationalised using marketing capabilities)	The challenge faced by Chinese multinationals is whether the capabilities developed at home are applicable to the international scene in the long term in terms of transferability and the existence of a suitable market for their propositions (He et al., 2019). Mainstream theories suggest that to upgrade and gain differentiation and brand advantage abroad, Chinese firms should develop a new set of capabilities to operate in diverse institutional environments and as a consequence strengthen their performance abroad (Cardoza & Fornes, 2013; Child & Rodrigues, 2005; Fornes et al., 2016) On the other hand, Mathews (2006), one of the authors who challenged Western-developed theories, explained that those firms which lack substantial prior resource in their home market, based their strategies on the Linkage, Leverage, and Learning (LLL) framework. The author emphasised the idea that traditional theories do not necessarily apply and that there might be the opportunity to adapt existing ones or even develop new ones All in all, although Chinese capabilities are still young, the literature shows that Chinese firms learn not only "through experience but also through knowledge transfers" (Lattemann et al., 2017, p. 155), but Chinese firms do possess dynamism and speed to absorb knowledge and practices, in the international context. The integration or the development of new capabilities, if needed, would depend on their visionary leadership, their creative learning abilities, but also on a stronger international human resource management and a more global perspective

firms with very few studies available for EM firms in general and from China in particular (Fornes et al., 2021; Mellahi et al., 2010; Mutlu et al., 2015; Williamson et al., 2013; Wu, 2013a, 2013b). In addition, scarce attention has been paid to understanding the development of capabilities of Chinese firms and the role of the home institutional framework in shaping these capabilities, including marketing, in the international scene outside China and mainly the EU (Haasis & Liefner, 2019). Within this, few works introduce both formal and informal institutions into the analysis and combine IT and the RBV (Kim et al., 2019).

China presents a unique institutional environment. This is evident considering the two main formal and informal institutional elements defined above: (i) the strong role of the Chinese government (Angulo-Ruiz et al., 2019) reflected in new and still developing domestic market institutions such as the "weak legal and regulatory frameworks, ownership patterns, public funding access, or government participation in firms" (Cardoza et al., 2015, p. 4) or in the definition of internationalisation policies, and (ii) the influence of informal institutions, in particular guanxi (vertical and horizontal relationships or political and business relations). In addition, Chinese culture and philosophy also seem relevant elements that might explain the unique strategic mindset of Chinese managers. In fact, it has been shown that these elements strongly influence Chinese business culture, strategic decisions as well as the decision-making process of Chinese managers. In this sense, the institutional environment has a relevant impact on strategy formulation and therefore on the development of capabilities of Chinese firms both at domestic and international level; an influence that might be different depending on the type of Chinese firm. Different types of companies may face different institutional environments and therefore might adopt different strategic positions (Lin, 2010; Peterson Institute for International Economics, 2023).

In this context, it seems necessary to understand how Chinese multinationals will adapt their business strategies and decision-making processes, especially their marketing capabilities to new institutional environments, or define new ones, in order to develop successful business and marketing strategies that will provide sustainable competitive advantage in the international marketplace. On the one hand, it might seem that strategy implementation, in particular the decisions from Chinese managers about marketing capabilities, would be unworkable or might become a challenge for Chinese firms competing in the EU (Liu, 2015). However, on the other hand, it would be interesting to analyse whether this uniqueness or "Chinese-ness" might be a unique capability explaining the success of many Chinese firms on the international scene. Following these ideas, the present study will focus on Chinese multinationals with domestic and further international experience, meaning that born globals (Lin et al., 2016) are not part of the study.

In this sense, the present study will attempt to address the following question:

> Q: How does the Chinese domestic business environment shape the development of capabilities, including marketing, of firms going abroad?

Within this, two sub-questions are identified:

> Qa: How do Chinese domestic institutional elements (formal and informal) influence the definition and development of marketing capabilities in the domestic market?
> Qb: To what extent are the marketing capabilities developed in the domestic market applicable and transferred to international markets with different institutional environments (mainly the EU)?

Combining Institutional Theory and the Resource-Based View of the firm, the main aim of this book is to analyse and understand how home formal and informal institutional elements (mainly government support, personal relations, and the Chinese culture and philosophy) influence the definition and development of Chinese firms' marketing capabilities at home, and whether and how these capabilities are applicable by these firms in a different environment (in this case the European Union (EU)). For this purpose, the study will analyse how Chinese institutional elements (formal and informal) influence the definition and development of marketing capabilities and how this differs depending on the type of company, providing useful insights about the Chinese business and institutional environment. Within this, the study will seek to understand how managers from different types of Chinese firms interpret marketing capabilities and define them in their companies. Following this idea, the influence of the domestic institutional environment in the application, development, and/or definition of marketing capabilities will also be critically analysed, providing an in-depth understanding of Chinese firms' business strategies, objectives, and competitive advantages at home and abroad in different environments. Finally, the study will analyse the marketing capabilities of Chinese firms transferred abroad, or the development, eventually, of new capabilities for international markets under different institutional environments, helping practitioners, academics, and policymakers to understand the rapid rise of Chinese multinationals in and outside China.

References

Adams, P., Freitas, I. M. B., & Fontana, R. (2019). Strategic orientation, innovation performance and the moderating influence of marketing management. *Journal of Business Research, 97*, 129–140.

Alon, I., Anderson, J., Ziaul Haque, M., & Ho, A. (2018). A review of the internationalization of Chinese enterprises. *Asia Pacific Journal of Management*. https://doi.org/10.1007/s10490-018-9597-5

Alqahtani, N., & Uslay, C. (2020). Entrepreneurial marketing and firm performance: Synthesis and conceptual development. *Journal of Business Research, 113*, 62–71.

Altamira, M., Fornes, G., & Mendez, A. (2022). Chinese institutions and international expansion within the BRI: Firm capabilities of Chinese companies in the European Union. *Asia Pacific Business Review*. https://doi.org/10.1080/13602381.2022.2093520

Angulo-Ruiz, F., Pergelova, A., & Wei, W. (2019). How does home government influence the internationalization of emerging market firms? The mediating role of strategic intents to internationalize. *International Journal of Emerging Markets, 14*(1). https://doi.org/10.1108/IJoEM-08-2017-0274

Barney, J. (1991). Firm resources and sustained competitive advantage. *Journal of Management, 17*(1), 99–120.
Barney, J., & Zhang, S. (2009). The future of Chinese management research: A theory of Chinese management versus a Chinese theory of management. *Management and Organization Review, 5*(1), 15–28.
Barrales-Molina, V., Martínez-López, F. J., & Gázquez-Abad, J. (2013). Dynamic marketing capabilities: Toward an integrative framework. *International Journal of Management Reviews*. https://doi.org/10.1111/ijmr.12026
Bellabona, P., & Spigarelli, F. (2007). Moving from open door to go global: China goes on the world stage. *International Journal of Chinese Culture and Management, 1*(1), 93–107. https://doi.org/10.1504/IJCCM.2007.016170
Boisot, M., & Meyer, M. (2008). Which way through the open door? Reflections on the internationalization of Chinese firms. *Management and Organization Review, 4*(3), 349–365.
Buckley, J. (2018). Internalisation theory and outward direct investment by emerging market multinationals. *Management International Review, 58*, 195–224. https://doi.org/10.1007/s11575-017-0320-4
Buckley, P., Clegg, J., Cross, A., Liu, X., Voss, H., & Zheng, P. (2007). The determinants of Chinese outward foreign direct investment. *Journal of International Business Studies, 38*(4), 499–518.
Buckley, P., Clegg, J., Voss, H., Cross, A., Liu, X., & Zheng, P. (2018). A retrospective and agenda for future research on Chinese outward foreign direct investment. *Journal of International Business Studies, 49*(1), 4–23.
Cardoza, G., & Fornes, G. (2011). National and international expansion of Chinese SMEs: A different story? In X. Fu (Ed.), *China's role in global economic recovery*. Routledge.
Cardoza, G., & Fornes, G. (2013). The international expansion of China's small and medium-sized business: Status today and future outlook. *Journal of Chinese Entrepreneurship, 5*(3), 252–273.
Cardoza, G., Fornes, G., Li, P., Xu, N., & Xu, S. (2014). China goes global: Public policies' influence on Small and Medium-size Enterprises' international expansion. *Asia Pacific Business Review*. https://doi.org/10.1080/13602381.2013.876183
Cardoza, G., Fornes, G., Li, P., Xu, N., & Xu, S. (2015). China goes global: Public policies' influence on small- and medium-sized enterprises' international expansion. *Asia Pacific Business Review, 21*(2), 188–210.
Cardoza, G., Fornes, G., & Xu, N. (2011). *Institutional determinants of Chinese SMEs' internationalization: The case of Jiangsu Province*. Paper presented at the Chinese Economic Association, Dublin.

Chen, C., Chen, X., & Huang, S. (2013). Chinese guanxi: An integrative review and new directions for future research. *Management and Organization Review, 9*(1), 167–207.

Chen, X., & Wu, J. (2011). Do different guanxi types affect capability building differently? A contingency view. *Industrial Marketing Management, 40*(4), 581–592.

Chenyan, Z., Wei, Z., Junjie, H., & Mario, K. (2022). The role of government policies in explaining the internationalization of Chinese firms. *Journal of Business Research, 141*, 552–563. https://doi.org/10.1016/j.jbusres.2021.11.056

Child, J., & Marinova, S. (2014). The role of contextual combinations in the globalization of Chinese firms. *Management and Organization Review, 10*(3), 347–371.

Child, J., & Rodrigues, S. (2005). The internationalization of Chinese firms: A case for theoretical extension? *Management and Organization Review, 1*(3), 381–410.

Cui, L., & Jiang, F. (2012). State ownership effect on firms' FDI ownership decisions under institutional pressure: A study of Chinese outward-investing firms. *Journal of International Business Studies, 43*(3), 264–284.

D'Oria, L., Crook, T., Ketchen Jr., D., Sirmon, D., & Wright, M. (2021). The evolution of resource-based inquiry: A review and meta-analytic integration of the strategic resources–actions–performance pathway. *Journal of Management, 47*(6), 1383–1429.

Darroch, J., Miles, M. P., Jardine, A., & Cook, E. (2004). The 2004 AMA definition of marketing and its relationship to a market orientation: An extension of Cook, Rayburn, & Abercrombie (1992). *Journal of Marketing Theory and Practice, 12*(4), 29–38.

Davis, L., & North, D. (1971). *Institutional change and American economic growth*. Cambridge University Press.

Day, G. (1994). The capabilities of market-driven organizations. *Journal of Marketing, 58*, 37–51. https://doi.org/10.1177/002224299405800404

Day, G. (2011). Closing the marketing capabilities gap. *Journal of Marketing, 75*, 183–195.

Day, G. (2013). Closing the marketing capability gap. *Journal of Marketing, 75*(4), 183–195.

Deng, P. (2009). Why do Chinese firms tend to acquire strategic assets in international expansion? *Journal of World Business, 44*(1), 74–84.

Deng, P. (2012). The internationalization of Chinese firms: A critical review and future research. *International Journal of Management Reviews, 14*(4). https://doi.org/10.1111/j.1468-2370.2011.00323.x

Deng, P., Yang, X., Wang, L., & Doyle, B. (2017). Chinese investments in advanced economies: Opportunities and challenges. *Thunderbird International Business Review, 59*(4). https://doi.org/10.1002/tie.21903

DeSarbo, W., Di Benedetto, C., Jedidi, K., & Song, M. (2006). Identifying sources of heterogeneity for empirically deriving strategic types: A constrained finite-mixture structural equation methodology. *Management Science, 52*(6), 909–924.

Du, J., & Zhang, Y. (2018). Does One belt one road initiative promote Chinese overseas direct investment? *China Economic Review, 47*(C), 189–205.

Elango, B., & Pattnaik, C. (2007). Building capabilities for international operations through networks: A study of Indian firms. *Journal of International Business Studies, 38*(4), 541–555.

Estrin, S., & Prevezer, M. (2011). The role of informal institutions in corporate governance: Brazil, Russia, India, and China compared. *Asia Pacific Journal of Management, 28*(1), 41–67.

European Union Chamber of Commerce in China. (2020). *The road less travelled: European involvement in China's Belt and Road Initiative*. https://reconasia.csis.org/road-less-travelled/

Fornes, G., & Cardoza, G. (2018). Internationalization of Chinese SMEs: The perception of disadvantages of foreignness. *Emerging Markets Finance & Trade*, 1–20. https://doi.org/10.1080/1540496X.2018.1518218

Fornes, G., Cardoza, G., & Altamira, M. (2016). *Informal structures and practices in the national and international expansion of SMEs from emerging markets: Evidence from Brazil and China*. Paper presented at the Academy of Management annual conference, Anaheim.

Fornes, G., Cardoza, G., & Altamira, M. (2021). Do informal business and political relations help SMEs from emerging markets in their national and international expansion? Evidence from Brazil and China. *International Journal of Emerging Markets, 17*(8). https://doi.org/10.1108/IJOEM-01-2020-0058

Fornes, G., Lopez, B., Bierens de Haan, M., & Blanch, J. (2018). Best practice example of CSR and S&E engagement in emerging economies: Analysis of a case study based in China. *Journal of Asian Business Studies, 13*(4). https://doi.org/10.1108/JABS-08-2017-0120

Ge, G. L., & Ding, D. Z. (2005). Market orientation, competitive strategy and firm performance: An empirical study of Chinese firms. *Journal of Global Marketing, 18*(3–4), 115–142.

Guenzi, P., & Troilo, G. (2006). Developing marketing capabilities for customer value creation through Marketing-Sales integration. *Industrial Marketing Management, 35*(8), 974–988.

Gundlach, G., & Wilkie, W. (2009). The American Marketing Association's new definition of marketing: Perspective and commentary on the 2007 revision. *Journal of Public Policy & Marketing, 28*(2), 259–264.

Haasis, T., & Liefner, I. (2019). Reviewing the research on the internationalization of Chinese firms: Thematic expansion, new impulses and potential future development. *International Journal of Emerging Markets, 14*(1), 24–50.

He, S., Khan, Z., Lew, Y., & Fallon, G. (2019). Technological innovation as a source of Chinese multinationals' firm-specific advantages and internationalization. *International Journal of Emerging Markets, 14*(4). https://doi.org/10.1108/IJOEM-02-2017-0059

He, X., K., B., & Filatotchev, I. (2012). Resource-based and institutional perspectives on export channel selection and export performance. *Journal of Management*. https://doi.org/10.1177/0149206312445926

He, X., & Wei, Y. (2011). Linking market orientation to international market selection and international performance. *International Business Review, 20*(5), 535–546.

Hernandez, E., & Guillen, M. (2018). What's theoretically novel about emerging market multinationals? *Journal of International Business Studies, 49*(1), 24–33.

Hofstede, G. (1981). Culture and organisations. *International Studies of Management and Organization, 10*(4), 15–41.

Hong, J., Wang, C., & Kafouros, M. (2015). The role of the state in explaining the internationalization of emerging market enterprises. *British Journal of Management, 26*, 45–62. https://doi.org/10.1111/1467-8551.12059

Hoskisson, R., Eden, L., Lau, C., & Wright, M. (2000). Strategy in emerging economies. *Academy of Management Journal, 43*(3), 249–267.

Huang, Y. (2016). Understanding China's Belt & Road Initiative: Motivation, framework and assessment. *China Economic Review, 40*(C), 314–321.

Hult, G., Ketchen, D., & Slater, S. (2005). Market orientation and performance: An integration of disparate approaches. *Strategic Management Journal, 26*(12), 1173–1181.

Johanson, J., & Vahlne, J. (1977). The internationalization process of the firm—A model of knowledge development and increasing foreign market commitments. *Journal of International Business Studies, 8*(1), 23–32.

Ju, M., Fung, H., & Mano, H. (2013). Firm capabilities and performance: Institutional perspective on foreign and local firms in China. *The Chinese Economy, 46*(5), 86–104.

Kamboj, S., & Rhaman, Z. (2015). Marketing capabilities and firm performance: Literature review and future research agenda. *International Journal of Productivity and Performance Management International Review, 64*(8), 1041–1067.

Katsikeas, C., Samiee, S., & Theodosiou, M. (2006). Strategy fit and performance consequences of international marketing standardization. *Strategic Management Journal, 27*(9), 867–890.

Kaufmann, L., & Roesch, J.-F. (2012). Constraints to building and deploying marketing capabilities by emerging market firms in advanced markets. *Journal of International Marketing, 20*(4), 1–24.

Khanna, T., & Palepu, K. (1997). Why focused strategies may be wrong for emerging markets. *Harvard Business Review, 4*(75), 3–10.

Khanna, T., & Palepu, K. (2010). *Winning in emerging markets: A road map for strategy and execution.* Harvard Business School Publishing Corporation.

Kim, K., Lattemann, C., Park, I., & Zhang, W. (2019). New international business theories for China goes global? The importance of institutions, innovativeness and learning. *International Journal of Emerging Markets, 14*(1), 2–5. https://doi.org/10.1108/ijoem-01-2019-574

Lattemann, C., & Alon, I. (2015). The rise of Chinese multinationals: A strategic threat or an economic opportunity? *Georgetown Journal of International Affairs, 16*(1), 168–175.

Lattemann, C., Alon, I., Spigarelli, F., & Marinova, S. (2017). Dynamic embeddedness in Chinese firm internationalization. *Thunderbird International Business Review, 59*(4), 547–559.

Li, S., & Li, S. (2000). The road to capitalism: Competition and institutional change in China. *Journal of Comparative Economics, 28*(2), 269–292.

Lin, S., Mercier-Suissa, C., & Salloum, C. (2016). The Chinese born Globals of the Zhejiang Province: A study on the key factors for their rapid internationalization. *Journal of International Enterpreneurship, 14*(1), 75–95.

Lin, X. (2010). State versus private MNCs from China: Initial conceptualizations. *International Marketing Review, 27*(3), 366–380.

Liu, H. (2015). *The Chinese strategic mind*. Edward Elgar Publishing Limited.

Liu, J., & Su, J. (2013). *How does market orientation affect product innovation in China's manufacturing industry: The contingent value of dynamic capabilities*. Paper presented at the International Conference on Education Technology and Management Science.

Luo, Y., & Child, J. (2015). A composition-based view of firm growth. *Management and Organization Review, 11*(3), 379–411.

Ma, H., Wu, X., Yan, L., Huang, H., Wu, H., Xiong, J., & Zhang, J. (2018). Strategic plan of "Made in China 2025" and its implementation. In *Analysing the impacts of industry 4.0 in modern business environments*. IGI Global.

Mathews, J. (2006). Dragon multinationals: New players in 21st century globalization. *Asia Pacific Journal of Management, 23*(1), 5–27.

Mellahi, K., Demirbag, M., Tamer Cavusgil, S., & Danis, W. (2010). Marketing strategies of MNCs for emerging markets: Internationalisation and market entry mode. *International Marketing Review, 27*(2), 267–271.

Meyer, K., Estrin, S., Kumar Bhaumik, S., & Peng, M. (2009). Institutions, resources, and entry strategies in emerging economies. *Strategic Management Journal, 30*(1), 61–80.

Meyer, K., & Peng, M. (2016). Theoretical foundations of emerging economy business research. *Journal of International Business Studies, 47*, 3–22. https://doi.org/10.1057/jibs.2015.34

Meyer, K. E. (2004). Perspectives on multinational enterprises in emerging economies. *Journal of International Business Studies, 35*(4), 259–276.

Morgan, N. (2012). Marketing and business performance. *Journal of the Academy of Marketing Science, 40*(1), 102–119.

Morgan, N., Douglas, W., & Mason, C. (2009a). Market orientation, marketing capabilities and firm performance. *Strategic Management Journal, 30*, 909–920. https://doi.org/10.1002/smj.764

Morgan, N., Slotegraaf, R., & Vorhies, D. (2009b). Linking marketing capabilities with profit growth. *International Journal of Research in Marketing, 26*, 284–296.

Mutlu, C., Zhan, W., Peng, M., & Lin, Z. (2015). Competing in (and out of) transition economies. *Asia Pacific Journal of Management, 32*(3), 571–596.

Narula, R. (2012). Do we need different frameworks to explain infant MNEs from developing countries? *Global Strategy Journal, 2*(3). https://doi.org/10.1111/j.2042-5805.2012.01035.x

Nee, V., & Opper, S. (2012). *Capitalism from below: Markets and institutional change in China*. Harvard University Press.

Noble, C., Rajiv, K., & Kumar, A. (2002). Market orientation and alternative strategic orientations: A longitudinal assessment of performance implications. *Journal of Marketing, 66*(4), 25–39.

North, D. (1990). *Institutions, institutional change, and economic performance.* Cambridge University Press.

OECD. (2018). China's Belt and Road Initiative in the global trade, investment and finance landscape. In *OECD Business and Finance Outlook 2018.* OECD Publishing.

Oliveira, R., Menzies, J., Borgia, D., & Figueira, S. (2017). Outward foreign direct investment from emerging countries: Theoretical extension and evidence from China. *The International Trade Journal, 31*(5), 402–428.

Otto, A. S., Szymanski, D. M., & Varadarajan, R. (2020). Customer satisfaction and firm performance: Insights from over a quarter century of empirical research. *Journal of the Academy of Marketing Science, 48*, 543–564.

Park, S., & Luo, Y. (2001). Guanxi and organizational dynamics: Organizational networking in Chinese firms. *Strategic Management Journal, 22*(5), 455–477.

Parmentola, A. (2017). Why Chinese companies go abroad? A theoretical model to explain the drivers of the internationalisation strategy of Chinese MNEs. *International Business Research, 10*(10), 82–93.

Pasa, M., & Shugan, S. (1996). The value of marketing expertise. *Management Science, 42*(3), 370–388.

Paul, J., & Benito, G. (2018). A review of research on outward foreign direct investment from emerging countries, including China: What do we know, how do we know and where should we be heading? *Asia Pacific Business Review, 24*(1), 90–115.

Peng, M. (2002). Towards an institution-based view of business strategy. *Asia Pacific Journal of Management, 19*, 251–267.

Peng, M. (2012). The global strategy of emerging multinationals from China. *Global Strategy Journal*. https://doi.org/10.1002/gsj.1030

Peng, M., Lebedev, S., Vlas, C., Wang, J., & Shay, J. (2018). The growth of the firm in (and out of) emerging economies. *Asia Pacific Journal of Management, 35*(4), 829–857.

Peng, M., Lee, S., & Wang, D. (2005). What determines the scope of the firm over time? A focus on institutional relatedness. *Academy of Management Review, 30*(3), 622–633.

Peng, M., & Luo, Y. (2000). Managerial ties and firm performance in a transition economy: The nature of a micro-macro link. *Academy of Management Journal, 43*(3), 486–501.

Peng, M., Wang, D., & Jiang, Y. (2008). An institution-based view of international business strategy: A focus on emerging economies. *Journal of International Business Studies, 39*, 920–936.

Peterson Institute for International Economics. (2023). China's state vs. private company tracker: Which sector dominates? *PIIE*. https://www.piie.com/research/piie-charts/chinas-state-vs-private-company-tracker-which-sector-dominates

PRC, T. S. C. (2017). *Made in China 2025*. http://english.gov.cn/2016special/madeinchina2025/

Ramamurti, R. (2012). What is really different about emerging market multinationals? *Global Strategy Journal, 2*(1), 41–47.

Ramamurti, R., & Hillemann, J. (2018). What is "Chinese" about Chinese multinationals? *Journal of International Business Studies, 49*(1), 34–48.

Rauch, J., & Trindale, V. (2002). Ethnic Chinese networks in international trade. *The Review of Economics and Statistics, 84*(1), 116–130.

Rottig, D. (2016). Institutions and emerging markets: Effects and implications for multinational corporations. *International Journal of Emerging Markets, 11*(1), 2–17.

Rugman, A., & Li, J. (2007). Will China's multinationals succeed globally or regionally? *European Management Journal, 25*(5), 333–343.

Scott, W. (1995). *Institutions and organizations*. Sage.

Shou, Z., Chen, J., Zhu, W., & Yang, L. (2012). Firm capability and performance in China: The moderating role of guanxi and institutional forces in domestic and foreign contexts. *Journal of Business Research, 67*(2), 77–82.

Slater, S., & Narver, J. (1993). Product-market strategy and performance: An analysis of the Miles and Snow strategy types. *European Journal of Marketing, 27*(2), 33–51.

Sun, F. (2017). Relationship versus transaction marketing in China: An institutional approach. *Business and Management Studies, 3*(2), 47–60.

Surdu, I., Mellahi, K., & Glaister, K. (2018). Emerging market multinationals' international equity-based entry mode strategies: Review of theoretical foundations and future directions. *International Marketing Review, 35*(2), 342–359. https://doi.org/10.1108/IMR-10-2015-0228

Tajeddini, K., & Ratten, V. (2020). The moderating effect of brand orientation on inter-firm market orientation and performance. *Journal of Strategic Marketing, 28*(3), 194–224.

Teece, D., Pisano, G., & Shuen, A. (1997). Dynamic capabilities and strategic management. *Strategic Management Journal, 19*(7), 509–533.

Tracey, P., & Phillips, N. (2011). Entrepreneurship in emerging markets: Strategies for new venture creation in uncertain institutional contexts. *Management International Review, 51*(1), 23–39.

Tripsas, M. (1997). Unraveling the process of creative destruction: Complementary assets and incumbent survival in the typesetter industry. *Strategic Management Journal, 18*(Summer Special Issue), 119–142.

Wang, B., & Gao, K. (2019). Forty years development of China's outward foreign direct investment: Retrospect and the challenges ahead. *China & World Economy, 27*(3), 1–24. https://doi.org/10.1111/cwe.12278

Wang, C., Hong, J., Kafouros, M., & Baoteng, A. (2012). What drives outward FDI of Chinese firms? Testing the explanatory power of three theoretical frameworks. *International Business Review, 21*, 425–438.

Wernerfelt, B. (1984). A resource-based view of the firm. *Strategic Management Journal, 5*(2), 171–180.

Williamson, P., Ramamurti, R., Fleury, A., & Leme Fleury, M. (2013). *The competitive advantage of emerging market multinationals*. Cambridge University Press.

Wright, M., Filatotchev, I., Hoskisson, R., & Peng, M. (2005). Strategy research in emerging economies: Challenging the conventional wisdom. *Journal of Management Studies, 42*(1), 1–33. http://search.ebscohost.com/login.aspx?direct=true&db=buh&AN=15645292&site=ehost-live

Wu, J. (2013a). Diverse institutional environments and product innovation of emerging market firms. *Management International Review, 53*(1), 39–59.

Wu, J. (2013b). Marketing capabilities, institutional development, and the performance of emerging market firms: A multinational study. *International Journal of Research in Marketing, 30*(1), 36–45.

Yan, H., He, X., & Cheng, B. (2017). Managerial ties, market orientation, and export performance: Chinese firms experience. *Management and Organization Review, 13*(3), 611–638.

Yang, X., & Stoltenberg, C. (2014). A review of institutional influences on the rise of made-in-China multinationals. *International Journal of Emerging Markets, 9*(2). https://doi.org/10.1108/IJoEM-09-2012-0095

Yang, Y., Wang, Q., Zhu, H., & Wu, G. (2012). What are the effective strategic orientations for new product success under different environments? An empirical study of Chinese businesses. *Journal of Product Innovation Management, 29*(2), 166–179.

Yao, K. (2020). *What we know about China's 'dual circulation' economic strategy*. https://www.reuters.com/article/china-economy-transformation-explainer-idUSKBN2600B5

Yau, O. (1988). Chinese cultural values: Their dimensions and marketing implications. *European Journal of Maketing, 22*(5), 44–56.

Yau, O., Chan, T. S., & Lau, K. F. (2009). Influence of Chinese cultural values on consumer behavior. *Journal of International Consumer Marketing, 11*(1), 97–116.

Yi, J., Hong, J., Hsu, W., & Wang, C. (2017). The role of state ownership and institutions in the innovation performance of emerging market enterprises: Evidence from China. *Technovation, 62*(63), 4–13.

Zhang, M., Qian, G., Wheeler, J. V., & Kwon, J. (2015). Institutional effect on born global firms in China: The role of Sun Tzu's The Art of War strategies. *Journal of Asia Business Studies, 10*(1), 1–19.

Zou, L., Shen, J. H., Zhang, J., & Lee, C.-C. (2022). What is the rationale behind China's infrastructure investment under the Belt and Road Initiative. *Journal of Economic Surveys, 36*(3), 605–633. https://doi.org/10.1111/joes.12427

4

A Narrative Inquiry Strategy to Analyse Capabilities of Chinese Multinationals

4.1 Introduction

The following chapter explains how the analysis was carried out. First, it defines the research philosophy. Second, it explains the research design adopted and the strategy (Narrative Inquiry), following the objectives of the study. Third, the chapter continues with the sample selection process and data collection methods, with a focus on how narrative interviews were developed. Fourth, it explains the challenges addressed during the data analysis process. It ends with a detailed explanation of the data analysis process.

4.2 Research Philosophy. Social Constructivism

The research design of the study assumes that reality is socially constructed and subjective and that knowledge is only of significance when developed through interaction with others (Easterby-Smith et al., 2002; Polkinghorne, 1988; Saunders et al., 2003). These assumptions

M. Altamira, *Chinese Firms in the Global Market*, Palgrave Macmillan Asian Business Series, https://doi.org/10.1007/978-3-031-59227-0_4

are based on the fact that the author is part of what is being observed, focusing on the meaning, and understanding of what is experienced by the managers of the companies that are part of the study. Other reasons supporting these ontological and epistemological assumptions are: (i) the research follows an inductive approach aiming at developing theory after the analysis of data, (ii) conclusions of the research are expected to be based on the observations and interpretations of the data collected, (iii) this data collection is based on narratives that present the story or personal experience of the interviewees on the topic being studied, and (iv) data analysis is developed through the research process, rather than being a separate activity (Polkinghorne, 1988; Saunders et al., 2003).

4.3 Research Design and Strategy

4.3.1 Narrative Inquiry

Following this framework, a suitable qualitative strategy should be defined in order to address the questions presented in Chapter 3. The table below shows the main characteristics and most relevant differences among the five main research strategies in qualitative inquiry according to Creswell (2009) in terms of the focus of the research and data collection methods (Table 4.1):

The selected research strategy should help the author to understand and analyse, from the Chinese managers' experiences working in the firms part of the study, the following ideas based on the objectives of the study as well as on the questions this study intends to address:

a. the Chinese domestic institutional environment where Chinese managers develop their decision-making processes, and the impact of the perceived relevant institutional elements, formal and informal, on them, especially on the definition and development of marketing capabilities,

Table 4.1 Characteristics and differences among qualitative research strategies

Research strategy	Focus of the research	Data collection method
Ethnography	Context and culture setting	Observations and interviews
Narrative Inquiry	Personal and individual experiences and sequence of events	Personal stories, narratives
Phenomenological approach	How a phenomenon is experienced and perceived at the time that it develops	Interviews
Grounded theory	Develop theory after the collection and analysis of data	Interviews and coding process
Case studies	The study of a case or cases that address a particular situation	Interviews, documents, reports, observations

i. within this, the definition and development of the marketing capabilities in the domestic market and how managers interpret these marketing capabilities, and

b. the definition and development of marketing capabilities in different business environments, mainly Western markets (the EU in particular), and the influence of the home institutional environment, as a result of the internationalisation expansion of the company.

Based on these ideas, a process and sequence of events related to the domestic development and further internationalisation expansion of each of the companies, described from the participant personal experience, will be key to the study. It is in this context that the vehicle selected to develop this work among the qualitative strategies described in Table 4.1 above is Narrative Inquiry.

Narratives are the representation of stories and Narrative Inquiry, the "storytelling methodology" (Kim, 2015, p. 118) through which the researcher studies the narratives based on the personal experiences of the storytellers. Several scholars have recognised the relevance of this research strategy in the field of Management and Organisational change (see for example Boje, 1994, 2001; Boyce, 1996; Gertsen & Soderberg, 2011; Rhodes and Brown, 2005). As mentioned by Rhodes and Brown (2005),

Narrative Inquiry provides a valuable source of insight in the context of organisations where stories are analysed in terms of how different people, in this case Chinese managers, subjectively make sense of the strategic choices, the definition and development of marketing capabilities in the present study, in relation to their organisations more broadly. In this sense, Narrative Inquiry is useful to bring the subjective element to the analysis of the study by listening to, documenting, analysing, and reporting the different stories that interviewees tell about their organisations and the processes in which they are involved (Rhodes & Brown, 2005). In addition, this type of strategy helps to recognise and see organisational change as a process to understand the paradoxes and complex causal relationships found in organisations rather than viewing them as homogeneous. This approach also considers different possible meanings of organisational action focusing on "the plurality of different possible stories and storytellers" (Rhodes & Brown, 2005, p. 177).

In international business research, there is a growing interest in recognising the value of qualitative methods and in claiming their place in the field lost in recent years over a more commonly used positivist approach (Birkinshaw et al., 2011; Fainshmidt et al., 2020). This represents new opportunities to develop Narrative Inquiry in international business and marketing studies (Gertsen & Soderberg, 2011; Liu et al., 2018). As shown by Gertsen and Soderberg (2011), stories are an "underutilized source of data in international business research, where quantitative approaches are dominant" (Gertsen & Soderberg, 2011, p. 802). The authors, based on their research about Intercultural Collaboration between a Danish and a Chinese company, showed that although the analysis of individual narratives is time-consuming, they provide a valuable insight difficult to obtain through other types of methods on organisational realities, individual experiences and personal interpretations while revealing ways in which these may correspond or differ among different actors. In addition, narratives about global strategies and their definition and development from managers and employees located in different environments offer "an understanding of the challenges headquarters meet when trying to build a common understanding of the global strategy and a commitment to develop it into new practices" (Gertsen & Soderberg, 2011, p. 802). Therefore, it seems that international business research might offer relevant material in the form of stories that are fundamental to the understanding of strategy implementation across borders.

4.3.2 Narrative Genre

The narrative genre is the type of form the text or collected data would take. Kim (2015) defined narrative research genres as the form that a Narrative Inquiry text would take, which may include: (i) autobiography, (ii) autoethnography, (iii) biographical research, (iv) oral history, (v), life story, (vi) personal growth life story, and (vii) arts-based narrative research. Thinking about the narrative genre or form helps the researcher to think about the final research text; this is how the storyteller represents the data or the collected stories. The definition of the narrative genre is an important step in the research design as it makes the analysis more distinct from other qualitative researches, and more importantly, it helps the researcher to determine the type of data, the method for data collection as well as the written form of the final research text (Kim, 2015; Riessman, 2005).

In this context, the present study fits within the biographical research genre. In other words, the study collects stories from others. This type of research focuses on personal lived experiences and on the meanings the storytellers give to their stories. More specifically in the context of the present research, it analyses the stories that storytellers, or the Chinese managers, tell from their personal point of view and experience about:

a. the Chinese domestic institutional environment where they develop their decision-making processes, and the impact of the perceived relevant institutional elements, formal and informal, on them, especially on the definition and development of marketing capabilities,
    i. within this, the definition and development of the marketing capabilities in the domestic market, and of how they interpret these capabilities, and

b. the definition and development of marketing capabilities in different business environments, mainly Western markets (the EU in particular), and the influence of the home institutional environment, as a result of the internationalisation expansion of the company.

Unfolding, therefore, sequences of events and experiences over time (Pentland, 1999), the resulting stories would be a source of insight in the context of the particular organisation where stories are analysed in terms of how Chinese managers subjectively: (i) perceive and interpret the influence of relevant institutional elements in their firm's definition and development of marketing capabilities, and understand marketing capabilities in the domestic market, and (ii) interpret the influence of the Chinese institutional environment on the definition and development of marketing capabilities outside China, mainly in the EU, while they identify the need to adapt, or otherwise, the marketing capabilities as a result of operating in a different institutional market.

Moreover, Narrative Inquiry and biographical research are concerned not only with the content of the narrative text but also with the social, historical, and cultural context in which stories are told and the influence of different groups and actors on the act of narration (Kim, 2015); that is, in the present study, with the particular institutional context that may influence the stories. This is especially relevant to the study because it has been shown that Chinese managers' decisions and therefore their experiences within their organisations and their resulting stories might be shaped by the institutional environment. It is expected that these narratives would help to develop explanations and interpretation that will lead to further theory. As mentioned in the previous chapter, a narrative is also a story that describes a process and connects cause and effect, being the core of good theory, that is, narrative texts contain indicators for an underlying process theory (Pentland, 1999).

4.4 Sample Selection

As explained above, the focus of this study is to develop theory rather than to test it, so it seems that theoretical sampling is the most appropriate technique for sample selection (Eisenhardt & Graebner, 2007). Theoretical sampling is a non-probability purposive sample technique (Saunders et al., 2003) that involves cases being selected because they are particularly suitable and convenient for the purpose of the work as well as for theoretical reasons, such as "revelation of an unusual phenomenon, replication of findings from other cases, contrary replication, elimination of alternative explanations, and elaboration of the emergent theory" (Eisenhardt & Graebner, 2007, p. 27). In addition, multiple case selection also allows a robust, generalizable, and testable theory to be built. Thus, in the particular context of the study, the goal of theoretical sampling is to extend emergent theory (Eisenhardt, 1989). Also, the "polar type" approach, or the selection of extreme cases, is followed to select the sample as it is useful to observe contrasting patterns across the sample and to recognise clear patterns of the central constructs and logic of the phenomenon under study (Eisenhardt & Graebner, 2007).

A two-stage sample is defined for the study. In a first stage, a preliminary analysis with a first sample is developed, and gaps are identified, while in a second stage additional companies to fill these gaps are selected and a further analysis complementing the first one is developed. In the first stage, the criteria to select the sample are based on the elements that are identified in the analysis and development of the theoretical framework to be relevant to the phenomenon under study. In this sense, the relevant role and the influence of the Chinese government in the business environment in terms of ownership patterns is identified as one key characteristic of the Chinese business environment with a relevant impact on strategy implementation. As introduced above, different types of companies and therefore Chinese managers taking decisions within the company may face different institutional environments and therefore might adopt different strategic positions (Lin, 2010). In addition, the role of the government in specific industries also seems relevant: Chinese authorities have been supporting strategic industries linked to their economic and political goals. Also, as mentioned in Chapter 2, the work is focused on Chinese firms that have internationalised or are internationalising to the EU. So, in this context, and with the purpose of finding patterns, similarities, and differences, companies in the sample represent a balanced combination of the following five criteria. Approximately 400 firms are currently in the EU fulfilling these criteria (Amendolagine et al., 2017; CEIC, 2020):

a. Types of firms:
   i. State-Owned Enterprises (SOEs): firms ultimately owned by the public and the domestic government who exercise the ownership rights and decisions (OECD, 2018),
   ii. National Champions (State-Owned National Champions (SO NCs) and Private National Champions (Private NCs)): firms aiming at supporting the government's strategic aims while in return receiving easier access to sources of finance and preferential contract bidding. Usually, SO NCs in particular hold a monopoly status in protected industries. These firms are usually state-owned, especially in China, but several are still in private hands (Hemphill & White III, 2013), but with a strong influence from the government, and
   iii. Other Private Firms (OPFs): firms privately owned.
b. Industries.
c. Enough experience of the firm in the EU. The experience abroad of the firms in the EU in number of years is also considered in order to test both the definition and the development of the capabilities and how they contribute to a sustainable competitive advantage abroad. In order to be significantly representative for the purpose of the study, firms should have at least two years' experience of operating in the European environment. All firms should have also developed enough experience in the domestic market before going abroad so the development of home marketing capabilities can be analysed; that is, Chinese born globals are not part of the present study.

d. Sales in the EU. % of sales in the EU is also considered. Firms should have a significant presence and activity in the EU, so to be significantly representative for the purpose of the work, firms should have at least 5% of sales in the EU.
e. Not be resource-seeking, in order to understand and test the marketing function of the firm.

Moreover, the work is focused on personal experiences and interpretations. As such, the profile of the participant is key, especially when dealing with Narrative Inquiry, in which interpretations, opinions, and points of view are at the core of the study. In this sense, participants should be Chinese managers from Chinese companies involved in the decisions regarding marketing in international markets but with enough experience in the domestic market as well. More specifically, they should have participated in the definition of the marketing strategy or have worked in the marketing department and have been involved in the international expansion of the firm to the EU, ensuring they have good knowledge about both markets. In this context, having the necessary business insights and knowledge is also ensured. Activities in other markets such as Latin America or other Asian countries from some companies in the sample are also considered in order to compare, contrast, and extend the findings. Finally, a good level of conversational English or Spanish (the author has a long experience working in Spain involved in projects with China) is required, as interviews are developed in these languages; the author does not speak Chinese, so in this sense the collaboration of a professional Chinese interpreter is also considered in some situations in which the participant has mentioned not feeling completely comfortable telling a story in English.

Following this framework, in a first stage a sample of twenty companies and an advisor for the Shanghainese government is selected. After a preliminary data analysis, the author identifies gaps and a second sample of nineteen additional companies (forty in total, 10% of the total population) is selected in order to fill these gaps and complement the analysis.

From the forty participants, seven work for SOEs, six for SO NCs, seven for Private NCs, and twenty for OPFs. The advisor for the

Shanghai government is included because of his extensive experience working within the Shanghainese government and because he previously worked for several Chinese state-owned firms. Also, nineteen different industries are represented in the sample. Details of the sample can be seen in the table below. Names of the firms are not shown in order to preserve the agreed anonymity of the participants (Table 4.2).

4.5 Data Collection

Data is collected through in-depth semi-structured interviews. The main benefit to conducting qualitative interviews is to understand how participants construct their meaning and the significance of their situations from the "complex personal framework of beliefs and values which they have developed over their lives in order to help explain and predict events in their own world" (Easterby-Smith et al., 2002, p. 73); a definition that fits within the objectives of the study. Furthermore, in the context of Narrative Inquiry, narratives can be collected from different sources, such as observations or reports, but also through narrative interviews in the form of texts, further analysed through narrative analysis which considers their content, form, and context (Lieblich et al., 1998; Riessman, 2008). In this context, the data collection process is based on narrative interviews in addition to the collection of second-hand information of each of the companies which is accessed through the Internet.

The intended focus of the narrative interviews is twofold, following the objectives and questions of the study. First is the understanding of the interpretation of Chinese managers of the influence of relevant Chinese institutional elements (formal and informal) on the development of their firms' marketing capabilities. This will seek to understand the different institutional elements (formal and informal) relevant for Chinese managers from different types of companies, and how they interpret the marketing capabilities and help to define them in their companies in China, so they can be compared with the capabilities that might be developed abroad. Second is the understanding of the interpretation of Chinese managers of the influence of Chinese institutional elements (formal and informal) on the development of the firm's

Table 4.2 Companies and managers interviewed

Firm	Industry	Size (annual in millions of RMB)	% of sales outside China	Type of firm
Co1	Hospitality	50–200	less than 5	SOE
Co2	Education	50–200	25–40	SOE
Co3	Trading	more than 5000	15–25	SOE
Co4	Real State	more than 5000	25–40	SOE
Co5	Education	non-profit	40–60	SOE
Co6	Automotive	more than 5000	40–60	SOE
Co7	Construction	more than 5000	40–60	SOE
Co8	Advisor for the Shanghainese government	n/a	n/a	SOE
Co9	Airline	more than 5000	25–40	SO NC
Co10	Telecommunications	more than 5000	05–15	SO NC
Co11	Banking	more than 5000	05–15	SO NC
Co12	Technology	more than 5000	40–60	SO NC
Co13	Consumer electronics	more than 5000	40–60	SO NC
Co14	Telecommunications	more than 5000	40–60	SO NC
Co15	Consumer electronics	1000–5000	40–60	Private NC
Co16	Consumer electronics	more than 5000	40–60	Private NC
Co17	Conglomerate	more than 5000	40–60	Private NC
Co18	Automotive	more than 5000	40–60	Private NC
Co19	Conglomerate	more than 5000	25–40	Private NC
Co20	Automotive	more than 5000	40–60	Private NC
Co21	Consumer electronics	1000–5000	40–60	Private NC
Co22	Technology	50–200	less than 5	OPFs
Co23	Technology	less than 50	less than 5	OPFs
Co24	Trading	less than 50	more than 75	OPFs
Co25	Fine Chemicals	more than 5000	more than 75	OPFs
Co26	Fashion	less than 50	25–40	OPFs
Co27	Supply Chain Services	1000–5000	05–15	OPFs
Co28	Consultancy and Manufacturing	1000–5000	40–60	OPFs
Co29	Trading	1000–5000	40–60	OPFs

(continued)

Table 4.2 (continued)

Firm	Industry	Size (annual in millions of RMB)	% of sales outside China	Type of firm
Co30	Consultancy and Manufacturing	200–500	40–60	OPFs
Co31	Trading	1000–5000	40–60	OPFs
Co32	Technology	Confidential	Confidential	OPFs
Co33	Technology	less than 50	40–60	OPFs
Co34	Technology	50–200	40–60	OPFs
Co35	Fashion	50–200	25–40	OPFs
Co36	FMCG	Confidential	Confidential	OPFs
Co37	Education	50–200	40–60	OPFs
Co38	Manufacturing and supplier	less than 50	15–25	OPFs
Co39	Consumer electronics	1000–5000	25–40	OPFs
Co40	FMCG	50–200	less than 5	OPFs

marketing capabilities outside China, in different institutional environments, mainly in the EU. That is, interviews would be divided into two different consecutive stories following the international expansion of the firm, representing two different narratives for analysis. Each interview is developed following the model of Jovchelovitch and Bauer (2000) which defines the main phases of narrative interviews in the following table (Table 4.3):

In practice, first, a pre-designed interview protocol (not shared with the participant) is developed and used only for the author's personal guidance purposes. This protocol is based mainly on the different phases of development of a company, from being domestic, including how the marketing function is developed in China to become international and on ideas and premises analysed in the theoretical framework. This is useful for the author in order to keep in mind the different ideas and areas that should be addressed during the interview. In the preparation phase, the author explains the context of the study, while defining some key concepts relevant to the project but not self-evident for the participant (institutional elements, or marketing capabilities, for example), and the procedure of the interview or how the interview will be structured (for example, that the two parts should be differentiated: first the story of

Table 4.3 Phases of narrative interviews

Phases of the narrative interview	Rules for the interview
Preparation	Exploring the field Formulating *exmanent* questions (questions emerging from the researcher's background)
Initialisation	Formulation of the initial topic for narration. Use visual aids
Main narration	No interruptions Only non-verbal or paralinguistic encouragement to continue telling the story Wait for signals of the end
Questioning phase	Only question: what happened then? No opinion or attitude questions No arguing on contradictions Do not ask: Why? Go from *exmanent* to *immanent* questions (questions emerging from the story)
Small talk	Stop recording Only question: why? Write up notes immediately after the interview

the company in China and second, after the company decides to expand abroad).

Then, in the initialisation phase, an explanation of the initial topic for each of the phases is introduced, with simple words and sentences. In this sense, and in order to encourage the participant to start with the storytelling, the author emphasises the idea that she wants to hear his/her own story in the company from his/her own experience, from the cultural, business, and social context in which the firm operates in China (i.e., the institutional context) and its influence on the activity the company develops in China, to the marketing function of the firm, and continuing with the internationalisation expansion in the second story. For example, the author encourages the participant to start the storytelling by asking for his/her opinion about the perceived Chinese environment and how or to what extent this affects or has affected the natural development of the company in China since its inception. In this part of the interview, the role of the government and informal relations (guanxi) are introduced by the author. This will help the participant to better understand the meaning of institutional elements. Also, from the research point of view this will help to test the perceived influence of these elements identified deductively in the theoretical framework on the development of marketing capabilities and inductively understand more specific elements within them. This step is very important for the participant to understand the interview as a story.

A required scenario to facilitate the individual storytelling is also needed. For the participant to feel comfortable, the author emphasises the confidentiality of the data collected as well as the fact that he/she will be the only one with access to the information and that it will only be used for the purposes of the particular study. Showing empathy with the participant as well as interest in the story is key in order to facilitate continuous storytelling. During the interview (the narration phase), most of the time the author just listens or asks clarifying questions intended to stimulate the storytelling; for example, "And, what about marketing?", "Could you further develop this idea?", "Why did you or the company decide to go abroad?". The author also encourages the participant to give specific examples of his/her experience, while avoiding making references to the official story of the company as previously known from secondary sources. That is, the author does not reveal any previous knowledge about the company, avoiding opinion or attitude questions, as well as argument and contradictions. Once the participant shows signs that the story has ended, the author asks some further clarifying questions, always considering the protocol. After the interviews, the author should take notes as soon as possible about the relevant points found. Thirty-five interviews were developed face-to-face while five were carried out using the Internet (Skype or WeChat video call). Thanks to the technology, the author has had access to relevant companies not accessible any other way. However, communication difficulties are evident, especially because of poor internet connections which make it very complicated to maintain the flow of the stories. In these cases, interviews are expected to be longer and more clarifying questions are needed as well as higher efforts to encourage the storytelling. In any case, even if interaction is crucial in such a context, these interviews are considered as they are worth including in the analysis.

Each interview lasts an average of 60–90 minutes and are all recorded with the permission of the participant. During the interviews, the author follows the guidelines recommended by Robson (2002):

- Appearance: dressed according to the context in which the interview is carried out (in the company, in a cafeteria, on the Internet, etc.) and as expected by the participant. For example, if the author is interviewing a Chinese businessman related to the government in the company's headquarters, the author should dress more formally (in a suit, for example) than if he/she is interviewing an entrepreneur working in a technology start-up in a cafeteria,
- Approach: being pleasant while making the participant comfortable. This is key to encourage storytelling. The participant needs to feel comfortable. In the context of the work, the author should make sure that he/she always has with him/her name cards and a small gift for the participant (the exchange of name cards as well as of presents is part of Chinese business culture). Of course, to thank the participant for his cooperation as well as of the gatekeeper before starting with the interview is a kind gesture, and
- Familiarity with the interview: showing sufficient knowledge of the topic under discussion and of the company, but never showing assumptions or making references to the official story of the company, as previously mentioned.

4.6 Challenges to be Addressed During the Study

The present strategy presents several limitations and challenges that should be addressed before starting with the research process. These challenges become even more relevant considering that very few studies in the context of international organisations and marketing had previously adopted qualitative approaches, especially Narrative Inquiry. In this context, it was difficult to find useful benchmarks and learn from past studies. The main challenges found during the study are as follows:

1. Access to a large and appropriate sample of participants. This challenge was known and considered by the author from the very beginning of the study. That is, it is important to evaluate the feasibility of the research strategy from the very beginning. In this case, the author had previous experience working in China, having developed a good network of contacts that would help her with the sample. Also, the support of a collaborator in China, who is Chinese with a relevant network of contacts for the interviews in China, is key in this aspect. However, the challenge was not the access to a large number of Chinese managers from Chinese companies, but the access to a balanced sample in terms of ownership structure, especially the access to managers working in state-owned companies. SOEs are usually very big and powerful corporations so the access to managers with relevant positions, usually government officials, is not easy. They usually do not speak good English, they are not comfortable talking to a foreigner and they do not want to share relevant information about the company. To solve this challenge, managers close to the collaborator or the author from public companies with a state-owned shareholder are included in the sample as well as managers who worked in the past for this type of company.
2. Stories as personal experiences. Finding patterns, differences, and similarities is not easy in the context of organisations where participants present diverse backgrounds and work for different types of companies. For the present study, a large sample is needed, and therefore a large number of stories, in order to develop sound conclusions. In the first stage, and after discussions with several experts in qualitative data, only twenty interviews are considered in order to develop a first analysis, draw a first set of conclusions, and identify uncovered gaps. Then, a new sample with new companies is defined. Moreover, participants sometimes find it difficult to articulate their personal thoughts, experiences, and beliefs, especially with a stranger. Out of the forty participants, the author only knew five previously; for the rest, the collaborator and a gatekeeper were needed. In the case of

Chinese participants, this challenge is even greater. In this context, it is important to note that in China, guanxi, which is defined as "the set of connections or ties to secure favours in personal and organisational relations" (Park & Luo, 2001), is considered one of the most relevant cultural values shaping relationships. This means that personal introductions by the gatekeepers were key so participants could trust the author and feel comfortable telling a story based on their personal experiences. This is crucial in order to obtain strong narratives, as well as to deal with potential sensitive issues that may arise during the interviews (i.e., corruption in the context of the companies in China, an important phenomenon in recent years that has been the focus of relevant policies defined by the current Chinese president) and which may incentivise ambiguous or unreal answers or stories.

3. The use of a foreign language in the development of the interview. To develop interviews in general, and narrative interviews in particular, in a foreign language is challenging; even if both the author and the participant are bilingual in the language used, the meaning we give to a specific word or sentence may be different. For this reason, it is important to work with a local professional interpreter, especially for the development of the transcripts in case the author does not understand some ideas in the texts.
4. The use of technology. Related to the previous point and the access to participants, thirty-five interviews are developed face-to-face while five are carried out using the Internet (Skype or WeChat), representing an additional difficulty. On the one hand, thanks to the technology, the author has access to relevant companies that could not be visited during her trips to China, but on the other hand, communication difficulties are evident, especially because of poor internet connections which make it very complicated to keep the flow of the stories. In any case, even if interviews are longer in these cases and the author should ask more clarifying questions or make more effort to encourage the storytelling, these interviews are worth including in the analysis. The recommendation from the author is to try to avoid video calls for narrative interviews, as interaction is crucial in such a context, unless the contact is worth the extra effort and a good level of conversation in the language of the interview is guaranteed.

5. Finally, a deep analysis of the context is necessary, especially of the development of the Chinese economy, since the reforms defined by the Chinese government in 1978—including awareness of: (i) key events in China's history, and the resulting institutional changes (Nee & Opper, 2012), and (ii) the unique Chinese strategic mind based on the Chinese tradition and philosophy and shaping Chinese managers' business decisions (Liu, 2015) in order to understand the foundations of the Chinese business environment and its unique institutional elements. In order to conduct Narrative Inquiry, especially in this cross-cultural Chinese-European context, it is imperative to understand these factors clearly and in detail as they have a strong influence on the stories. This becomes even more relevant by the fact that the analysis is focused on Chinese companies internationalising to the EU where, apparently, the home and distinctive Chinese business environment is no longer valid or contrasts with the Western management style.

4.7 Data Analysis

After the narrative interviews are developed, the next step is data analysis. This is the process of converting the raw data collected through interviews into a research text, engaging in analysis and interpretation (Kim, 2015). In Narrative Inquiry, and more specifically in the context of biographical narrative research, the author should focus on interpreting the meanings storytellers give to their experiences through an analysis of a plotline, categories, and themes that emerge in the stories, while considering the context of the story (Kim, 2015). The analysis of the interviews in the study is carried out in two stages. The first twenty interviews are used to develop a first analysis and find unfilled gaps, while the rest of the interviews are developed to complement and strengthen the initial findings. In both sets of analyses, the following procedure and method of analysis is followed.

In the first place, every story is transcribed with the help of the same professional Chinese interpreter who helped the author during some interviews. The Chinese interpreter has been very helpful with the verbatim transcription (the text is captured exactly as uttered) while developing interpretations of sentences that are unclear due to the use of a non-native language during the interviews. If some doubts are found during the transcription process, the interviewee is contacted, and the issue is discussed with him/her in Chinese.

Following the questions, objectives of the study as well as the narrative genre, the goal of the analysis is to find similarities, differences, and patterns across storytellers in order to develop theory. The focus should also be on the content rather than on the form of the text; this is on the "told" of the story (Riessman, 2008). In this context, a thematic analysis following the method of Saunders et al. (2003) and the narrative analysis of Polkinghorne (1995) in the context of biographical narrative research are considered as the most appropriate methods of analysis (Kim, 2015). However, it is also important to know how and why things happened according to a specific context, or why and how the storyteller is behaving in a certain way regarding a specific situation, so the "telling" should also be considered, adopting a narrative mode of analysis to show the significance of the storyteller's experience (Polkinghorne, 1995).

As explained above, the narrative interviews are divided into two different stories, representing two different narratives for analysis: (i) the understanding of the interpretation of Chinese managers of the influence of relevant Chinese institutional elements (formal and informal) on the definition and development of their firms' marketing capabilities, and (ii) the understanding of the interpretation of Chinese managers of the influence of Chinese institutional elements (formal and informal) on the development of the firm's marketing capabilities outside China, in different institutional environments, mainly in the EU.

The process of analysis is developed as follows. First, the first narrative is analysed across all participants. With the purpose of finding patterns, similarities, and differences, a multilevel unit of analysis is defined that considers: (i) different types of firms and ownership and (ii) different industries. That is, first, the transcripts from SOEs are analysed together taking into account the different industries, second NCs (SOs and Private) and finally transcripts from OPFs are considered.

For each of the narratives and units of analysis, the text is reduced to the relevant content while all non-narrative passages are eliminated. This is useful to focus on the relevant parts while facilitating further analysis. The resulting material is then read several times trying to keep an empathetic and open-minded approach to identify emerging patterns in the stories within each of the units. At this moment, the initial and global impressions are put in writing. For this, the author just uses a Word document where she writes her impressions and thoughts for each of the stories and writes the first findings in another Word document while she identifies initial patterns. It is in this part of the analysis where the author pays more attention to the mood and personal evaluation of each of the participants, adding comments in the margins of each of the stories. For this, the author needs to listen again to some of the interviews, in addition to reading the transcripts. This was done through a deep engagement with the relevant literature, especially with the literature about the government policies, the incentives for each type of firm and their timeline as well as secondary data about the companies.

In parallel, a coding process identifying conceptual groupings from the transcripts or themes is carried out, considering different aspects, such as where and when the theme appears, the context for each of the themes or the transition between them. That is, the author analyses each of the narratives and units of analysis individually identifying themes to then be able to compare them considering the information given by the participants. Then, Pentland (1999) features of narratives that would help interpretation are considered, which are: (i) the sequence in time, (ii) the different actors involved in the story, (iii) the narrative voice reflecting a point of view, (iv) an evaluative frame of reference, like meaning and cultural value, and (v) further indicators of content and context relevant to the study and for the interpretation of the events.

Some themes are identified deductively based on the theoretical framework and the structure of the interview in order to test the application of theory while others are developed inductively while going through the stories. For this part of the analysis, NVivo is used. This tool is chosen mainly for data management as it is very useful to analyse rich-text-based information where deep levels of analysis are required.

Findings are then written in a separate document, organised by units of analysis, structure of the interview and themes that are common across the stories while considering the timeline of each of the stories. In a second stage, the same process is developed for the second narrative, resulting in two different sets of narratives and two different conclusions. The author identifies gaps that should be covered with the second round of interviews. In this sense, after the first analysis of the first twenty interviews is developed and gaps are identified, a new sample of companies is defined, and the same process developed again.

This combination of the following elements, (i) theoretical selection of case studies, (ii) in-depth interviews, (iii) pattern matching with relevant literature and secondary data, (iv) to include and keep verbatim descriptions of participant´s views, (v) use respondent validation, by contacting participants to discuss whether the themes and concepts reflect their narratives, (vi) engaging with other researchers, scholars and lecturers to reduce the researcher bias and (vii) the coding process using NVivo, aimed to provide reliability, internal construct, and external validity to support the findings of the analysis (Morse et al., 2002; Silverman, 2015). In addition, throughout the development of the text, the issue of validity is further considered using the approach defined by Lieblich et al. (1998) for the analysis of narratives as presented in the previous chapter. Following the model, validity in the study is ensured through the evaluation and application of the four following criteria:

1. Width: quality of the interviews and the proposed interpretations and analysis are ensured by detailed explanations of the sample and participants (including verbatim descriptions of participants' views), as well as by the use of a Chinese interpreter. Participants' perspectives are also clearly and accurately presented. Finally, quotations, or alternative explanations for the reader's judgement of the evidence are included in the data analysis of the narratives.
2. Coherence: data analysis shows a meaningful and relevant picture as shown in the discussion parts of Chapter 6 that can be evaluated internally and externally. References to the literature and other sources, especially regarding government policies and their timeline, are included in Chapters 5 and 6 to double check participants'

narratives. Participants' views and perspectives are validated using respondent validation.

3. Insightfulness: originality in the presentation of the study and of the analysis are considered throughout the development of the text.
4. Parsimony: focus on the ability of providing an interpretation and analysis based on a small number of concepts as well as an aesthetic appeal are considered throughout the development of the text.

4.8 Conclusion

The aim of this chapter was to explain and discuss the research strategy followed in the present study. In addition, the chapter presented how companies in the sample were selected and how data was collected and further analysed. The following chapter will present the results of the data analysis.

References

Amendolagine, V., Amighini, A., & Rabelloti, R. (2017). Chinese multinationals in Europe. In *Understanding China Today*. Springer International Publishing.

Birkinshaw, J., Brannen, M., & Tung, R. (2011). From a distance and generalizable to upclose and grounded: Reclaiming a place for qualitative methods in international business research. *Journal of International Business Studies, 42*, 573–581. https://doi.org/10.1057/jibs.2011.19

Boje, D. M. (1994). Organizational storytelling: Struggles of pre-modern, modern and postmodern organizational learning discourses. *Management Learning, 25*(3), 433–461.

Boje, D. M. (2001). *Narrative methods for organizational and communication research*. Sage.

Boyce, M. E. (1996). Organizational story and storytelling: A critical review. *Journal of Organizational Change Management, 9*(5), 5–26.

CEIC. (2020). https://www.ceicdata.com/datapage/en/country/china

Creswell, J. W. (2009). *Research design: Qualitative and quantitative approaches.* Sage.

Easterby-Smith, M., Thorpe, R., & Lowe, A. (2002). *Management research; an introduction* (2nd ed.). SAGE.

Eisenhardt, K. (1989). Building theories from case study research. *Academy of Management Review, 14*(4), 532–550.

Eisenhardt, K., & Graebner, M. (2007). Theory building from cases: Opportunities and challenges. *Academy of Management Journal, 50*(1), 25–32.

Fainshmidt, S., Witt, M. A., Aguilera, R. V., & Verbeke, A. (2020). The contributions of qualitative comparative analysis (QCA) to international business research. In (Vol. 51, pp. 455–466). Springer.

Gertsen, M., & Soderberg, A. (2011). Intercultural collaboration stories: On narrative inquiry and analysis as tools for research in international business. *Journal of International Business Studies, 42*, 787–804.

Hemphill, T., & White III, G. (2013). *China's national champions: The evolution of a national industrial policy—Or a new era of economic protectionism?* Wiley Online Library.

Jovchelovitch, S., & Bauer, M. W. (2000). Narrative interviewing. In M. W. Bauer & Gaskell, G. (Eds.), *Qualitative researching with text, image and sound: A practical handbook* (pp. 57–74). Sage.

Kim, J. (2015). Narrative data analysis and interpretation. In *Understanding narrative inquiry: The crafting and analysis of stories as research.* Sage.

Lieblich, A., Tuval-Mashiach, R., & Zilber, T. (1998). *Narrative research: Reading, analysis and interpretation* (Vol. 47). Sage.

Lin, X. (2010). State versus private MNCs from China: Initial conceptualizations. *International Marketing Review, 27*(3), 366–380.

Liu, H. (2015). *The Chinese strategic mind*. Edward Elgar Publishing Limited.

Liu, Y., Oberg, C., Yedidia Tarba, S., & Xing, Y. (2018). Brand management in mergers and acquisitions: Emerging market multinationals venturing into advanced economies. *International Marketing Review, 35*(5), 710–732.

Morse, J. M., Barret, M., Mayan, M., Olson, K., & Spiers, J. (2002). Verification strategies for establishing reliability and validity in qualitative research. *Evidence Based Nursing, 1*(2), 13–22.

Nee, V., & Opper, S. (2012). *Capitalism from below: Markets and institutional change in China.* Harvard University Press.

OECD. (2018). *Ownership and governance of state-owned enterprises: A compendium of national practices.* https://www.oecd.org/corporate/ca/Ownership-and-Governance-of-State-Owned-Enterprises-A-Compendium-of-National-Practices.pdf

Park, S., & Luo, Y. (2001). Guanxi and organizational dynamics: Organizational networking in Chinese firms. *Strategic Management Journal, 22*(5), 455–477.
Pentland, B. T. (1999). Building process theory with narrative: From description to explanation. *Academy of Management Review, 24*(4), 711–724.
Polkinghorne, D. (1988). *Narrative knowing and the human sciences.* State University of New York Press.
Polkinghorne, D. (1995). Narrative configuration in qualitative analysis. *International Journal of Qualitative Studies in Education, 8*(1), 5–23.
Rhodes, C., & Brown, D. (2005). Narrative, organizations and research. *International Journal of Management Reviews, 7*(3), 167–188.
Riessman, C. K. (2005). Narrative analysis. *Narrative, memory & everyday life* (pp. 1–7). University of Huddersfield.
Riessman, C. K. (2008). *Narrative methods for the human sciences.* Sage.
Robson, C. (2002). *Real world research a resource for social scientists and practitioner-researchers* (2nd ed.). Blackwell.
Saunders, M., Lewis, P., & Thornhill, A. (2003). *Research methods for business students.* FT Prentice Hall.
Silverman, D. (2015). *Interpreting qualitative data.* Sage.

5

A Narrative Analysis of Chinese Managers' Personal Experiences

5.1 Introduction

The data analysis is divided into two main parts following the structure of the narratives explained in the previous chapter. The first part analyses the first narrative, which is related to the domestic environment and the capabilities developed by Chinese firms to compete in this context. The second part then analyses the second narrative, which is related to the international environment with a focus on the EU along with the capabilities developed and applied in that context. The data analysis is developed around the themes identified in the personal narratives of the interviewees.

M. Altamira, *Chinese Firms in the Global Market*, Palgrave Macmillan Asian Business Series, https://doi.org/10.1007/978-3-031-59227-0_5

5.2 Analysis of the First Narrative. The Domestic Environment and the Development of Capabilities in China

In the first narrative, managers talked about the environment in which they developed their activities in China and their perceived marketing capabilities. The objective was to understand how Chinese firms developed their competitive advantages and to what extent the environment and market institutions influenced this development.

5.2.1 The Domestic Environment

A Huge, Dynamic, and Fast-Changing Market

a. A Perceived Fierce Competition in a Huge Market

Participants started their narrative with their perception of the environment in which they were operating. During the interviews, there was a shared feeling among participants that the Chinese business environment presented unique characteristics (in comparison with Western economies) that defined the way of doing business in their companies. China presented the characteristics of an EM (interviewees described China, for example, as a "developing country" (Co12), an "emerging economy" (Co16), or an "emerging market" (Co22) that had been experiencing a rapid/well above average pace of economic development, sustained during a long period, together with a relatively fast liberalisation and adoption of a free market system; that is, the consequence mainly of the Open Door policy defined in 1978 and the subsequent more than 40 years of reforms (Hofman, 2018). Following this context and related to this evolution, there was also a shared perception that China was a fast-changing market along with an increasing middle class (although still with relatively low income) representing a large customer and profit base. As explained by Co1, Co2, Co6, Co15, and Co30, "there are many different markets in terms of level of education, culture, and income, but all of them willing to progress"; "now they have money to spend, at least if compared to only some years ago", "there are different markets in China. It is like different countries in one country", "the domestic market is very dynamic with the demand changing every day, with new consumers accessing the market every day", and "at the bottom of the pyramid, there is a mass population of Chinese people who are low income or middle income, so, quite different from developed countries, where it is more like an olive. But these people are getting more and more money, so the demand is continuously increasing, meaning that there are more and more opportunities for companies". Participants perceived this environment as in a constant state of flux where change is constant and ambiguous, a consequence of "extraordinary past growth rates and investments that were, and somehow are still constantly attracting new firms, both domestic and international. Everything is very fast, quite unpredictable" (Co12).

In this context, and as a result of the rapid economic growth and the rapid and ambiguous changing environment of the past decades, participants explained that they had the feeling of defining and developing their activities in a very crowded market with a lot of participants offering the same products/services, to the same target market, at the same time. This was a shared perception from every participant, especially from those working in private companies (private National champions (Private NCs) and other private firms (OPFs)), less obvious in stories from participants working in State-owned enterprises (SOEs) and State-owned National Champions (SO NCs) since the environment faced by these firms was more stable, controlled by the government and with fewer players. This situation was having a direct effect on the scope of their strategic decisions; managers described their strategic planning based mainly on what competitors were doing (i.e., a reactive strategy), especially on their pricing strategies focused on the short term. Even though they were operating in this context and reacting to competitors, participants' companies were growing and making profits.

For example, managers from Co18 and Co19 described the situation as follows: "China's market changes every day. New companies are entering the market every day with new and different products; so in this sense the competition in the domestic market is fierce, although this also means that we have more opportunities" (Co18), "this environment with lots of competitors offering the same at the same time to the same mass market affects our business culture, business strategy, and of course business decisions. The market changes very fast, new products are in the market every day. The environment is very dynamic and unpredictable. So, our strategy, actions and decisions should be developed for the short term, we cannot plan beyond that because everything changes very fast" (Co19).

b. No Equal Footing for Every Type of Company, Regulations Evolving at a Slower Pace

Despite the perceived opportunities to develop a business as a result of the increasing demand, managers from OPFs stated that they were feeling uncomfortable and at a disadvantage operating in an environment characterised by regulations that poorly deal with the increasing and fierce competition. In this sense, participants, especially managers from medium-large private firms, expressed a negative feeling by highlighting the weak regulatory framework and poor legal enforcement by Chinese authorities that was making it difficult to compete in China. Their perception was of not competing on an equal footing as OPFs were operating in a very crowded and uncertain environment, while the environment for the other firms (SOEs and NCs) was more stable and safer. According to managers, a stronger enforcement would help "to regulate or to control the competition in the Chinese business environment" (Co22). Words like "war" (Co25), "no rules" (Co27), and "steal consumers" (Co32) appeared in their accounts.

This perceived regulatory uncertainty was mainly due to a young legal and judicial system while the market had been evolving faster than institutions. Also, managers hinted at a link between ownership, the influence of the government in Chinese firms, and opportunities in the market. They argued that different types of companies were subject to different environmental effects: "In the end, SOEs and SO NCs are the ones that receive the help and support to develop their operations" (Co35), "private firms should deal with many inconveniences in the market, especially because of the poor support of the government, and the poor legal protection, and no rules. It is even worse if you compete with firms close to the government. You will always be at a disadvantage" (Co38), "Protection and support is always for firms close to the government. The rest we need to compete in a completely different scenario. Much more complex, with no rules. We are alone in this sense in China" (Co28). According to their narratives, managers perceived different opportunities to operate among types of firms, reflected in a negative discriminatory government support for OPFs.

Discriminatory Government Support

The influence of the government in shaping the environment was pointed out by most interviewees as a strong and unique characteristic of China's business environment. Examples from the interviews were "the majority of the companies in China are owned by the government" (Co15), "government defines the activity in the market" (Co26), "the Chinese government has more power in the economy and the society that in other countries" (Co14), or "Chinese companies need to deal with the government in order to grow" (Co36). Indeed, it is important to note that during the '90s, the phase of market building reforms, the Chinese government continued to develop privatisations, although only a few of them were allowed to be totally private, meaning that the majority of them remained in state hands (Spar & Oi, 2006), a situation that continued during the market enhancing reforms phase (Hofman, 2018), from 2003 onwards, and where *lishu* relationships still are the norm.

a. Positive Influence for Managers Working in SOEs and NCs (SO and Private)

The perception of the government influence differed depending on the ownership structure of the firm. Managers from SOEs and NCs explicitly recognised that the government facilitated their access to preferential conditions and sources of funding, privileged information about the market, and access to main actors in the supply chain. In addition, decisions were made by the government while managers were just following their guidelines and plans: "I just followed the plan; it was a good opportunity at that time. We were responding to new plans, meaning new business, new demand. Very positive and easy for the company" (Co5). The government appeared as a facilitator for the companies' expansion and success. Another manager added "working with the government provides security and is a guarantee of success as it supports and eases business decisions providing good opportunities to access the market and resources" (Co3), while other participants emphasised the positive efforts made by the government: "government is fighting for corruption, which will enhance better competition and new foreign capital entry" (Co1). The perception was of a safe environment, the reason why managers showed a low-risk mindset developed in China. Managers were used to working in a controlled environment with positive support from government officials, with few players in the market, meaning many opportunities to develop business with low risk.

This same argument can also be valid for managers from private NCs; however, this was not explicitly mentioned, only some implicit ideas could be identified from their narratives. For example: "it is a stable market, we have a very good position, so it is like we have a stable demand" (Co15) or "we are very big, no huge competition, the market is quite easy" (Co17). These quotes contrasted with the feelings of managers from OPFs. The reason might be that private NCs, even though they have benefited from government support to reach their leadership position in China, were not feeling comfortable showcasing the preferential support received. They probably wanted to avoid mentioning that this support was part of their success.

b. Negative Influence for Managers Working in OPFs

On the other hand, participants from OPFs showed a negative perception of the government's influence in their firms, considered as weak support to develop their business and sometimes a barrier. They explained that "in China, there is a difference between being private or having some kind of relationship with the government. If you do have this, you will succeed" (Co24), "the rest of companies (*non-government related firms*) need to deal with the government to access distribution channels, to access the media, to do any paperwork, and many other activities. That is a nightmare for private firms, the processes are very long. But if you are an SOE, everything is done" (Co35), "There are difficulties in China for private companies to develop business due to government power always positively influencing state-owned firms, being actually one of the main motivations of private companies to go abroad" (Co40). The feeling was that they were "out of the system" and did not have the same opportunities as SOEs or NCs. In addition, as already introduced in the first part of the narrative, managers observed a poor enforcement of regulations; they perceived a weak legal protection and weak application of competition rules: "The government only protects their companies, their firms" (Co30), "it is not fair for every company, for us, we need to go through a lot of obstacles every day" (Co31). "SOEs do not face competition, for them it is fine, but we do face it. Lot of competitors doing the same and it is like if anything is allowed. Copying, stealing consumers, offering lower and lower prices, more and more aggressive marketing campaigns. It is like a war" (Co36). "In China all the resources are for the SOEs, resulting in a very negative scenario for private companies, that need to fight every day to get access to financial resources" (Co38), "SOEs are the ones who received all the support and the ones strong in the market, private companies need to make more efforts to compete" (Co40), and "Competition in China is so huge that it very often pushes companies to do unethical things. Our product has two copies, you know. Which is very niche product, like for international trades, there are competitors that have already two copies. So, competition is very tough and there is little protection" (Co39).

In this sense, it seemed that managers from OPFs were feeling that SOEs and SO NCs were the ones dominating the market (the government might be using SOEs/NCs to deploy their policies) while working close to the government benefited the business development thanks to an easier access to relevant resources. According to their comments, the government was supporting these types of firms, being responsible for the perceived unlevel playing field found in the Chinese market: "for some industries, which might need some licenses, for example, like fire extinguishers, this is high margin. But the government only gives licenses to certain companies. Not because their technologies are advanced, but because they have good relationships" (Co36). The shared feeling was that there were opportunities to develop business and growth, but these opportunities were not the same for everyone; managers emphasised the negative discriminatory support from the government in terms of ownership and type of operation (strategic sectors aligned with government plans are the key here). This supports the idea that managers from private firms need to make more efforts to operate in China, implying that they would be able to develop stronger market-oriented capabilities than SOEs and NCs.

At this point of the narrative, some differences can also be identified within different types of industries of OPFs. The above-mentioned perceptions were mainly described by managers working in industries not supported by government policies. In other words, managers working in technology, consumer electronics, or education (industries included in the government initiatives presented in Table 2), did not explain or imply a negative perception of the government influence.

Intensive Use of Personal Relations

Following the narrative and the strong relevance given by participants to the influence of the government, informal institutions in the form of personal relations and connections came up in the interviews. All interviewees perceived informal institutions as the key asset to ease business development in China as they facilitated access to market opportunities and reduced the impact, in private firms, of negative discriminatory government support. Examples from the interviews were: "Guanxi is a method to ease business development" (Co18), "Guanxi helps business development through relationship development securing favours" (Co20), "There is huge importance for relationships for business in China" (Co28), and "The ones that have the best connections have the best opportunities" (Co32). Two types of personal relationships were identified: (i) political relationships with government officials or political relations and (ii) business relationships with business partners including clients, distributors, and buyers. Both were perceived as a determinant in providing preferential access to relevant resources.

a. Intensive Use of Political Relations

Managers working in SOEs and NCs (SO and private) showed a positive expected perception of the government influence while they explained that personal relationships with government officials were part of their daily tasks and strategy. "Our culture of working closely with the government helps us to develop. We have been growing in recent years with hard work and also thanks to big plans from the government based on very good relationships" (Co2). "We are very close to the government, we have very good relationships with the local authorities" (Co4).

According to participants, being close to the government was synonymous with power, growth, and security. Also, in the case of some participants, they recognised the preferential support or access to some resources they received; thanks to these relationships. This reinforced the idea of the positive differing institutional support and how useful it was to be aligned with government plans as well as the low business risk mindset developed by managers working in these types of firms: "working with the government provides security in this complex market and is a guarantee of success as it supports and eases business decisions providing good opportunities to access the market and resources" (Co3), "Chinese companies need to deal with the government in order to grow" (Co6), and "In our case it is easier, in the end, SOEs are the ones that receive the help and support to develop their operations because we follow the plans of the government. We respond to them" (Co7).

In the case of private NCs and OPFs from specific industries or sectors supported by the government, similar to their comments on the influence of the government, they did mention links with the government, but not in an explicit manner nor with much emphasis. For example, a manager from Co16 said: "usually we have some help, maybe some support (laughs), but not much. We are very big", while another participant mentioned: "we are independent, we do have our strategy, our board, our guidelines" (Co15), avoiding mentioning that the owner was a former government official. Even if their strong position in the market was partially achieved due to the support they had received, they preferred not to mention it as it might be considered that they had other more important competitive advantages. It seemed they preferred to emphasise that they had achieved their strong position with their own efforts regardless of the help received.

On the other hand, the shared perception about the government influence shown by managers from OPFs was of "the need to be friends" (Co24) or "we do not want to be in trouble" (Co25). They agreed on the need to work on developing personal relationships with government officials but by way of not being at a disadvantage regarding other types of firms (SOEs, SO NCs, NCs). Managers included the development of personal relationships with government officials as part of their daily tasks and strategy, even when they did not want it: "It is part of what we should do" (Co26), "the rest of companies (*private companies, non SOEs*) we need to deal with the government, develop the links, work hard on it, to access distribution channels, to access the media, to do any paperwork, and many other activities. Sooner or later, we should do it if we want to progress" (Co28). For managers from OPFs, it was very important to be close to the government while developing a good relationship with government officials, as in the end, their success in the market would depend on them. The development of close links appeared as a way to minimise the impact of the negative discriminatory support, a way to speed up the process to get access to relevant resources while obtaining preferential support that would facilitate the development of the business. The access to resources was perceived as not being the same for every type of company or industry, prevailing in some cases the personal relations among the government and companies. For example, managers explained: "And from my personal opinion, the government in China has a much stronger influence on the companies, on the business. The government in China is everywhere, as most of big IT companies are from the Chinese Government, so this makes even more restrictive their influence on us. We should deal with it, but the less the better. We do not want to get in trouble" (Co38), or "We must have the government on our side and do not make much noise. Sooner or later, we will need their support. So, it is better to have a good relationship" (Co40).

All in all, the Chinese government appeared in the stories as the main actor designing and defining actions, rules, and policies in China. This is not surprising considering the evolution of the country since 1978, especially since the opening of the economy in 1979, an evolution guided by the different plans and actions defined by the Chinese government; China is considered an institution-led market, created, and strategically defined by the government (Wei et al., 2020). In this sense, political relationships, based on personal ties linked to the positional power of the politician, meant that managers' personal connections with government officials were the basis for mutual trust that led to successful business relations. Due to this, the development of these ties had also become a common practice among managers from private firms, not only SOEs and NCs, representing a valued asset or relational capital for the success of business operations. However, political relations were more relevant and more valued in a positive way by managers from SOEs and NCs; managers from OPFs considered them a "mechanism of protection" (Co26), "just in case" (Co28) it is needed, as, in the end, the government is everywhere" (Co30) and "sooner or later we have to deal with it" (Co31).

b. Intensive Use of Business Relationships

Continuing with the relevance of personal relations, most of the managers from private NCs and OPFs mentioned that the development of business relations, both within the company with colleagues and outside the company with business partners, in addition to the relationships with the government mentioned earlier, were key to define and develop their decision-making processes in the domestic market. They were perceived as a very important asset to compete in the rapidly developing market described at the beginning of the narratives. These relations were not mentioned in the narratives from managers working in SOEs and SO NCs, probably because they were not needed due to the business conditions in which they operate; that is, a stable, safe, and controlled business environment with a strong influence from the government.

In the case of managers from private NCs, business relationships appeared relevant when they talked about the first steps of the company, as they considered they were useful to find new opportunities while reducing uncertainty, similar to what was found in stories from managers from OPFs. However, a lower emphasis was perceived in interviews with managers with extensive experience, probably because the firm had already a strong position in the market thus business relationships were no longer needed.

In addition, for managers working in OPFs, during the first years of activity business relations provided trust to find the right partner to develop a business in China. According to them, trust was a key asset to establish a new venture in China, especially in order to protect the business idea from potential competitors. "My partners are friends. My friend put in the money. My operation manager was my MBA classmate. And my sales manager, she was my classmate at university. And my production manager has worked for me for the last ten years. It looks like a family company because are all related. It is very important, as my feeling is of trust. But how to work it out with guanxi is very important to set up the rules and discipline. I do not want to share my idea with anyone else" (Co22) or "I need to trust the person first. I need to know he will stay with me and will not go tomorrow to the competitor. For this reason, I spend time knowing the person, inviting him to dinner, knowing his family. Only after this we can do business" (Co31).

Moreover, personal relations were also perceived as a tool to access market opportunities and speed up the processes, as dealing with the administration was perceived to be slow and inefficient. Chinese managers relied on friendship to get access to customers, partners, and private sources of funding while avoiding banks that might offer different support or different conditions depending on the type of firm. Business relationships provided support to navigate through the administrative processes and avoid red tape. Managers explained that: "Guanxi is a way to speed up the process of developing a business. You need to be quick, you need to respond, you need clients, you need partners, etc.…but then you need to stay there" (Co22), or that "They also help get some money support from the family, so we don't need to borrow the money from the bank to pay the interest" (Co36).

This suggested that private firms, including private entrepreneurs and start-ups, were able to develop their businesses thanks to innovative informal arrangements within networks that provided the necessary business norms and helped to overcome the barriers to enter the market (for example, getting loans from banks, for which they would need to pay very high interest), overcoming thus the absence of defined formal rules supporting the development of this type of new company structure while suffering at the same time from competitive exclusion from SOEs (Nee & Opper, 2012). Through the personalised exchange, multiplex relationships, information sharing, joint market development, and short-term financing, managers from private firms found ways to reduce uncertainty while enhancing sustainable development. Also, to work with the "right" Co33 persons helped to protect jointly against untrustworthy competitors.

5.2.2 Marketing Capabilities

Starting Point

This part of the narrative was more devolved by managers from private NCs and OPFs than by managers working in SOEs and SO NCs. This was not surprising as SOEs were making less effort to develop their business and sell their products or services. In fact, it could be perceived in the narrative that managers from SOEs and SO NCs gave lower emphasis to their perceived necessary marketing actions. These types of firms were focusing their efforts on just satisfying the given demand while responding to the stable and controlled market: "We just need to sell what they say we need to sell. The demand is given. Of course, we need to grow, but it is easy because we are getting bigger and bigger and in more cities in China. No big marketing efforts are required" (Co4).

Managers from private NCs and OPFs considered marketing as tactical, pointing out a list of different activities focused on the short term, defined to reach new clients and increase market share fast. For example, the manager from Co23 said that "we do some advertising to raise our brand awareness, do some market research, talk to the users to understand our brand's weaknesses, and then we also do online marketing, for example, Weibo, WeChat, some social networking, social marketing to spread out the words. And then we have some exhibitions, some conferences we should attend, so we prepare for the booths, activities. And, we have, for example, some operations of the products. We may have some campaigns, we have some activities in which users can participate, either online or off-line, mostly online. A lot of things. We need to sell (laughs)". Also, another manager mentioned different activities to increase their sales, "local social media, market with local partners, we will have billboards by the freeways, where people will try to buy. We will also hire people distributing flyers on the street to pull people to take a look at our project. We need to be present where the people are and where people are going to buy, the hot places" (Co26). Participants described the marketing they were doing in China as focused on sales, emphasising the tactical focus of the activity, while they described their sales teams as multifunctional, polyvalent, doing several activities at the same time with the main goal of increasing sales: "My department is called marketing, but I just need to complete KPIs related to sales, we do sales basically. There is no difference" (Co33). "We don't even have the marketing department. Because we have very short history, we just have 10 years, and we grow up very fast. Because we need to make them sell, we need to reach their sales objectives. So, everyone does a lot of things to reach this" (Co31). Managers showed a reactive behaviour as they were passively responding to customers' demands and not anticipating them.

In addition, managers from most companies described the Chinese domestic consumer as price sensitive; his purchasing decisions were based on price. Due to this, firms have adapted their pricing strategies to Chinese consumers' expectations, focusing on defining the best function-price balance always based on competitors: "People in China do not care too much about the service, it is mainly price, because there are many options which are similar" (Co22), "So I sell, in China. We have Taobao, right? Everything. I will do some, I'll check the price on Taobao, similar products, to decide my price" (Co31), "In China margins are not important, just low prices, to sell more and have more clients, stealing them from competitors" (Co32). In this sense, it could be said that in China consumers were not demanding, mainly because they did not have a legacy, meaning that they did not know what they wanted because they hadn't been exposed to other options in the market, they had grown as consumers in this context. So, it is the mentality of just trying new products that the increasing middle class can afford. In addition, consumers could find so many different options that they go for the less expensive ones: "a basic quality is fine, if the purpose is achieved, it is fine.

Chinese would go for the price, among all the options" (Co34), "So, if the product does not work, it is ok, they can easily change. In Europe it is a combination of price, quality and the perceived added value" (Co35), "So, price was all definitely based on competition, not depend on the cost" (Co38). There were too many options in China so switching and trying new and different products was easy. The manager from Co23 explained: "if your products are good, very solid, and the price is very competitive, you can easily find the proper partners, to start from small size to medium to big one. Price is one of the most important factors that influence to decide whether you can succeed or not". In this context, sales promotions appeared as the most relevant action to attract new consumers. For example: "It is what works in China. Why do we have the Singles day? It is the most popular sales day not only in China, but worldwide. Chinese people get crazy with promotions" (Co21) or "every week we should be aware of the promotions of the competitors and react accordingly, we need to be better (laughs)" (Co23).

Furthermore, aggressive mass publicity campaigns, including deep engagement with social media due to the extended use of mobile phones and the internet, were considered the most important communication means. In fact, the shared belief was that the bigger the impact, the better because "it is the only way consumers can know you" (Co19). No comments regarding loyalty or long-term strategic actions were identified in the narratives. Some examples from the interviews were: "The more potential customers we can reach the better, we can have access to different mechanisms. But the bigger impact the better. China has places full of people. There we are" (Co16), "The internet, mobile phones are our best channels" (Co29), "Big publicity, a lot of ads in social media. WeChat is very important, the best way to reach your consumers" (Co34). Indeed, managers invested less once the intended positioning had been reached; managers explained that no big resources were needed nor dedicated to their perceived marketing function (i.e., sales). "Of course, we do online, but consumers are already aware of the brand, we don't spend much. We are already big" (Co20). "It's too slow to do marketing I think; in the Chinese market we have to start from the promotion, attending the fairs doing the advertisement of your production, products and explain what the competitive part of your products is. After, it is fine, no more big efforts. We already have our network" (Co19) or "In China, we spend very few in marketing. We select the big actions, very big time to time, and that is it. The cost compared with the other foreign companies is very low" (Co36). These quotes reinforced the idea that sales-oriented actions were mainly considered in the first stages of development of the firm, with the main purpose of reaching consumers in the short term. Also, this seems to confirm that private NCs may not need to do huge investments in terms of marketing as their sales are done and their market share guaranteed.

Finally, several managers from private NCs and OPFs considered relationships as key to achieve their sales goals. They described their sales teams' objectives as "getting the right contacts" (Co21) or "developing relationships are finding the right network" (Co25). This idea was also emphasised by other managers who explained that one of the key activities of the sales team was to attend fairs with the only purpose of making friends: "Firstly, we have some salespersons, if they want to sell something, our product, to a company, the first step is trying to get the right contacts. We go to fairs, we increase our network" (Co31), "And the social network is very important. They usually use a lot of guanxi in the sales and marketing" (Co34). The development and use of personal relations also helped managers to get preferential access and conditions in distribution and advertisement channels. "My friend was working in the advertising company, we got for free the space in the metro" (Co39). This confirmed how business relations helped managers find new opportunities and navigate through processes in which they would suffer from the negative discriminatory support mentioned above. For example, the main advertising channels or main locations for these advertisements (metro, airport, train stations, etc.) would probably depend on the Chinese government.

Definition and Development of Products and Services

a. Reactive Innovation Strategy as Key in the Domestic Market

Innovation, considered as new product development, appeared in most of the narratives when managers explained how new products and services were defined and developed in China. Two different perspectives could be identified. On the one hand, managers from SOEs and NCs (state-owned and private) explained how the Chinese government was pushing innovation by providing firms with financial help and investments in R&D. This government strategy was responding to plans defined and promoted with the goal of enhancing innovation while developing the domestic market. In particular, from the 2000s, the Chinese government decided to focus on innovation and technology policies, moving from market-oriented policies towards a strong intervention of the government in these sectors (Ling & Naughton, 2016). Policies and government interventions continued in this direction with the new measures adopted in the 13th Five-Year Plan, the Made in China 2025 Strategy defined in 2015 by President Xi Jinping, and the most recent 14th Party Congress on productivity and innovation.

These plans were considered in the narratives, especially from managers working in technology, consumer electronics, and telecommunications (in SOEs, NCs, and even OPFs), as clear indications for new developments and opportunities to define new businesses: "The government wants to develop this region, so we need to go to this region, and we need to go first" (Co13). Another manager explained that "We should be aware of what the government wants to do next to be there and get this business" (Co16). Without the pressure to compete and with the support of the government in terms of access to relevant resources, such as financial support or other resources, such as R&D funds, managers could define their activities in a low business risk environment. This reinforced the low business risk mindset identified in managers from SOEs and NCs (SO and private). Other examples were: "Another depends on the technologies. Last maybe is competition. But I think this is not very important, because we are already No. 1 in the world, so what we need is to be very, very clear, or need to listen more to the customers' needs and need to research for the technologies and we have the support to do that, the support from the government" (Co15). "If China should be the leader in a specific technology, this is decided and supported by the government, in 3G, 4G, so we need to go for it" (Co10), "Right, in a lot of levels, and they are in control of a lot of resources for the next five years of development, and they will relocate a lot of resources in a lot of areas, so it means in China, we should have a deep understanding of the government's future plan and the focus" (Co12), or "Well, we do not define the industries in which to invest. We need to listen to the trends, what would be important in China for the coming months, years, and then we look for the best partners to invest in, and this at the end of the day is defined by the government plans" (Co17). Innovation, or what was considered by managers as new products and market development, was based on the push of the government; in other words, narratives showed that an institution-led market, created and strategically defined by the government, promotes growth by enhancing technological development, positively affecting the catch-up of Chinese firms (Wei et al., 2020).

On the other hand, managers from OPFs considered innovation as key to compete in China's domestic market. Copying and imitating appeared in most of the stories from participants working in private firms as a daily issue they had to deal with. For example: "Every year, every month we have a different new item for promotion. Otherwise, we will always have a trouble to speed up the growth of the company. Because in China, imitation is tolerable, right? Today, you invent one thing, tomorrow someone will copy you. So, what you need to do and what I did is to have a standard, which is IEC standards, IEC international electrical community standards" (Co38). In this context, innovation was considered by managers as launching something new to the market faster than competitors in order to defend themselves as well as to survive and protect them from weak enforcement of competition and other regulations. Innovation was conceived as the key activity to survive in the market. That is, rapidly launching new products or adapting existing ones as a response to the huge market rapidly developing. Managers were following a reactive rather than an active innovation strategy. Examples were: "I think, most of the Chinese companies are pretty tough in terms of the business strategy. Because of the competition and because of the hotness of, you know, earning money from the users, so I think that China is more innovative than any other country in terms of the business model. For example, high discounts or offering free products, in China this is very common, but you have to be innovative in terms of how you can make money. Also, because probably competitors will copy you, so we need to be very innovative" (Co31).

In this sense, it seemed that Chinese managers had developed innovative skills and were developing innovative business models. They needed to find a way to survive in China. In fact, lately, Chinese firms have demonstrated how to be innovative and are evolving from copying to being copied, leading the innovation of products, technologies, and business models (Hsu, 2017). A reason for that would be not to depend on legacy, with the Chinese building new and innovative business ideas from zero. In any case, and for every type of firm, innovation appeared as relevant when it came to develop new products, markets, or regions, but it was always considered a reactive strategy, rather than active. In the case of SOEs and SO/private NCs as well as in some OPFs from strategic industries, this was because the government was pushing innovation with strong investments, especially in R&D, and in the case of OPFs, they were reacting from or preparing for misleading competition.

b. An Increasingly Well-Prepared and Large Labour Force Working Long Hours

Finally, managers from most large firms in the sample (SOEs, NCs, and OPFs) emphasised the idea that Chinese firms had succeeded in China due to the increasingly well-prepared and large labour force working long hours. According to participants, thanks to this perceived unique domestic advantage, firms had been able to achieve a shorter time to market, and offer shorter product life cycles while increasing cost efficiency. This domestic advantage, considered part of the Chinese mentality and Chinese "way of thinking" (Co7), explained why Chinese firms could offer the right function-price balance to target the increasing middle class while adapting fast to the continuous and ambiguous changes. A manager from Co10 explained that "At the same time, in the [company] they have time to discover new software, launch a new phone… China has been built with the effort of millions of Chinese, working extremely hard, many hours. It is also the mentality". Also, the manager from Co12 said that: "the big companies like Sony, Bosch, Siemens, GE, they also produce security. But they need two years to develop new products, new generation products. We just do it in a maximum of 6 months. The real reason is that in Chinese companies we have a lot of human resources. This human resource is not just unskilled workers, but mostly highly educated engineers. Last year in China, more than maybe 6 or 7 million students graduated from universities. So, for engineers, we can hire the Chinese students, their skill is very good, they are high-quality workers who can compete with the rest of the world". Finally, "China has a huge workforce, that enables us to do too many things, quicker. We are very hardworking (working longer hours and with much less holidays than say Europe)" (Co9).

In conclusion, according to participants, new product and service development was closely related to the development of new innovative ideas, products, services, and business models, but it appeared as a reactive rather than an active strategy. In the case of SOEs, NCs, and OPFs from strategic industries, innovation was promoted and supported by government plans, which were the main source of new ideas and developments. In the case of OPFs, innovation appeared because of their need to differentiate from competitors that use imitation and copying, as well as to survive the weak enforcement of regulations. In addition to innovation, a large labour force for execution and with good leaders on the top of the pyramid guiding this execution appeared as a unique domestic advantage that had been supporting large firms' business success and growth.

5.2.3 Summary of the Findings of the First Narrative

The chart below summarises the findings of the first narrative analysed above. Findings are summed up in the themes identified in the experiences described by the managers working in the firms in the sample. Firms can be divided into three groups according to the development of their capabilities: (i) SOEs (including SO NCs), (ii) Private firms aligned with the government (Private NC and OPFs from strategic industries or sectors), and (iii) OPFs. At the end of the chart, a closure and brief discussion is included, which is further developed in the next chapter (Chart 5.1).

Main themes in the story	Domestic Environment		
	A huge, dynamic, and fast changing market	Discriminatory government support	Intensive use of personal relations
Main findings	▪ General perception of a huge market very rapidly changing. ▪ Managers consider change as continuous and ambiguous. ▪ This huge market provides a very large customer and profit base. ▪ Managers, mainly from private firms (NC and OPFs) perceive very high competition (many players offering the same at the same time to the mass market). ▪ Short-term planning and focus on competitors. ▪ The perception of this situation is positive, as there are business opportunities. ▪ However, managers from private firms (not NC), feel uncomfortable working in this type of environment as they consider they do not compete on an equal footing: – ▪ No similar opportunities due to the perceived negative discriminatory government support depending on the type of firm and industry (see next).	▪ Managers from SOEs and SO NCs: – ▪ Perceive positive influence from government officials. – ▪ Perceive a safe environment to develop their business. – ▪ Show low business risk mindset. – ▪ Managers from SOEs: – – ▪ Explicitly recognise that the government has facilitated their access to preferential conditions and sources of funding, privileged information about the market, and access to main actors across the supply chain. – – ▪ For this reason, they consider China as a safe environment with good opportunities and low business risk. ▪ Managers from private NCs and OPFs from strategic industries: – ▪ Implicitly accept the positive support received. – ▪ Seem not comfortable showcasing the preferential support received by the government. – ▪ May want to avoid showing that this support is part of their success. ▪ Managers from OPFs. – ▪ Feel weak support from government. – ▪ Observe poor enforcement of regulations. – – ▪ Perceive negative influence of the government. – – – ▪ Emphasis on negative discriminatory government support. – – – ▪ Perceive a weak legal protection and weak application of competition rules – – – ▪ Feel that do not have the same opportunities as SOEs or NC	▪ Managers from SOEs/ SO NCs: – ▪ Include development of personal relationships with government officials as part of their daily tasks and strategy. ▪ Managers from private NCs and OPFs from strategic industries: – ▪ Include development of personal relationships with government officials as part of their daily tasks and strategy. – ▪ Include development of business relationships to support their firms: – – ▪ Although less emphasis and need due to an already strong position in the market. ▪ Managers from OPFs: – ▪ Both business and political relations are part of their tasks and strategy. – ▪ Business relations: – – ▪ Help to find new opportunities within the industry and reduce uncertainty. – – ▪ Provide trust to find the right partner (trust considered a key asset) and protect the business idea – – ▪ Help access to private sources of funding – – ▪ Provide support to navigate through the administrative processes and avoid red tape. – – ▪ Help to protect jointly against dodgy competitors. – ▪ Political relations: – – ▪ Managers include development of personal relationships with government officials as part of their daily tasks and strategy, even when they do not want it. – – ▪ They try to minimise the impact of the negative discrimination through these relations.

Chart 5.1 Summary of the findings of the first narrative

Main themes in the story	Marketing capabilities		Closure/discussion of the first narrative
	Starting point	Definition and development of products and services	

Main findings	▪ Managers from SOEs/SO NCs:
	  ▪ Perceive marketing mainly as the increase of sales, i.e., only commercial focus.
	▪ Managers from Private NCs and OPFs:
	  ▪ Consider marketing mostly tactical
	  ▪ They have multifunctional and polyvalent sales teams. Focus on sales.
	  ▪ Are reactive to customers' demands.
	    ▪ Define domestic (Chinese) consumer as price sensitive.
	    ▪ Define price based on competitors.
	      ▪ Consumers look for the right function-price balance. Too many options. Easy to change.
	    ▪ Consider sales' promotions as the most relevant actions.
	  ▪ Consider most relevant communication means as very aggressive mass publicity campaigns including deep engagement with social media
	  ▪ Invest less once the intended positioning has been achieved.
	  ▪ Consider relationships as key to achieve their sales' goals, especially in private firms. (e.g., managers use their relationships to get preferential access and conditions in distribution and advertisement channels).
		▪ Managers from SOEs, NCs (state-owned and private) and OPFs from strategic industries:
		  ▪ Put emphasis on innovation pushed by the government with financial help and investment in R&D.
		  ▪ Consider plans from the government as clear indications for new developments.
		  ▪ Perceive policies/plans from the government as opportunities to develop business.
		    ▪ This means low business risk to develop a new business.
		▪ Managers from OPFs:
		  ▪ Consider that innovation is key to compete in China's domestic market:
		    ▪ To protect from competitors.
		    ▪ To survive and protect from weak enforcement of competition and other regulations.
		    ▪ Follow a reactive rather than active innovation strategy.
		▪ Several managers (from all types of firms, although mainly from big firms) find that the domestic advantage of an increasing well prepared and large labour force working long hours are key to:
		  ▪ Achieve a shorter time to market
		  ▪ Offer shorter product cycles
		  ▪ Increase cost efficiency
			▪ SOEs/SO NCs:
			  ▪ A resource-bridging capability (Chen & Wu, 2011) with government officials is key to operate in China.
			▪ Private NCs and OPFs from strategic industries:
			  ▪ A resource-bridging capability with government officials is key to operate in China.
			    ▪ Firms benefited from the positive discriminatory support of the government and therefore they have become leaders with low business risk.
			  ▪ A resource-bridging capability with business partners supports the growth of the firm.
			  ▪ An adaptive capability (Chen & Wu, 2011) is developed:
			    ▪ Due to a huge market rapidly developing and the perceived continuous and ambiguous changes faced in the first stages of development.
			    ▪ Due to the weak institutional environment faced in their first stages of development.
			    ▪ Rooted in the Chinese culture: competitor orientation, agility, and stratagem.
			▪ OPFs:
			  ▪ A resource-bridging capability with government officials helps to avoid being at a disadvantage.
			  ▪ A resource-bridging capability with business partners helps to face the negative discriminatory support from the government.
			  ▪ An adaptive capability is developed:
			    ▪ Due to a huge market rapidly developing and the perceived continuous and ambiguous changes.
			    ▪ Due to the weak institutional environment faced in their first stages of development.
			    ▪ Rooted in the Chinese culture: competitor orientation, agility, and stratagem.

Chart 5.1 (continued)

5.3 Analysis of the Second Narrative. Operating in an International Environment

In the second narrative, managers talked about their experience in the European market and how they had been developing their business activities in this environment. This narrative was divided into two main parts. In the first part, experiences from managers talking about the first stage of their firms in the EU were considered; that is, how/why the company decided to go to Europe as well as how the first activities were defined before entering the market and during the first years of operation/introduction. In the second part, the focus was on the medium term, considering the narratives of managers from companies with more than three years of experience in the EU in the sample, and on how they adapted to the new market.

5.3.1 First Stage

Drivers to Go Abroad

Most of the participants started this part of their narrative by explaining why their companies decided to enter the European market. Most of the participants from every type of company (SOEs, SO NCs, private NCs, and OPFs) emphasised the influence of the domestic government on their firms' internationalisation plans and decisions, in addition to other motivations to go abroad. However, the perception of this influence was different depending on the type of company.

a. The Positive Influence of the Chinese Government in SOEs, SO NCs, and private NCs

Managers from SOEs and SO NCs perceived a positive influence of Chinese government plans for internationalisation, being the main driver for going abroad. More specifically, they explained that the internationalisation of the firm was the result of government-to-government deals and government-strategic and economic plans outside China. The Chinese government facilitated the international expansion of these firms by providing strong support, for example, in the form of financial help (mainly through loans with preferential conditions from state-owned banks) or access to information about international markets. In this sense, the manager from Co6 explained that: "the firm was following government-to-government deals in other emerging countries when we first went abroad. We received a lot of support. I remember the links between the two governments and the financial support. Of course. It was a very important plan for the Chinese government". The manager from Co7 reported that: "our presence in Spain was due to the government-strategic decisions of the firm in Spain and Europe. The government needed us to be here; they facilitated a lot of information about the market". Also, the manager from Co9 explained that the company was responding to the government policies of going abroad when they first internationalised at the beginning of the 2000s, an expansion promoted by the government after China's accession to the WTO in 2001. More examples from the stories were: "We received financial support from the Chinese state development bank" (Co4) or "First of all, I have to say we are here (in Europe) because of the government, they want to open the Madrid hub, and they can support our company with money for every flight. If we fly, they can support for three years" (Co9).

Managers working in private NCs also mentioned the financial support received by the government in the form of preferential access to special funding conditions through state-owned banks. In this case, firms were following internationalisation policies and other government initiatives while taking advantage of the incentives received. However, in contrast with SOEs and SO NCs, managers working in these firms did mention that their internationalisation plans were also a result of their growth objectives. The manager from Co16 explained: "of course, it is clear that there is an interest from the Chinese government, but we also want to grow, expand our business, so there is an effort from the firm's perspective". These firms had a large customer and profit base at home, so international expansion was part of their natural plans to grow.

Finally, some managers from OPFs also explained that different in contrast with the negative support felt at home, the Chinese government was supporting them to go abroad. This could be identified in narratives from managers working in strategic sectors/industries like consumer electronics and technology. Managers showed a positive perception of these government initiatives that were helping firms to expand abroad. These initiatives included financial support to attend international fairs as well as tax refunds. Examples from the narratives include: "The Chinese government has some plans for exports, for exhibitions outside, actions outside" (Co22), "The government helps firms to go abroad, also for small companies, so if you can benefit then you can go outside" (Co32), "Because the labour cost was low, China was the factory of the world, government was pushing exports with a lot of incentives like tax refund or giving credits to the manufacturers" (Co34), "they (government officials) are supportive. And if the company wants to apply for some trade shows overseas the government also helps and offers some subsidy. Financial support to go to the fairs. And if you do export business, we also got some tax refund" (Co37), and "So we have tax refund, you know, there is something called exportation tax refund. So today if you want to export electronic products or high-end products, the tax refund is higher. If you want to export textile, the tax refund is like 5%, versus like 15% for energy-saving products or any high-tech products" (Co39).

These plans and incentives mentioned by the interviewees are aligned with the different internationalisation policies defined by the government since 1978 and are detailed in Table 2. Firms in the sample that internationalised in the 2000s were benefiting, as mentioned by interviewees in the narratives, from the promotion of the government of light industries, reduction of custom duties, and financial aids to support exports (Bellabona & Spigarelli, 2007). Other firms, which started their internationalisation process in recent years, mainly after 2010, may be responding to the increasing support of the Chinese government to domestic firms with a focus on innovative products as a result of different initiatives like Made in China 2025 or the Belt and Road Initiative; these firms in the sample belong to industries such as technology, telecommunications, and automotive (energy efficient and new-energy automobiles) (OECD, 2018; Oliveira et al., 2017). The government was promoting the expansion of these firms to developed regions with the purpose of improving the positioning of Chinese firms, both at home and abroad, representing new opportunities for Chinese firms and their managers to develop new businesses (OECD, 2018).

b. The Negative Influence of the Chinese Government on OPFs

In the case of managers working in OPFs from different industries to those mentioned above (i.e., Technology or automotive), the government had an impact on their internationalisation plans, but mainly because of the negative discriminatory influence in the domestic market, being one of the drivers for their internationalisation. Managers from OPFs considered Western markets, the EU in particular, as markets that would enhance their development and growth without the disadvantages faced at home. They perceived the EU as a safer and freer market to operate as explained by Co25, Co27, and Co35 respectively: "The government influence is one of the reasons we go abroad, to compete more freely without restrictions. It would be much easier", "More restrictive policies in China. And the company income tax is high, like twenty-five per cent. As a result, companies want to keep the benefit out of China", and "All the resources and help from the government are for SOEs. Private companies need to operate in a negative environment, where we need to fight every day to get access to capital. That is why many private companies go abroad; to look for new capital, better and easier options to grow".

c. Other Motivations for Private NCs and OPFs

In addition to the support from the government, government initiatives to promote internationalisation, or the government negative discriminatory influence at home, private firms (NCs and OPFs) explained additional motivations for international expansion. First, a motivation shared by several managers was their willingness to learn and bring this knowledge back to China. Managers perceived the European market as "better prepared, more mature" (Co31) or "with mature knowledge that we can acquire and develop at home" (Co38). The goal was to find new business practices that could be developed and applied in the Chinese domestic market to increase the company's domestic competitiveness. This confirms the findings from Ramamurti and Hillemann (2018): "We want to learn like this kind of standardised things. We want to build in China. But now we want to fully understand this regulation, this standardisation in Europe and in the US. Then we can build in China... So that is our big chance. So that's why we want to cooperate with foreign companies to fully understand how to do it and then develop it in China" (Co40).

Second, some managers also explained that firms were looking for new markets to avoid dependence on a market with lowering margins due to the increasing competition explained in the first narrative. Co33 stated this very clearly: "One main reason is to expand the brand outside China. That is because in China the penetration is also very high now. A lot of efforts to compete affecting our business objectives. So for us this is a need, the need to continue growing". Even if the domestic market was full of business opportunities, as explained in the first narrative, huge competition seemed to make operating in China difficult in the sense that firms developed their business strategies in a very crowded market and were usually forced to lower prices according to competitors, meaning lower margins. It is in this context that they think the EU may be a new market opportunity for new business developments that would complement domestic growth.

Finally, managers from OPFs also explained their desire to develop internationally well-known brands as a positive endorsement for their development in the domestic market. They considered that if the brand could be successful in the EU, it would be better accepted in China. The reason for this would be that Chinese consumers still perceive foreign brands as "of better quality" (Co32). If the product or service was accepted by European consumers, this would be a very positive endorsement for the firm in the domestic market: "the reason is the strategy to upgrade the brand, and second is to enter high-profile markets like Europe. If the brand is successful in here, it's a huge endorsement in China" (Co39).

All in all, internationalisation strategies of SOEs, SO NCs, private NCs, and OPFs from strategic industries were responding to the positive support received by the government. However, in the case of private NCs, managers also showed growth motivations, international expansion being a natural step in the development of the firm. Finally, for private firms in general (NC and OPFs), the reasons to go abroad seemed to be a combination of reactive strategies to escape from the negative discriminatory support from the Chinese government at home, and additional motivations such as knowledge acquisition, firm's development in a perceived less crowded market and brand awareness development.

Companies and Managers' Assumptions in the First Stage in the International Market

a. The Adoption of a Similar Business Model and Marketing Approach as in the Domestic Market

Managers from private NCs and OPFs explained that when the firm first entered the EU, they defined and applied the same marketing approach as in the domestic market. In this sense, the same competitor orientation was found in the narratives. Managers explained that they first focused on what Western competitors were doing with the purpose of "beating them" (Co19) and "positioning ourselves as the best new option" (Co21). In this sense, the same as they did in China, they also defined very aggressive publicity campaigns with the same purpose of increasing sales with a special focus on the very short term. Also, they expected that the European consumer would be price sensitive, and therefore their actions should be focused on the best function-price balance. Finally, rather than thinking of the consumer and adapting the offer to the host market, managers defined the same product and service portfolio for the European market. Examples from the stories were: "When we started in the UK, we just defined the lower price, as in China. Now we should elevate it step by step" (Co33), "First the firm wanted to fight against its main competitor, Cisco. The firm defined prices 30 or 40% lower. A huge advertising campaign was launched. This did not work. A war started. And the firm learnt. It learnt to find partners" (Co34), "we entered Europe with the same product and price, with a very clear focus on the main competitors in Europe" (Co36), or "We entered Europe because we wanted to sell the same product as in China. We thought we would also be the best in Europe" (Co38).

The manager of a mobile phone company (Co39) also described how his company's strategy was also based on price in the EU but with some differences. His perception was that Chinese brands were not considered to be as good as home-based brands, so he decided to establish a very high price expecting that the European consumer would identify the brand as of high quality. He soon realised that the European consumer did not understand their positioning and strategy: "We recently launched a flagship phone last month, June 19th, in Paris, Louvre, and the price was 999 Euro. And another special edition of Lamborghinis version, priced €1999 and €1699. These two prices are super high. We received lots of doubts and questions like who are you like a new brand or why do you position yourself like this? Why is your product worth such a high price? We were shocked at the beginning. For us it was clear".

The decision of going abroad and the market selection seemed to be an opportunistic and short-term decision, with poor previous market research. In the case of SOEs, SO NCs, and private NCs, the decision was made because of government decisions or because they just found it was a good moment to do so but without a deliberate strategic plan within the firm. In the case of OPFs, it seemed that the decision was adopted because managers perceived it was a good moment, a decision adopted quickly, with no previous planning, in addition to their desire of operating in a less restrictive environment. It was not considered nor defined as a strategic decision, similar to the decision-making process defined for the domestic market and linked to the particularities of the Chinese environment explained by managers in the first narrative. Some examples from the managers' experiences were: "We look for similarities and learning opportunities. What is the market for this? If we do phones, we go to Finland (when Finland was a reference in the mobile phone industry), or we choose the US because we work on technology. It was like the good moment for this product" (Co22), "When we started in the European Union, we didn't have any deliberate plan... we just wanted to go to Europe because it is a large market outside China and many renowned companies are from there" (Co32), or "It is just learning by doing completely, just go abroad, just try with whoever does business in your sector" (Co38).

Furthermore, it is interesting to note that many of the managers explicitly mentioned that they expected to have the same results as in China. "We had a leading position in China. So why not being the best in Europe? Then you realise that this is not the way it works here (in Europe)" (Co16). A feeling of naivety (or presumptuousness) could be unfolded from the narratives. Participants seemed to think that if they had been successful in China, they could be successful anywhere. This perception was especially relevant in SOEs, SO NCs, and private NCs, probably because of the low business risk mindset shown by their managers and developed at home due to the strong support from the government and the poor international business knowledge, an attitude already identified in the first narrative.

b. An Expected Similar Environment to that in the Domestic Market and the Development of Personal Relationships

Managers from all firms in the sample expected a similar business environment to that in China and as a consequence, they acted similarly when they first entered the market: "we acted as we know when we entered Europe, as we had to enter another city in China. As if it was another decision for the domestic market" (Co26).

Managers from SOEs, SO NCs, and private NCs showed that they were used to the support received. This was evident when they explained the reasons why the firm went abroad, but also when they emphasised that the development of political relationships with Chinese government officials, arranged before going abroad, was key in the decision-making process. The development of these links had clear similarities with the relevance of political relationships in the domestic market that were part of their daily tasks and activities and facilitated their business operations in China. In this sense, these types of firms relied on the same resource-bridging capability when deciding to enter a new market, but both with government officials from the home and host country. Managers showed that they were comfortable also operating in the EU, in an environment with a perceived low business risk, as they would be protected by both home and host governments.

Similarly, several managers from private NCs and OPFs looked for relations with potential business partners before going abroad based on trust. In this context, alliances and partnerships seemed to be the most popular ways to enter the European market, with relationships playing a fundamental role. Managers were looking for the most suitable partner to work with, following the same behaviour as in China. These business relationships in the host market were considered useful to find new opportunities within the industry while reducing the possible uncertainty that could be found in the new business environment. Examples from the narratives are: "We look for the right partner and we cooperate together to learn how to do things in Europe" (Co21), "Guanxi is important at the beginning, is the only way to start in a different country. It is a matter of trust to do business with someone you know and also because they already know how things work" (Co24), "We go where access is easy and where we already have some business relationships" (Co30), or "So that's why every time we go to different trade shows, we will look for the best ones and talk with them and look for some opportunities to cooperate. It is the only way to know the market" (Co31).

Managers from private NCs and OPFs also relied on local friends and their recommendations to have easier access to the market and reduce the uncertainty when doing business in a new business environment for the first time. Managers relied on Chinese lawyers, Chinese friends with previous experience in the sector or recommendations from the Chinese diaspora. In addition, they made efforts to develop a strong business network by finding support in local contacts, establishing local offices or teams with local employees. This was also considered as the most trusted option to start a business in the EU, based on the resource-bridging capability with business partners developed at home: "We have that establishment, we will establish that company in each country, then we will recruit local talent, and we will understand how to do that skill transfer, and we will do whatever it needs with the local partner to improve culture, that is, to work on cross-cultural management" (Co19) and "We hire the most experienced persons in the industry. We only hire them. And of course, trusted workers" (Co21). Through partnerships and local teams, Chinese managers had access to key information about the market, the local consumer, and distribution channels while they minimised the barriers in terms of cultural distance, language, and the understanding of local practices. Some managers looked for these links before going abroad, as a premise to develop a new business in the new market, while others found these links useful to overcome the initial wrong assumptions in the international market.

Finally, another reason to develop local relationships that was mentioned in the narratives was that cooperating with a local company would help to overcome the challenge of the negative perception of Chinese products and services; even today, the European consumer perceives Chinese products as of low value-added or low quality. Some managers in the sample explained that in the first stage, their brand was not used, "until at least the market and the consumer know that if a European company trusts a Chinese one, this means that we are also good" (Co34). If personal networks helped managers in the domestic market to develop their business in order to overcome the perceived challenges, as explained in the first narrative, networks, or personal relationships also seemed to be relevant in the first stage of the internationalisation of the firm. Chinese managers relied on the same factors that seemed to be successful in the domestic market.

c. Expected Friendlier Environment in the Case of OPFs

Managers from OPFs also expected less regulations and a friendlier business environment in the EU. This was one of the motivations for these firms to go abroad as a consequence of their desire to operate far from the negative discriminatory support from the Chinese government enjoyed at home. However, participants realised right after they entered the EU that they were working in a very different market with a different structure and institutional elements; the first feeling was that they should understand, follow, and comply with many perceived requirements and rules; very different to the perceived non-existent regulations in the domestic market. They were not suffering from discriminatory government support, but they found a different institutional environment, with more formal institutions being the norm. European authorities seemed, according to managers' perceptions, more demanding, perceiving a much stronger legal enforcement. The feeling was that this was very new for them; elements such as "pay commissions to all your business partners as in the contract" (Co24), "deal with garbage (in reference to environmental initiatives)" (Co25), or "security requirements for employees" (Co38) were new to them. They seemed surprised about the new rules, but they did not perceive them as constraints; some managers even considered that they would have a positive effect in their domestic operations, as they understood they could be good for the business.

These misunderstandings (probably based on the lack of experience of operating in a different environment) showed a poor international business knowledge as well as little access to information about markets outside China; it might be important to note here that managers lacked access to international communication sources like TV or the Internet and that international business had recently been introduced in universities or business schools. Some examples from the narratives are: "We don't have a very strict or clear idea in terms of marketing strategy or how to build a brand here. We just decided to come" (Co21) and "I set up the UK company by myself; I came Europe five years ago. I know nothing about this market, business in Europe" (Co34). The manager from Co37 explained: "Business schools in China are something relatively new and international business is a subject that has been introduced only recently. We don't have the proper knowledge to go abroad, you know, the English is still very poor, including a lot of start-ups, let's say, all the start-up I meet, maybe 10%, the top management can speak very average English. So that's a very big limitation if you want to go global. So, these start-ups are struggling, even if they have a lot of subsidies. They are struggling because, you know, the market moves very fast, they have a lot of competition".

All in all, in the first stage of the internationalisation process, managers deployed the same business model and marketing approach as in the domestic market as well as the same decision-making process. In addition, managers from all types of firms expected a similar environment to that in China and therefore acted similarly. Only some managers, mainly from OPFs suffering from the negative discriminatory support at home and not linked to strategic industries, expected a friendlier market to operate.

5.3.2 Second Stage

Mistakes and Challenges Identified After the First Steps in the EU

As introduced in the preceding section, after the first steps in the EU, managers realised that mistakes were made and that several challenges should be faced. Some differences were found depending on the type of firm. Managers from SOEs and SO NCs found some challenges once they entered the market, but they were not considered as big issues affecting their activity. Managers reported mainly language issues, cultural differences, and some difficulties in finding the right team, challenges usually faced by any type of firm or individual when going abroad to a new market for the first time: "The culture, the language, the habits, everything is different. We need to get used to it" (Co7), "the mentality is different, we come here to work and work" (Co10), "of course the language, but that is why we have local persons, although it is not easy to find the right ones. They also should understand our culture, our goal, be trustable" (Co11), or "I realised that working and the entrepreneurial mind-set of working hard and making easy money, currently the norm in China, is not valid when going abroad" (Co14).

For managers working in private NCs and OPFs, challenges were more evident and affected their activities and strategy in the EU. They realised about the mistaken assumptions and actions from the first stage. More specifically, managers considered the development of the firm harder than expected, mainly due to a more mature market than predicted before going to the EU. This was evident in two main areas: (i) the European consumer behaviour and consumption patterns found, and (ii) the perceived different "rules of the game" as already introduced above.

On the one hand, consumption patterns were different from the ones expected, very different from the ones they were used to in

China working with the Chinese consumer. The main challenge was to understand that the focus in Europe should not be only on increasing sales (sales orientation, as it is in China). The key point was about educating the consumer, understanding first his needs: "So for the Chinese company to go international, the most important challenge is still to understand the way of our customer thinking. The culture, history, even philosophy. That's very important. We should understand more about our customer. It's not only to sell, as in China" (Co22). Managers understood that the competitor orientation leading to low prices adopted at the very beginning was not successful in Europe. Similarly, managers also perceived that Europeans were less affected by mass publicity or sales promotions: "The European consumer has usually a knowledge of the product, the quality, the market. He knows what he wants. In this sense, he is less affected by commercial initiatives" (Co16), "People are more mature in terms of what they see and what is appearing in the media or other commercial channels. So, we won't do it this way" (Co17).

Moreover, managers found that the European consumer gave a higher importance to quality beyond only a suitable function-price balance, which was also important, but not that determinant as in China. The point, and the challenge, was to develop a good enough product, with good quality, matching European standards: "later we found our product cannot match customer requirement, then we found, okay, our competitor is different, they are more leading in technology, quality... different from us" (Co22), "Chinese people, the customers, are very easy. They like to try but they do not mind buying new things every time. Good is enough. In Europe they are more conservative, they spend more time choosing, comparing. It is also true that there are less options" (Co34). Another manager emphasised the quality perception: "It is cost leadership in China vs technology leadership in Europe. Now we will advertise, or we will mention more about our technology leadership" (Co39). In this case, the firm showed that it learnt from the experience and understood the need to adapt to consumers' expectations. Another manager had the feeling that to match European standards would make the firm better in terms of product and service development. "Even if we think our product and service meet their requirements, it is not perfect, something is wrong. We do not match consumers' expectations. We need to improve and be better. Here quality is more important than in China" (Co23).

Another challenge was the perceived lower importance given to online marketing activities if compared to the online efforts made in China. "People have different tastes and different habits, and also in terms of the virtual marketing, the culture is different. So, first of all, we need to understand what is more popular in Europe, among, for example, their young consumers. Store is still more important here and social networks are different" (Co26), "Alibaba is even bigger than Amazon, right? If you compare Black Friday in the US in the shops, few people go to shops in China. Now in China, almost no one goes to, you know, stores" (Co28), "In China everyone buys on the Internet. Alibaba, Taobao. In Europe the store is the place to be" (Co35), "First we should focus on the physical channel, when we first came to UK, different from China, we thought the online channel marketing was the most effective way to approach our potential customers here. Today we combine it with the use of social media to market our channel products, and channel events" (Co40).

In this sense, most of the managers used similar terms to define the actions they should develop in the EU, if compared to the ones in China. The shared perception was that the actions to attract European consumers were of "higher order" (Co24), "more demanding" (Co29), or "of higher level" (Co34). Usually, these actions meant higher investments than predicted: "When we know the rules, how much money I need to keep in my pocket so that I can have the money to do lots of marketing, the print marketing, the social media marketing. So, I realised that this would have an impact on firm performance" (Co36). As a consequence, a short-term mentality, as applied in China and in the first stage in Europe, was not valid anymore. Chinese managers were forced to think more about the consumer and plan their activities with a medium- to long-term focus.

On the other hand, managers found different "rules of the game". More specifically, most of the managers working in private firms mentioned they had to face different economic and judicial systems as well as a stronger enforcement of regulations. "We found much more rules, much legal requirements than in China when it comes to operating here. Pay different taxes, garbage, security legal requirements" (Co17), "we call PPE, personal protection equipment, we gave all the PPEs to our employees, ask them to put on the mask, helmet, the glasses, the breath is not very free, they say they don't want to put it on. And we just do not, like, yell to them, you have to wear it. And the customer said this is your responsibility, company responsibility, to be responsible for your employees, to let them wear the glasses, masks. So, this is a very big difference. Here we would even have legal problems" (Co19), "it is the law, and we need to follow it. Because the domestic customer, they only focus on their product itself, they do not care about your operators. The partner (in Europe) will say, if there is no change, then no orders will be placed. So that is why we change to train our operators, workers [because] this is good for you" (Co38).

Finally, cultural aspects affecting their way of doing business in Europe were found as, for example, the importance given to contracts in Europe, different to China, where trust and relationships are more important: "Business environment in general is very different. When you understand how it works, it is easy. They really like to follow the contract. They are very picky or very serious when discussing the contract with us, but once the terms of the contract are clearly defined, they would just do according to what the contract says" (Co29).

All in all, (i) the different consumer behaviour and consumption patterns found in Europe and (ii) the different "rules of the game" clearly affected their activities' definition as well as their profit and growth expectations. Managers were over-optimistic on prospects. After the first stage, they realised that they got lower margins than predicted as well as lower growth rates. Managers explained how they needed to adapt to consumers' behaviour as well as to new rules of the game that had an impact on their costs as well as on their pricing strategy, which could no longer be the same as in China, based on competitors. This was exemplified by the following quotes: "It's a different way here, we are still competitive, but you don't need to be very much cheaper than others. If you are much cheaper, as we wanted to be in China or here, 50% cheaper than your rival, lots of the partners will not sell you, they think you are, how to say, you are destroying the system" (Co20) or "we need to make more efforts to sustain office operations, to pay the salary commissions of merchandisers who are visiting on our behalf. And even to deal with the garbage, etc. lots of unexpected costs, so we must set up the price much higher than usual, as in China and as considered at the beginning" (Co36).

In sum, it could be concluded that the main challenges and differences perceived by the participants were found on: (i) the maturity of the market: the EU was perceived as a sophisticated market with demanding consumers showing experience, knowledge and interest about the product or service; that is, with different consumption patterns to the ones developed in China, as identified by participants, whereas the Chinese market presented an uncertain environment and a rapidly changing demand, (ii) the legal and regulatory frameworks; while in China participants, as explained in the first narrative, especially by managers from private firms, found lack of transparency and protection from the government, in the EU they found a more demanding and much stronger legal enforcement, with different "rules of the game", and (iii) business knowledge and management style: participants realised they lacked business experience and knowledge as they faced more sophisticated management practices while they perceived in their European partners a larger experience working in business. Finally, Chinese managers should understand the different cultural behaviours, and how to behave in mature business contexts, especially on the different importance given to personal relationships. In this sense, it seems to be confirmed in the narratives that Chinese managers needed to rely on local managers and staff to overcome these disadvantages and adapt to the new local environment.

In any case, managers showed quick learning abilities to adapt to the European context based on their flexibility and agility developed at home. They found challenges, but managers did not show a feeling of failure or the willingness to drop the decision of going abroad. Mistakes did not prevent them from continuing in the EU.

Success Factors

In the medium and long term, different success factors were identified from managers' narratives depending on the type of firm. Managers from SOEs and SO NCs showed that they were able to face the few initial challenges thanks to the backup of the government. In this sense, it seemed evident that firms became tools for the government's international plans. The few challenges found, and the poor importance given to them, showed that managers were benefiting from a low business risk mindset inherited from home. The feeling was that the firm would be successful no matter what may happen, as the government will always be there: "we have its support; we are very strong because of that. As something from the government, it will not let it fall" (Co2). A different language or not finding the right partner at the beginning were not perceived as relevant problems by managers working in these firms as they knew that with the backup of the government, business will develop smoothly: "it is fine, we do not have too many troubles, nothing relevant" (Co5). They felt safe operating outside due to the support from the government: "I'll give you money to grow better and do better marketing and get famous in the international market. But I control the company. Yes, but once the company is going down, they will help, they will put money and they will help. There was support, yes. For example, one firm from solar energy, they were going down for five years and then the government decided to support them, to keep the position" (Co6). Even if firms were not economically or financially successful, the government would support them as strategic assets and tools for its internationalisation plans.

On the other hand, private NCs and OPFs showed the ability to develop innovative ways to use their home-developed adaptive capability adapted to the European market. A resource-bridging capability with business partners was useful to face the initial challenges, but this capability seemed to fade in the medium term. In general, managers explained that in the medium term, they identified the need to adapt and include some changes while trying to keep some of their home-developed advantages. Adopting the reactive behaviour that characterised managers in the sample, they understood, after the initial mistakes and challenges, that the European consumer was completely different and that a competitor orientation was not valid anymore. More importantly, they were able to identify several strengths unique to them and very positively perceived by Western consumers and partners. Consequently, they focused on building upon them. For example, some managers found that combining their low-cost strategies, perceived as an advantage in a mature market affected by a global crisis, with efforts in new innovative breakthroughs and product customisation, was a successful strategy in the EU. European consumers benefited from lower prices with a good enough quality adapted to European standards. Some Chinese firms that implemented their home strategy of targeting unfulfilled needs and markets also realised they were successful. These strategies seemed to be possible thanks to the adaptive capability developed at home with the ability to target the right segment while identifying unfulfilled needs.

Also, a common pattern found in most technology, telecommunication, and consumer electronics firms was that managers invested huge amounts of money in R&D centres in Europe, in which managers and their teams could get new knowledge through the collaboration with Western partners, which could then be developed at home thanks to the domestic advantages (i.e., with a large workforce, extensive working schedules and short product cycles and time to market), upgrading the domestic R&D capacity. As explained by several managers, it was taking around half the time to develop and improve a new technology in China. With this cost efficiency, Chinese firms would stay competitive in the EU, while also spreading their improved R&D capacity globally. "I think, compared to the companies in the US or the European companies, our advantage, it's the speed, the faster speed, the better sense of the users' experience and also the Internet, so that we are more like Internet companies instead of software companies, right? We can collect user feedback faster and then develop it faster, and on the other hand, we have more flexible business models" (Co21).

Chinese firms were then able to launch new, innovative, and cost-efficient products in Europe and more competitive than their Western competitors: "Another point is that no company can provide so quickly what we provide, with such good technologies, because we can change and adapt very quickly, meeting their needs" (Co34) or "now we compete with quality and service. So, for example, the high-level, top, Bosch, they have high price, and then there is Da Hua, is this price very low. We sell the prices much higher that Da Hua, more than any other Chinese company, but of course, it is much lower than Bosch. It is like finding a position not covered in this market. Lower prices but providing good local service to the customers. We are able to do that, and we are successful" (Co34).

In this sense, flexibility and efficiency, leading to innovative developments, seemed to be success factors for the medium and long term in the EU. According to managers, these were positive elements perceived by European partners and one of the reasons they usually decided to cooperate with Chinese firms, in addition to the access to the large Chinese market: "Efficiency developed at home that can help partners to reduce costs with processes not previously known by them. This is our added value as well. Because they are engineers, they know their products very well. But they might not be as good as us to know the manufacturing process of the product. At unit price, we are higher; but the total operation cost for them will be lower, so that is our innovation and development. And I feel that Western companies may not have the same capability to do innovation and development, so they would pay the bill. They would like to buy this" (Co16). This is, private NCs and OPFs improved their adaptive capability based on home-based advantages.

Furthermore, the strong customer base at home seemed to have a positive impact on the survival of the firm in Europe due to the financial resources that managers could get. The fact that they could still support low margins might also be explained by their strong domestic business as well as by their perseverance and main motivations to be in Europe which could only be reached with a sustainable presence in the continent. In other words, private firms secured a long-term presence in the EU by using resources from their strong domestic customer base despite the poor performance, at least in the first years of activity.

Finally, managers from private NCs showed that their firms secured their long-term presence in the EU through strong support from the Chinese government as their firms were considered strategic assets. From their narratives, it could be perceived that Chinese big companies with extensive experience outside China were companies that had received the support of the government to become global players. Several managers mentioned in their interviews that the government's goal was to "become more and more involved in the private sector and not only lead SOEs as it wants to be part of the success and not failures" (Co17). So, with its involvement, it would support firms to continue being successful in the international scene while "showing the increasing power of China worldwide despite the slowdown of the domestic market" (Co19). Managers from private NCs recognised that the government was an active participant in the company's management: "I know that the government wants to take shares and increase its power in the management roles" (Co18). According to managers in the sample, this influence and support of the government was evident in the easy access they had to financial sources through state-owned banks with "pretty good conditions and high subsidies" (Co20). Also, as explained by Co21's manager: "There are many high regulations to control private firms, especially since President Xi is in power, including the establishment of party branches within the firms. In return, firms will receive state investments". Other managers also confirmed the strong power of the government: "I would not say the government would let the firm down. Because the firm is facing big challenges now, but I would say the government would help the firm to go through that challenge. They would even talk with Mr. Trump if needed" (Co15), "The firm is not a public company. They do not have the stock, but they have virtual stock to, like, give bonuses to stimulate their employees. If other companies are doing that virtual stock, the law says no. But why can (the firm) do this? Because Mr. Zhu Rongji, the former Premier of China, gave them this exclusivity, saying they can do the virtual stock to incentivise their employees. So, this is one very obvious case, how the government is supporting them. Other companies doing this virtual stock, no way. But the firm can do this. This is an obvious case of how government supports them" (Co17).

All in all, thanks to strong government control and support (SOEs, SO NCs, and private NCs, as well as OPFs from industries supported by the government) and the development of an improved adaptive capability with home-based advantages (private NCs and OPFs), Chinese firms could secure their long-term presence in the EU.

5.3.3 Summary of Findings of the Second Narrative

The chart below summarises the findings of the first narrative analysed above. Findings are summed up in the themes identified in the experiences described by the managers working in the firms in the sample. Similar to the first narrative, firms can be divided into three groups according to the development of their capabilities: (i) SOEs (including SO NCs), Private firms aligned with the government (Private NC and OPFs from strategic industries or sectors), and OPFs. At the end of the chart, a closure and brief discussion is included, which is further developed in the next chapter (Chart 5.2).

<table>
<tr><th>Main themes in the story</th><th>Drivers to go abroad</th><th>Companies' and managers' assumptions in the first stage in the international market</th></tr>
<tr><td></td><td colspan="2">First stage</td></tr>
<tr><td>Main findings</td><td>
<ul>
<li>Managers from SOEs/SO NCs:
<ul>
<li>Follow the guidelines of the government: government-to-government deals and government strategic/economic plans.</li>
<li>Perceive high relevance of Chinese government policies for internationalisation.</li>
<li>Receive high support in the form of financial help and access to information about the international market.</li>
</ul></li>
<li>Managers from private NCs and OPFs from strategic industries:
<ul>
<li>Follow policies and other government initiatives and take advantage of the incentives received, in addition to their objectives of growth.</li>
<li>Consider that firms have a large domestic customer base supporting their international expansion, also perceived internationalisation as a natural step in the firm's expansion.</li>
</ul></li>
<li>Managers from OPFs:
<ul>
<li>Consider the negative discriminatory government support felt at home as a driver to go abroad.</li>
<li>Expect to learn from international firms to apply the learning at home.</li>
<li>Look for new markets/avoid dependence on a perceived saturated domestic market with lowering margins.</li>
<li>Want to develop brands recognised internationally, as a positive endorsement for their development in the domestic market.</li>
</ul></li>
</ul>
</td><td>
<ul>
<li>Managers from all types of companies:
<ul>
<li>Deploy the same business model and marketing approach as in the domestic market:
<ul>
<li>Focus only on increasing sales and price from competitors. Same competitor orientation (especially in private firms).</li>
</ul></li>
<li>Apply the same decision-making process as in the domestic market:
<ul>
<li>Opportunistic decision.</li>
<li>Short-term planning.</li>
</ul></li>
</ul></li>
<li>Managers from all types of firms expect a similar environment to that in China and therefore act similarly, i.e.:
<ul>
<li>Managers from SOEs/NCs:
<ul>
<li>Are used to the support received from the Chinese government and the low business risk.</li>
<li>Rely on relations with Chinese and host governments, arranged before going abroad.</li>
</ul></li>
<li>Managers from private NCs and OPFs from strategic industries:
<ul>
<li>Are used to the support received from the Chinese government and the low business risk.</li>
<li>Rely on relations with Chinese and host governments, arranged before going abroad.</li>
<li>Look for relations with potential business partners based on trust.</li>
<li>Rely on local friends/recommendations to have easier access to the market (Chinese lawyers, Chinese friends with previous experience in the sector, recommendations from Chinese diaspora).</li>
</ul></li>
<li>Managers from OPFs:
<ul>
<li>Look for relations with potential business partners based on trust.</li>
<li>Rely on local friends/recommendations to have easier access to the market (Chinese lawyers, Chinese friends with previous experience in the sector, recommendations from Chinese diaspora).</li>
</ul></li>
</ul></li>
<li>Managers from OPFs expect less regulations/a friendlier business environment in Europe.
<ul>
<li>Show a poor business knowledge as well as little access to information about international markets.</li>
</ul></li>
</ul>
</td></tr>
</table>

Chart 5.2 Summary of the findings of the second narrative

Main themes in the story — Second stage

Mistakes and challenges identified after the first steps in the EU

Main findings:

- Managers from SOEs/ SO NCs:
  - Find some challenges, but not considered as big issues.
  - Mainly face language issues, cultural differences, and difficulties in finding the right team.
- Managers from private NC and OPFs:
  - Realise the mistaken assumptions and actions from the first stage in the international market.
  - Consider the development of the firm in Europe harder than expected.
  - Find a more mature market than expected.
  - More mature consumers. Different consumption patterns. Should be consumer oriented.
  - Perceive different 'rules of the game'. i.e., Different social, economic, judicial systems as well as strong enforcement of regulations.
  - Were over optimistic on prospects:
    - Lower margins than predicted.
    - Lower growth rates achieved.
  - Show quick learning abilities, based on their flexibility and adaptive capability developed and acquired at home.
    - The challenges found do not prevent them from continuing in Europe.

Success factors

Main findings:

- Managers from SOE/SO NCs:
  - Deal with the challenges with support from the government.
  - Firms become tools for the government's international plans.
  - Benefit from a low business risk.
  - Feel safe operating outside due to the perceived backup of the government.
- Managers from Private NCs and OPFs from strategic industries:
  - Secure the long-term presence in Europe through strong support from the Chinese government.
    - This is more evident in the case of NCs, as they are considered strategic assets for the Chinese government.
- Managers from Private NCs and OPFs:
  - Show the ability to develop innovative ways to use their home-developed adaptive capability adapted to the European market.
  - Improve the adaptive capability based on home-based advantages.
  - Secure the long-term presence in the EU using resources from their strong domestic customer base despite the poor performance.

Chart 5.2 (continued)

Main themes in the story	Closure and discussion of the second narrative

Main findings	First stage in the EU:
	▪ SOEs and SO NCs:
	  ▪ A resource-bridging capability with Chinese government officials and host governments is crucial in the first steps abroad.
	▪ Private NCs and OPFs from strategic industries:
	  ▪ A resource-bridging capability with Chinese government officials and host governments is crucial in the first steps abroad.
	  ▪ A resource-bridging capability with business partners in Europe acts as the starting point when entering new markets.
	▪ OPFs:
	  ▪ A resource-bridging capability with business partners in Europe acts as the starting point when entering new markets.
	▪ Second stage in international market:
	▪ SOEs and SO NCs:
	  ▪ A resource-bridging capability with Chinese government officials is crucial in the second stage to provide firms with resources to outcompete local firms.
	▪ Private NCs and OPFs from strategic industries:
	  ▪ A resource-bridging capability with Chinese government officials is crucial in the second stage to provide firms with resources to outcompete local firms, more evident in the case of NCs.
	  ▪ The strength of the resource-bridging capability with business partners fades in the second stage as the company becomes stronger.
	  ▪ Their learning abilities underpin their adaptive capability to operate in different institutional environments.
	  ▪ Their adaptive capability is reinforced based on domestic advantages.
	▪ OPFs:
	  ▪ The strength of the resource-bridging capability with business partners fades in the second stage as the company becomes stronger.
	  ▪ Their learning abilities underpin their adaptive capability to operate in different institutional environments.
	  ▪ Their adaptive capability is reinforced based on domestic advantages.

Chart 5.2 (continued)

5.4 Conclusion

The objective of this chapter was to report and analyse the experiences shared by the participants in the study, following the structure of the two narratives. Graphs at the end of the analysis of each narrative presented a summary of the findings. The following chapter will present the results of the analysis, leading to the development of a framework to understand the development of capabilities of Chinese multinationals, with a focus on marketing capabilities.

References

Bellabona, P., & Spigarelli, F. (2007). Moving from open door to go global: China goes on the world stage. *International Journal of Chinese Culture and Management, 1*(1), 93–107. https://doi.org/10.1504/IJCCM.2007.016170

Hofman, B. (2018). *Reflections on forty years of China's reforms*. Fudan University's Fanhai School of International Finance.

Hsu, S. (2017). Foreign firms wary of 'Made in China 2025,' but it may be China's best chance at innovation. *Forbes*.

Ling, C., & Naughton, B. (2016). An institutionalized policy-making mechanism: China's return totechno-industrial policy. *Research Policy, 45*(10), 2138–2152.

Nee, V., & Opper, S. (2012). *Capitalism from below: Markets and institutional change in China*. Harvard University Press.

OECD. (2018). China's Belt and Road Initiative in the global trade, investment and finance landscape. In *OECD Business and Finance Outlook 2018*. OECD Publishing.

Oliveira, R., Menzies, J., Borgia, D., & Figueira, S. (2017). Outward foreign direct investment from emerging countries: Theoretical extension and evidence from China. *The International Trade Journal, 31*(5), 402–428.

Ramamurti, R., & Hillemann, J. (2018). What is "Chinese" about Chinese multinationals? *Journal of International Business Studies, 49*(1), 34–48.

Spar, D., & Oi, J. (2006). China: Building "capitalism with socialist characteristics". *Harvard Business School*.

Wei, J., Cong, S., Wang, C., & Pan, Q. (2020). The critical role of the institution-led market in the technological catch-up of emerging market enterprises: Evidence from Chinese enterprises. *R&D Management, 50*(4), 478–493.

6

A Framework to Understand the Development of Capabilities of Chinese Multinationals

6.1 Introduction

The chapter presents a summary of what has been developed in this project in terms of data analysis and findings from the previous chapter. It is structured into three main sections: Sect. 6.1 provides a summary of the data analysis process, Sect. 6.2 discusses the findings and presents the different propositions of the study that address the questions presented in Chapter 3, and finally, Sect. 6.3 presents the introduction of the framework.

6.2 Summary of the Data Analysis Process

This section presents a summary of the methodology applied in the study and the process of data analysis of forty interviews with Chinese managers about their personal points of view and experience regarding the influence of the domestic business and institutional environment on the development of capabilities at home and abroad. In particular, the study helps to understand and analyse the following ideas based on the objectives of the study as well as on the questions in the study:

M. Altamira, *Chinese Firms in the Global Market*, Palgrave Macmillan Asian Business Series, https://doi.org/10.1007/978-3-031-59227-0_6

i. the Chinese domestic institutional environment where Chinese managers develop their decision-making processes, and the impact of the perceived relevant institutional elements, formal and informal, on them, especially on the definition and development of marketing capabilities,
    a. within this, the definition and development of the marketing capabilities in the domestic market and how managers interpret these marketing capabilities, and
ii. the definition and development of marketing capabilities in different business environments, mainly Western markets (the EU in particular), and the influence of the home institutional environment, as a result of the internationalisation expansion of the company.

Interviews developed in the study represented sequences of events and personal experiences and representations over time; in other words, personal accounts or stories from managers working in the firms in the sample. It is in this context that the strategy defined for the study was Narrative Inquiry, an uncommon strategy in the field of management and international business, but relevant as it helps to provide a valuable source of insight in the context of organisations where narratives are analysed in terms of how different people, in this case, Chinese managers, subjectively make sense of the strategic choices (Rhodes & Brown, 2005). The forty firms in the sample, which were divided into State-Owned firms (SOEs), National Champions (state-owned or SO NCs, and private or Private NCs), and Other Private Firms (OPFs), represented different industries and had enough and substantial experience and percentage of sales in the EU. In this sense, this study gains relevance in the current business scenario in which the EU is the main trade partner of China (European Commission, 2019). The work builds upon the literature in the field and considers narrative interviews for data collection. Narrative interviews were divided into two different stories, representing two different narratives for analysis: (i) the understanding and interpretation of Chinese managers working in the firms in the sample of the influence of relevant Chinese institutional elements (formal and informal) on the development of their firms' marketing capabilities and (ii) the understanding and interpretation of Chinese managers of the influence of Chinese institutional elements (formal and informal) on the development of the firm's marketing capabilities outside China, in different institutional environments, mainly in the EU.

The goal of the analysis was to find similarities, differences, and patterns across interviewees in order to develop theory while focusing on the content rather than on the form of the text, that is, on the "told" of the story (Riessman, 2008). In this context, a thematic analysis following the method of Saunders et al. (2003) and the analysis of Polkinghorne (1995) of narratives in the context of biographical narrative research was considered as a method of analysis (Kim, 2015). A coding process was followed and categories and themes for each of the narratives identified. Findings were analysed and reported by themes as developed in the previous chapter; graphs included at the end of the analysis section of each of the narratives showed the main findings by themes.

6.3 Discussion

In this section, the author discusses the findings presented in the previous chapter. Following the structure of the interviews and the findings, the discussion is divided into two. The first discussion considers the findings of the first narrative and therefore attempts to answer the first sub-question of the study. The second discussion considers the findings of the second narrative and addresses the second sub-question.

6.3.1 Discussion of the First Narrative

Qa: How do Chinese domestic institutional elements (formal and informal) influence the definition and development of marketing capabilities in the domestic market?

As analysed in the first narrative, the Chinese environment presents unique characteristics that shape the capabilities developed by Chinese firms in the domestic market. Two areas are identified in this context: (i) a huge, dynamic, and fast-changing market and (ii) the role of market institutions. Within the latter, there are three main institutional elements: (a) a discriminatory government support, (b) the intensive use of personal networks, and (c) a unique strategic mindset embedded in the Chinese culture and philosophy; while the first two emerged as themes in the narratives, the third one appears after the analysis and interpretation of managers' experiences.

Thirty years ago, and especially between Deng Xiaoping's open door policy at the end of 1978 and the WTO accession in 2001, the Chinese domestic market started to: (i) get competition from both domestic and international players, (ii) grow very rapidly along with the country's economy (especially on the East Coast), and (iii) nurture companies that grew opportunistically (mainly SOEs) which after a few years became dominant players in their sectors. The combination of these three main points meant that: (i) companies that were allowed to produce and access the market (mainly SOEs and NCs as not all companies in China at that time were allowed to sell in the domestic market) grew tremendously fast, selling everything they produced, supplying a hungry Chinese market with new goods and services and (ii) that consumers were buying in a kind of trial and error exercise as moving from a centrally planned economy to one based on a free market, meaning that they didn't have the motivations, perceptions, learnings, and memories (Kotler & Keller, 2011) to inform their purchase decisions. That is, there was no legacy, meaning that consumers and firms were starting from zero in the adoption of new products and services and were acquiring new purchasing behaviour. After this first period, and especially during the market-enhancing reforms phase, from 2002 until 2020 (Hofman, 2018), domestic companies continued their growth based on an almost endless internal market full of consumers hungry for new products with an increasing but (still) relatively low purchasing power. This performance that started mainly in the Eastern part of China continued in the West of the country, mainly with the development of the West of China, a result of the 2000 Go West Policy, a campaign launched by the government to develop the Western territories, moving from the prosperous eastern coastal regions, focus of the first twenty years of reforms, to the less developed ones in the West of China, although very rich in terms of natural resources (Singh, 2002).

This background underpinned the marketing activities of Chinese firms developed in China. It is in this context that Chinese managers participating in the study showed a reactive behaviour towards demand, rather than active and forward-looking strategies aimed at educating consumers as is the case in markets with legacies and more developed institutions. Managers referred to their teams as multifunctional and polyvalent sales teams, and participants described their marketing activities mainly as tactical rather than strategic, pointing out a list of many and different activities aimed mainly to reach new clients and get market share. These activities were defined and developed with a short-term focus and usually reacting to competitors' actions (especially to their pricing strategies).

This growth was fuelled mostly by consumers without prior knowledge or perceptions of products and services, therefore less demanding and basing their consumption decisions on the strength of the endorsement (usually by a well-known local celebrity) or on the price-function relation. As a consequence, Chinese managers considered sales promotions as the most relevant action and aggressive mass publicity campaigns (including deep engagement with social media) as the main communication means. In addition, these Chinese consumers were found to be highly sensitive to price, therefore managers defined their pricing strategies by reacting to what competitors were doing. As there were several options in the market, firms sought to differentiate by lowering prices creating thus a race to the bottom in many markets.

At the same time and mainly as a result of the reforms and policies defined by the government, China had been experiencing constant and rapid changes in social, economic, and political institutions, making market institutions relevant elements influencing the development of capabilities in Chinese firms. China's government (at the central, provincial, city, or prefecture level) played a fundamental role in Chinese firms' strategic options; managers' decision-making processes, and therefore the firm's capabilities, were influenced by an institutional environment with a strong government presence felt not only in SOEs and NCs but also felt by managers from OPFs. However, within this, SOEs, NCs, as well as OPF from strategic industries and sectors, on the one hand, and the rest of OPFs on the other, were subject to different environmental effects in China and therefore to a different government influence (Lin, 2010). This situation resulted in a positive discriminatory government support perceived by managers working in SOEs, NCs, and strategic OPFs, and a negative one perceived by the rest of the managers from OPFs.

In this context, political as well as business relations were identified as relevant to the successful development of Chinese firms (Buckley, 2018; Fornes et al., 2021; Nee & Opper, 2012; Yi et al., 2017). Similar to what was found in previous studies, political relationships helped companies and managers in the sample to gain political legitimacy and avoid uncertainty while they provided shortcuts to government-related resources such as bank loans, tax payments, government support plans (Buckley, 2018; Fornes et al., 2021; Park & Luo, 2001), and industry trends (Chen & Wu, 2011; Fornes et al., 2016). Due to this, managers showed that the development of personal ties with government officials became common practice not only in SOEs and NCs but also among private firms to avoid being at a disadvantage. In addition, business relationships were a key valued asset for managers working in OPFs in the sense that they helped to face the negative discrimination from the government by facilitating the navigation through the administrative processes while avoiding red tape. They also helped to find new opportunities in the market while reducing uncertainty and protecting them from unfair competitors.

At this point, it is worth asking: how were Chinese firms able to grow and be successful in their domestic market? The answer seems to be in the development of capabilities that are relevant to, and are shaped by, the domestic business and institutional environment. Chinese firms developed a very strong and profitable domestic base that enabled them to develop their areas of strength as they were growing and to build their brands basing their current (and probably future) competitiveness on capabilities, namely: (i) adaptive capability and (ii) resource-bridging capability. There were four main elements influencing the development of these capabilities present in the domestic market, an influence that was different depending on the type of firm: (1) a huge market rapidly developing, (2) discriminatory government support, (3) the intensive use of personal networks, and (4) a unique strategic mindset embedded in the Chinese culture and philosophy.

The Development of the Adaptive Capability

Managers from private firms (OPFs in the sample) were shown to be successful at developing new products, services, and business models. These firms had developed innovative abilities following reactive innovation strategies as a response to: (i) the huge dynamic and fast-changing market, and the continuous and ambiguous changes faced: firms adapted quickly to the ever-changing business environment and demand, while developing the necessary flexibility to react to external signals and competitors and (ii) the weak institutional environment: private firms faced very high competition with weak legal protection and enforcement of competition policies. In this context, Chinese firms (OPFs) were exposed to imitation and copying from competitors, and innovation only appeared in the narratives as the way to survive and protect the development of new ideas from the perceived weak enforcement of market regulations. In addition, the negative discriminatory support from the government was evident in the narratives. Managers felt they did not have the same opportunities as SOEs or NCs and that they made more efforts to develop their business in a domestic market dominated by firms aligned with the government. As a result, firms developed the adaptive capability, the firm's ability to respond and adapt to market changes and maintain its competitive advantage over time.

Furthermore, the development of this capability could be explained by the unique Chinese strategic mindset identified from managers' experiences. On the one hand, the development of short-term strategies was supported by dialectical thinking, in which change is expected and is constant (Nee & Opper, 2012). Chinese managers explained that due to the continuous changes in the market, they developed their strategies with a short-term focus while at the same time they were more flexible. On the other hand, managers adopted a competitor orientation (rather than the consumer orientation usually found in Western firms) that allowed them to face competition with the idea that the competitor was the one to beat (i.e., the consumer is not usually the main priority). Therefore, they defined actions based on competition rather than on consumers, being reactive rather than active. This competitor orientation along with stratagems may also explain the extended and socially accepted imitation in China in which the achievement of a strategic objective through the unorthodox is embedded in the culture and philosophy. Finally, among managers working in private firms, agility was at the core of their mindset. This element explained why private firms were in a good competitive position (even beating larger companies) supported by the development of the adaptive capability that Chinese firms adopted in order to quickly adapt to the continuous and unpredictable changes in the market.

Managers from SOEs and SO NCs clearly benefited from domestic scale and size advantages, with the guidelines and directions of the government leading the execution of their plans and activities. In this sense, managers showed that they tended to be less flexible or adaptive (than what was found in managers in private firms, private NCs, and OPFs) due to the business and institutional elements they were operating in. That is, a stable, safe, and controlled environment with few players and with strong support from the government. In this context, their development was based on and supported mainly by an environment with little business risk, a consequence of: (i) very high growth rates of the market (especially until 2020) and (ii) positive discriminatory government support, with access to preferential resources from the government (funding, research, legal protection, etc.). Managers followed the plans of the government for product and service development and received financial support, legal protection, and other preferential access to resources needed to develop their business in China, a positive discriminatory support that has resulted in a low business risk mindset.

Government policies during more than 40 years of reforms are behind these findings. The three main phases of reforms—moving from a planned to a market-oriented economy, including the opening up of the economy during the 2000s, the development of the private sector (Hofman, 2018) or the decision to develop the West of the country through the Go West campaign—were driven by strong policies and incentives to firms. The main goal of the Go West policy was to promote "marketisation in the western region, attracting foreign investments and mobilising investments from the prosperous eastern provinces through preferential policies, including incentives in taxation and bank credits" (Singh, 2002, p. 122).

During the 2000s, the Chinese government decided to continue developing and implementing strong policies to support domestic growth, especially promoting strategic industries, moving from market-oriented policies towards a stronger government intervention (Ling & Naughton, 2016). In fact, in recent years, policies and government interventions have remained in this direction with the new measures adopted at the 14th Party Congress on productivity and innovation, the 13th Five-Year Plan, and finally the most recent Made in China 2025 Strategy defined in 2015 by President Xi Jinping. During the 18th Party Congress in 2014, market-oriented initiatives were still considered key for the country's development; however, the government also stated that an economic system with state ownership predominance should have a key role in the future development of the country. This government-led market (Wei et al., 2020) benefited SOEs, NCs, and any firm from strategic sectors or industries creating new demand and influencing the strategic behaviour of firms through favourable initiatives and positive support.

As a result, managers working in these firms, especially SOEs and SO NCs, showed a lower market orientation, as they were not motivated by economic reasons but by the political goals of the Chinese government. Within this and considering their strategic mindset, neither competitor orientation nor agility were identified as elements defining their business strategies. The two identified guiding principles of their decision-making process were: (i) short-term planning within dialectical thinking (they followed the government plans that usually had to be adopted very quickly) and (ii) "Tao" (which is associated with "greatness", a value identified in some narratives when managers talked about the growth and success of their firms and the power of the Chinese government, a presumptuous attitude identified in several narratives). Consequently, an adaptive capability was not identified in SOEs and SO NCs.

Finally, managers in private NCs and OPFs in strategic industries and sectors showed a combination of the capabilities, skills, and knowledge shown above. On the one hand, these firms had grown and developed their business in an environment similar to that faced by OPFs, facing the same challenges, and therefore developing the adaptive capability strengthened by the support received by the government because of their potential strong position within their industries in recent years. In particular, China's government was putting a lot of resources into the development of innovation and technology, as conceptualised by the publication of the Medium-Term Strategy for Science and Technology and the development of the 16 Megaprojects in innovation and technology (Hofman, 2018) as well as with the new measures and policies mentioned above on productivity and innovation, especially the recent Made in China 2025 Strategy. Firms in these sectors became strategic companies for the government and therefore they received similar preferential support as SOEs and SO NCs. Private NCs and OPFs aligned with the government, usually market-oriented and non-resource-seeking firms, were characterised by an adaptive capability supercharged by strong support from the government (mainly in terms of financial resources) and favourable policies that facilitated their operations in the domestic market. This made for very strong firms, usually leaders within their industries.

The Development of the Resource-Bridging Capability

The intensive use of personal networks also shaped the definition of managers' activities and capabilities in the domestic market. Both the development of personal networks with government officials and with business partners appeared in the narratives as very important for managers.

The Chinese government emerged as the main actor dictating actions, rules, and policies, and for this reason, the development of personal relationships with government officials was proved to be key to operating in China. On the one hand, the development of these ties was perceived as very positive both for managers working in SOEs, NCs, and OPFs from strategic industries in the sample, due to the strong support received during the development of their activities, mainly since the 90s and during the 2000s, the third phase of the reforms and onwards. Personal relations with government officials were part of their daily activities and firm strategy and were the basis for successful business development through the policies defined by the government. On the other hand, for managers in OPFs not operating in strategic industries, this influence was perceived as a barrier to growth. They included the development of personal relationships with government officials as part of their daily tasks and strategy, even when they did not want it, to try to minimise the impact of negative discrimination.

In any case, the development of personal ties with government officials based on personal relations (linked to the positional power of the politician) was a common practice among managers from every type of firm, representing a valued asset for mutual trust leading to successful business relations. However, political relationships were more relevant and more valued in a positive way by managers looking to secure an advantage to access resources controlled by the government or when doing business in strategic industries directly controlled by it. In addition, personal relationships with government officials also benefited private NCs in the sense they had taken advantage of positive discriminatory support from the government, which helped them to become leaders within their industry. Finally, the strong reliance on these ties explained the perceived safe environment and therefore the low business risk mindset developed by managers.

Personal networks with business partners were also important mainly for managers working in private firms, both NCs and OPFs, as a mechanism to facilitate their operations in a context characterised by negative discriminatory government support and a weak regulatory framework, felt by private NCs in their first stages of development, evident in every OPF regardless of its stage. OPFs still face challenges in an environment dominated by the government and SOEs and NCs, where preferential access was given to these firms as explained above. Through the development of business personal relations, managers from private firms found ways to detect new opportunities within the industry while they reduced the uncertainty caused by the continuous changes in the environment and the huge competition, which as a consequence supported continuous growth. In addition, personal networks with business partners were a mechanism that facilitated the development of business operations providing trust, a relevant and needed asset in China to find partners and develop long-term relationships, while at the same time helping to protect the business idea against dishonest competitors. In fact, a lack of trust is a characteristic of the stratagem culture. At the core of the stratagem is the achievement of a strategic objective through the unorthodox (Liu, 2015); taking the competitor by surprise is a way of understanding the unorthodox and a tactic usually developed by Chinese firms. In this sense, it might be possible to say that social networks and relationships, developed and used with the aim of developing trust and protecting business ideas from misleading competition, were a reactive behaviour or appeared because of the stratagem culture, and were therefore embedded in the Chinese culture and philosophy.

It is in this context that firms in the sample developed a resource-bridging capability, with both government officials and business partners: a firm's ability to access or obtain access to relevant and critical resources to secure sustainable competitive advantage (Chen & Wu, 2011). This resource-bridging capability with government officials was key to successfully operating in China for SOEs, NCs (SO and private), and OPFs from strategic industries, while it helped OPFs to avoid being at a disadvantage. In addition, the resource-bridging capability with business partners supported the growth of private NCs, especially in their first stages, and helped OPFs to face the negative discriminatory support from the government while dealing with the changing and ambiguous business environment and the perceived weak legal protection.

Concluding Remarks From the Analysis and Propositions

The Resource-Based View of the firm (RBV) (Barney, 1991) states that in order to achieve sustained competitive advantage, a firm should accumulate unique tangible and intangible resources or capabilities that are heterogenous and immobile as well as valuable, rare, and costly to imitate. In addition, and probably more importantly, the firm should be organised to capture the resulting value (Barney, 1991; Ju et al., 2013; Wernerfelt, 1984) of the resources or capabilities. On the other hand, marketing literature shows that a company that has adopted the marketing concept[1] will place its customers at the top of the organisation's list of priorities and will focus on capturing and satisfying them in order to create a sustainable and profitable relationship (Darroch et al., 2004; Day, 1994). A firm implementing this marketing concept is said to be market-oriented or to have adopted market orientation as an asset or capability. In this context, marketing capabilities are defined as complex bundles of skills and accumulated knowledge, exercised through organisational processes, that enable firms to coordinate activities and make use of their market-based knowledge and assets (Day, 1994).

As seen in this narrative, Chinese firms were reactive rather than active and proactive when responding to customers' demands; in the case of SOEs and SO NCs because the demand was given while in the case of private firms, especially OPFs, they were focused on dealing with a run to the bottom price war with competitors. This suggests that they did not adopt the marketing concept, at least in the way defined by received theories based on Western companies, and therefore that they were not basing their competitive advantages on the marketing capabilities seen in incumbent international companies, which, as defined by Morgan et al. (2009), can be grouped into two distinct sets: (i) specialised marketing capabilities: functionally focused capabilities built around the integration of the specialised knowledge held by the firm's marketing employees and the communication of benefits to current and potential customers (Day, 1994; Slater & Narver, 1993; Tripsas, 1997) and (ii) architectural marketing capabilities: capabilities that give strategic focus to the specialised marketing capabilities and drive the deployment of resources to achieve strategic goals.

In this context, the following propositions can be developed in order to address the first sub-question:

- Proposition 1: Chinese firms in the sample develop, by chance or by design in a reactive way, capabilities that are relevant and specific to them and are shaped by the huge domestic market rapidly developing, discriminatory government support, the intensive use of

[1] Marketing is defined as "Marketing is the activity, set of institutions, and processes for creating, communicating, delivering, and exchanging offerings that have value for customers, clients, partners, and society at large." (Gundlach & Wilkie, 2009, p. 260).

personal networks and a unique strategic mindset embedded in the Chinese culture and philosophy, mainly focused on the short term and competitors' actions.

- Proposition 2: The competitor vs. the consumer orientation, which may be the major difference between Chinese firms and firms from developed countries, might represent the biggest challenge for managers and companies going to Western countries to expand their activities, to the EU in particular.
- Proposition 3: An adaptive capability and a resource-bridging capability with both government officials and business partners are the relevant marketing capabilities at the core of the firms in the sample.
- Proposition 4: Private firms (including private NCs and OPFs) develop their competitive advantage around both an adaptive and a resource-bridging capability and base their resource-bridging capability on both their political and business connections.
- Proposition 5: SOEs and SO NCs develop their competitive advantage around the resource-bridging capability only, and within their political connections.

Finally, these findings suggest that SOEs and SO NCs may lack other marketing capabilities, such as adaptive capabilities, as they base their competitive advantage mainly on the support received by the government. This is in line with some previous studies showing that an overreliance on government support may weaken the company's competitiveness in the long term (Cardoza et al., 2016; Porter, 2008).

6.3.2 Discussion of the Second Narrative

Qb: To what extent are the marketing capabilities developed in the domestic market applicable and transferred to international markets with different institutional environments (mainly the EU)?

In other words, how have Chinese firms been competing and deploying their strategic options in markets with different institutional frameworks and therefore developing their capabilities? Narratives confirmed that the home environment played a fundamental role in the internationalisation strategies of Chinese firms in Europe (Lattemann et al., 2017). On the one hand, formal institutions, especially policies defined by the Chinese government, played a direct influence on the internationalisation decisions and processes of Chinese companies. Policies such as the "Go Global" strategy, or more recently "Belt and Road" or "Made in China 2025", were examples of the efforts of the Chinese government to enhance the internationalisation of Chinese companies (Lattemann et al., 2017; Zou et al., 2022). Not only were SOEs and SO NCs actively responding to this support but also non-state firms (NCs and OPFs in specific strategic industries) were especially active as they were benefiting from special conditions to go abroad (Du & Zhang, 2018). This supports the argument that Government Specific Advantages (GSA) (Ramamurti & Hillemann, 2018) are one of the most important factors enhancing the international competitiveness of Chinese firms.

On the other hand, informal institutions also played an important role in the international development of Chinese firms. Similar to what happened in the domestic market and given the strong support received from the Chinese government, the development of personal relationships with home government officials seemed crucial as well as the relationships between Chinese and host government officials, as they facilitated the first steps of the firm in the host market. Also, business relationships with local partners or local teams in the host market were determinant for Private NCs and OPFs in the choice of the market and when entering the EU as they facilitated the process in the first stage by reducing uncertainty and the access to relevant resources (Fornes et al., 2016; Lin et al., 2016; Oliveira et al., 2017).

Furthermore, narratives showed how the home environment and institutions had a great influence on the development of the capabilities of Chinese firms in the EU. The development and application of the capabilities differed depending on the stage in the internationalisation process as well as on the type of firm. On the one hand, during the first stage, Chinese firms relied on the resource-bridging capability developed at home. More specifically, a resource-bridging capability with home and host government officials was key for SOEs, NCs (SO and private) while a resource-bridging capability with business partners in the host country acted as a starting point for private NCs and OPFs. On the other hand, during the second stage, a resource-bridging capability with Chinese government officials was crucial for SOEs, NCs, and OPFs in strategic sectors. Finally, the adaptive capability developed at home as a consequence of the huge market rapidly developing, the continuous and ambiguous changes faced as well as the weak institutional environment, reinforced by domestic advantages and profits they were making in China, became key for NCs (SO and private) and OPFs to create sustainable competitive advantage in Europe in a second stage of their internationalisation process.

First Stage in the EU

During the first stage of the internationalisation process in the EU, Chinese firms in the sample deployed the same business model and marketing approach as in the domestic market, with a focus only on increasing sales and defining actions and prices based on Western competitors. They applied a similar decision-making process as in the domestic market while showing a similar behaviour taking decisions for the short-term and only because the opportunity appeared, i.e., an opportunistic decision-making process.

In this sense, SOEs and SO NCs were responding to government-to-government deals and government-strategic and economic plans, these government strategies and initiatives being their main motivation for going abroad. A list of detailed actions, initiatives, and incentives from the Chinese government to promote internationalisation, and from which firms in the sample could have benefited, can be found in Table 3.2. This strong support of the government explained the same low business risk mindset developed in the domestic market and shown during the first steps in the EU. Managers were used to the government backup and even if challenges appeared, they were not considered big problems affecting their operations. Different from managers from other types of firms, mainly private, managers did not seem to worry about business results or the future of the firm as they felt the firm would always be successful, even when positive results were not clear in the first stage. This was evident in the presumptuous attitude transmitted by several managers in the narratives. In this sense, the cultural aspects of dialectic thinking (firms followed the government plans, which usually changed often and were adopted very quickly) and "Tao" (which was associated with "greatness"), identified in the first narrative, also explained the business model adopted in the EU. In this context, SOEs and SO NCs, similar to what they were doing at home, relied on political relations with home and host government officials arranged before going abroad to look for the right opportunity for doing business and entering the market. The resource-bridging capability with Chinese government officials and host governments was crucial in the first steps abroad.

In the case of private NCs, they were also following policies and other government initiatives while taking advantage of the incentives received. Similar to SOEs and SO NCs, managers showed the same low business risk mindset as in the domestic market, developed as a consequence of the strong support received as well as their leading position in the market. The resource-bridging capability with Chinese government officials and host governments was also crucial in their first steps in the EU. This was also evident in the narratives from OPFs from strategic industries.

However, even if in most of the cases the decision to go abroad was because of the government decision, managers also considered the opportunity within their objectives of growth and as a natural step in their development, taking a more active role in the internationalisation process and decisions. In this sense, they showed a similar behaviour to the rest of the OPFs. The implementation of the same business model and marketing approach was evident in the adoption of the competitor orientation developed in China. Actions and objectives were developed for the short term with a focus on increasing sales while beating the competitor rather than focusing on the new consumers' needs.

Also, as in the domestic operations, they looked for relations with potential business partners. Some managers in the sample contemplated this option before going abroad while others decided to look for new partners once they realised there were unpredicted challenges in the new environment; a context characterised by political stability and mature institutions that contrasted with the less developed and more immature institutions found in China, especially in terms of: (i) the maturity of the market, (ii) the enforcement of legal and regulatory frameworks, and

(iii) the experienced business knowledge and management style (Child & Marinova, 2014).

Narratives made evident that managers, especially managers from OPFs with any kind of support from the government, faced challenges and made mistakes during their first steps in the EU because of: (i) poor business knowledge and experience in international markets, (ii) little access to information from the outside when they first decided to go to the EU, and (iii) wrong expectations about a more friendly and easier environment in which to operate.

In this sense, managers looked for relations based on trust while they relied on local friends and recommendations to have easier access to the market. For example, they previously contacted recommended Chinese lawyers, Chinese friends with previous experience in the sector, or considered recommendations from the Chinese diaspora in the host country. The resource-bridging capability with business partners in the EU acted as the starting point when entering new markets. That is, Chinese firms showed familiar behaviours and looked for similar environments during the first stage in the EU, acting as if they were at home, before acquiring learning to move to unfamiliar territories; guanxi, not just in China but abroad, was considered crucial for market selection and first entry into new markets.

Second Stage in the International Market

During the second stage in the EU, SOEs and SO NCs realised that they faced several challenges, but they were not considered as disadvantages. This shows again the low business risk environment in which managers felt they were operating and the feeling of safety that characterised their experiences. Therefore, to maintain the strong position, it was evident in the narratives that managers still relied on the resource-bridging capability, especially with home government officials, to get relevant resources, mainly financial support, to support their competitiveness against local firms. The same capability was identified in private NCs and OPFs from strategic industries as these firms were considered strategic assets for the Chinese government.

However, in the case of private NCs and OPFs (from strategic and non-strategic industries), the strength of the resource-bridging capability with business partners that proved to be relevant in the first stage in internationals markets seemed to fade in the second stage. Firms had become strong and even if they continued to rely on local partners or local teams, these relations did not appear as a competitive advantage in the medium and long term. Instead, managers showed strong learning abilities that underpinned their adaptive capability developed at home to operate in different institutional environments. In particular, managers faced and adapted very quickly to the challenges found in terms of: (i) the maturity of the market: the EU was perceived as a sophisticated market with demanding consumers showing experience, knowledge, and interest about the product/service; that is, with different consumption patterns to the ones developed in China; (ii) the legal and regulatory frameworks; while in China participants, as explained in the first narrative, especially by managers from OPFs from non-strategic industries, found lack of transparency and protection from the government, in the EU, they found more demanding and much stronger legal enforcement, with different "rules of the game"; and (iii) business knowledge and management style: participants realised they lacked business experience and knowledge as they faced more sophisticated management practices while they perceived a more extensive experience working in business in their European partners.

Eventually, Chinese managers understood the different cultural behaviours, especially how to behave in these mature business contexts, while understanding the different importance given to personal relationships. It seemed to be confirmed in the narratives that Chinese managers needed to rely on local managers and staff to overcome these disadvantages and adapt to the new local environment. More importantly, managers showed the ability to adapt their cultural values and switched from a competitor orientation to a consumer one, shaped, in any case, by Chinese unique cultural elements. In this sense, the flexibility and agility (Nee & Opper, 2012), another relevant cultural value inherited from home, helped Chinese managers to overcome the challenges and solved the mistakes made in the first stage.

Furthermore, in the medium and long term, this adaptive capability was reinforced in the EU based on the advantages developed in the domestic market; mainly the increasingly well-prepared and large labour force working long hours, shorter times to market, shorter product cycles, and an increase in cost efficiency. These factors, together with a large customer and profit base at home able to support the lower results in the host market, were key for a sustainable presence in the EU. Chinese firms were able to offer their local partners strong advantages to compete with their Western counterparts, while successfully targeting European consumers' unfulfilled needs. After the 2008 crisis, price and value-for-money consumers made up a significant and rising segment in developed markets representing a major opportunity for Chinese firms. Also, the increasing volatility in the global environment is demanding ever-greater flexibility, agility, and risk tolerance from managers and companies.

Concluding Remarks From the Analysis and Propositions

All in all, the domestic environment that shaped the capabilities developed by firms in the domestic market had a great impact on the capabilities developed and applied by Chinese firms in the EU. Managers showed that they learnt how to adapt the capabilities developed at home, shaped by: (i) a huge, dynamic, and fast-changing market, and (ii) distinctive market institutions, to the new environment to create sustainable competitive advantage also in different institutional environments.

The impact of the home and host institutional environment and the influence on the development of the capabilities of Chinese firms have been studied by several authors based mainly on mainstream theories. For example, Child and Marinova (2014) suggested that Chinese firms investing in countries with low political risk and mature institutions as, for example, the EU, find the highest challenges when operating in these environments, turning Chinese institutional and firm-level characteristics into firm disadvantages. Other authors argued that to upgrade and gain differentiation and brand advantage abroad, Chinese firms had to develop a new set of capabilities to operate in diverse institutional environments and as a consequence to strengthen their performance abroad (Cardoza & Fornes, 2013; Child & Rodrigues, 2005; Fornes et al., 2016).

Narratives showed that Chinese firms faced initial challenges and apparently made some wrong decisions during the first steps of their internationalisation process. Managers acted as if they were in China, influenced by several unique cultural factors and demonstrated a "learning by doing" behaviour. For example, one of the most relevant decisions, based on what they were used to doing at home, was the application of the competitor orientation which represented the main challenge during the first steps in the EU. However, far from coming back home and considering the European adventure a failure, managers in the narratives showed how challenges did not prevent them from growing and even developed a successful competitive advantage in Europe. That is, narratives confirmed that firms quickly learnt from the experience and the environment, and switched from a competitor to a customer focus strategy based on their home-developed capabilities, which were not a disadvantage in the Western market, as suggested by Child and Marinova (2014) nor new capabilities as proposed by other authors (Cardoza & Fornes, 2013; Child & Rodrigues, 2005; Fornes et al., 2016). Instead, these capabilities developed at home and embedded in the Chinese unique institutional environment became the source of competitive advantage of Chinese firms in the host institutional environment.

Mathews (2006), in his analysis of Dragon Multinationals, already anticipated the idea that traditional theories do not necessarily apply as Chinese companies have distinctive characteristics compared to incumbent firms. In fact, Chinese firms have developed new and different capabilities to the ones defined in Western environments as concluded from the narratives. The resource-bridging capability developed at home helped them to successfully select the market and partners, as well as enter the EU and outperform incumbent firms in the medium and long term (the latter mainly in the case of SOEs and NCs). In the case of private NCs and OPFs, managers integrated the knowledge acquired in the host market and, with flexibility and agility, they were able to improve the adaptive capability with Country-Specific Advantages (CSA) (Oliveira et al., 2017), confirming that Chinese firms not only possess dynamism and speed to absorb knowledge and practices (Lattemann et al., 2017) but that they are able to build on their home-developed capabilities thanks to visionary leadership, most of the time reinforced with government support, agility, and rapid learning abilities.

In this context, the following propositions can be developed in order to address the second sub-question:

- Proposition 1: In the first stage in the EU, SOEs and SO NCs base their competitive advantage on the resource-bridging capability developed at home with Chinese government officials and host governments.
- Proposition 2: In the first stage in the EU, private NCs and OPFs from strategic industries base their competitive advantage on the resource-bridging capability developed at home with Chinese government officials and host governments. A resource-bridging capability with business partners in Europe acts as the starting point when entering new markets.
- Proposition 3: In the first stage in the EU, OPFs base their competitive advantage on the resource-bridging capability developed at home with business partners in Europe, which acts as the starting point when entering new markets.
- Proposition 4: In the second stage in the EU, the resource-bridging capability with Chinese government officials is crucial to provide SOEs and SO NCs with resources to outcompete local firms.
- Proposition 5: In the second stage in the EU, the resource-bridging capability with Chinese government officials is crucial to provide private NCs and OPFs from strategic industries with resources to outcompete local firms, more evident in the case of NCs. In addition, the strength of the resource-bridging capability with business partners fades in the second stage as the company becomes stronger. Their learning abilities underpin their adaptive capability to operate in different institutional environments, which is reinforced based on domestic advantages.

- Proposition 6: In the second stage in the EU, the strength of the resource-bridging capability with business partners in OPFs fades as the company becomes stronger. Their learning abilities underpin their adaptive capability to operate in different institutional environments, which is reinforced based on domestic advantages.

6.3.3 A Framework to Understand the Development of Marketing Capabilities of Chinese Multinationals

Figure 6.1 illustrates the main findings of the research, which is a framework to understand the definition, development, and application of two marketing capabilities that are relevant to the Chinese business and institutional environment, the adaptive capability and the resource-bridging capability, following the analysis of a process and sequence of events related to the domestic development and further internationalisation expansion of Chinese companies in the EU. First, it presents the elements influencing the development of capabilities in the domestic market as well as the marketing capabilities defined and developed by each type of firm in China, corresponding to the first narrative and therefore addressing the first sub-question. The figure then shows, following the internationalisation path of each type of firm, the capabilities applied in the first stage of the internationalisation expansion in the EU (i.e., during the three first years of activity in the market) followed by those developed in a second stage (i.e., after three years of experience in the market), addressing therefore the second sub-question. Firms can be divided into three groups according to the definition, development, and application of their capabilities during their national and international expansion: (i) SOEs (including SO NCs), Private firms aligned with the government (Private NC and OPFs from strategic industries or sectors), and OPFs. Finally, findings show how firms are applying and developing the same capabilities developed at home and that these home-developed capabilities have become the source of competitive advantage of Chinese firms in the EU as discussed throughout this chapter. The study links capabilities and sustainable competitive advantage in the long term and applies firms' survival and maintenance of the activities in the EU as a proxy for performance. It does not consider marketing or financial performance as claimed by IT and the RBV, being an opportunity for future research in order to complement, enrich and expand the findings of the present study.

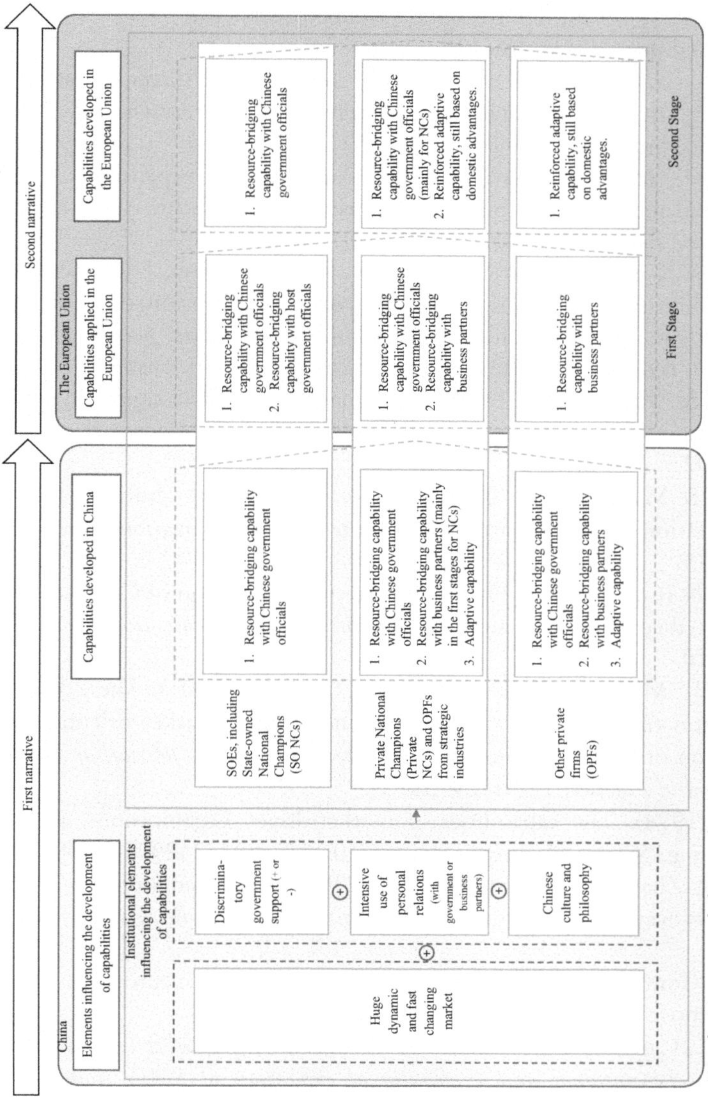

Fig. 6.1 Marketing capabilities developed by the three different types of firms in China and the European Union

References

Barney, J. (1991). Firm resources and sustained competitive advantage. *Journal of Management, 17*(1), 99–120.

Buckley, J. (2018). Internalisation theory and outward direct investment by emerging market multinationals. *Management International Review, 58*, 195–224. https://doi.org/10.1007/s11575-017-0320-4

Cardoza, G., & Fornes, G. (2013). The international expansion of China's small and medium-sized business: Status today and future outlook. *Journal of Chinese Entrepreneurship, 5*(3), 252–273.

Cardoza, G., Fornes, G., Farber, V., Duarte, R., & Gutierrez, J. (2016). Barriers and public policies affecting the international expansion of Latin American SMEs: Evidence from Brazil, Colombia, and Peru. *Journal of Business Research, 69*(6), 2030–2039. https://doi.org/10.1016/j.jbusres.2015.10.148

Chen, X., & Wu, J. (2011). Do different guanxi types affect capability building differently? A contingency view. *Industrial Marketing Management, 40*(4), 581–592.

Child, J., & Marinova, S. (2014). The role of contextual combinations in the globalization of Chinese firms. *Management and Organization Review, 10*(3), 347–371.

Child, J., & Rodrigues, S. (2005). The internationalization of Chinese firms: A case for theoretical extension? *Management and Organization Review, 1*(3), 381–410.

Darroch, J., Miles, M. P., Jardine, A., & Cook, E. (2004). The 2004 AMA definition of marketing and its relationship to a market orientation: An extension of Cook, Rayburn, & Abercrombie (1992). *Journal of Marketing Theory and Practice, 12*(4), 29–38.

Day, G. (1994). The capabilities of market-driven organizations. *Journal of Marketing, 58*, 37–51. https://doi.org/10.1177/002224299405800404

Du, J., & Zhang, Y. (2018). Does One Belt One Road initiative promote Chinese overseas direct investment? *China Economic Review, 47*(C), 189–205.

European Commission. (2019). *EU-China trade*. https://ec.europa.eu/trade/policy/countries-and-regions/countries/china/

Fornes, G., Cardoza, G., & Altamira, M. (2016). *Informal structures and practices in the national and international expansion of SMEs from emerging *markets: Evidence from Brazil and China*. Paper presented at the Academy of Management annual conference, Anaheim.

Fornes, G., Cardoza, G., & Altamira, M. (2021). Do informal business and political relations help SMEs from emerging markets in their national and international expansion? Evidence from Brazil and China. *International Journal of Emerging Markets, 17*(8). https://doi.org/10.1108/IJOEM-01-2020-0058

Hofman, B. (2018). *Reflections on forty years of China's reforms*. Fudan University's Fanhai School of International Finance.

Ju, M., Fung, H., & Mano, H. (2013). Firm capabilities and performance: Institutional perspective on foreign and local firms in China. *The Chinese Economy, 46*(5), 86–104.

Kim, J. (2015). Narrative data analysis and interpretation. In *Understanding narrative inquiry: The crafting and analysis of stories as research*. Sage.

Kotler, P., & Keller, K. (2011). *Marketing management* (14th ed.). Pearson.

Lattemann, C., Alon, I., Spigarelli, F., & Marinova, S. (2017). Dynamic embeddedness in Chinese firm internationalization. *Thunderbird International Business Review, 59*(4), 547–559.

Lin, S., Mercier-Suissa, C., & Salloum, C. (2016). The Chinese born globals of the Zhejiang Province: A study on the key factors for their rapid internationalization. *Journal of International Enterpreneurship, 14*(1), 75–95.

Lin, X. (2010). State versus private MNCs from China: Initial conceptualizations. *International Marketing Review, 27*(3), 366–380.

Ling, C., & Naughton, B. (2016). An institutionalized policy-making mechanism: China's return totechno-industrial policy. *Research Policy, 45*(10), 2138–2152.

Liu, H. (2015). *The Chinese strategic mind*. Edward Elgar Publishing.

Mathews, J. (2006). Dragon multinationals: New players in 21st century globalization. *Asia Pacific Journal of Management, 23*(1), 5–27.

Morgan, N., Douglas, W., & Mason, C. (2009). Market orientation, marketing capabilities and firm performance. *Strategic Management Journal, 30*, 909–920. https://doi.org/10.1002/smj.764

Nee, V., & Opper, S. (2012). *Capitalism from below: Markets and institutional change in China*. Harvard University Press.

Oliveira, R., Menzies, J., Borgia, D., & Figueira, S. (2017). Outward foreign direct investment from emerging countries: Theoretical extension and evidence from China. *The International Trade Journal, 31*(5), 402–428.

Park, S., & Luo, Y. (2001). Guanxi and organizational dynamics: Organizational networking in Chinese firms. *Strategic Management Journal, 22*(5), 455–477.

Polkinghorne, D. (1995). Narrative configuration in qualitative analysis. *International Journal of Qualitative Studies in Education, 8*(1), 5–23.

Porter, M. (2008). *On competition* (Updated and Expanded ed.). Harvard Business School Publishing.

Ramamurti, R., & Hillemann, J. (2018). What is "Chinese" about Chinese multinationals? *Journal of International Business Studies, 49*(1), 34–48.

Rhodes, C., & Brown, D. (2005). Narrative, organizations and research. *International Journal of Management Reviews, 7*(3), 167–188.

Riessman, C. K. (2008). *Narrative methods for the human sciences*. Sage.

Saunders, M., Lewis, P., & Thornhill, A. (2003). *Research methods for business students*. FT Prentice Hall.

Singh, A. (2002). Understanding China's 'Go-West' campaign. *China Report, 38*(1), 121–127.

Slater, S., & Narver, J. (1993). Product-market strategy and performance: An analysis of the Miles and Snow strategy types. *European Journal of Marketing, 27*(2), 33–51.

Tripsas, M. (1997). Unraveling the process of creative destruction: Complementary assets and incumbent survival in the typesetter industry. *Strategic Management Journal, 18*(Summer Special Issue), 119–142.

Wei, J., Cong, S., Wang, C., & Pan, Q. (2020). The critical role of the institution-led market in the technological catch-up of emerging market enterprises: Evidence from Chinese enterprises. *R&D Management, 50*(4), 478–493.

Wernerfelt, B. (1984). A resource-based view of the firm. *Strategic Management Journal, 5*(2), 171–180.

Yi, J., Hong, J., Hsu, W., & Wang, C. (2017). The role of state ownership and institutions in the innovation performance of emerging market enterprises: Evidence from China. *Technovation, 62*(63), 4–13.

Zou, L., Shen, J. H., Zhang, J., & Lee, C.-C. (2022). What is the rationale behind China's infrastructure investment under the Belt and Road Initiative. *Journal of Economic Surveys, 36*(3), 605–633. https://doi.org/10.1111/joes.12427

7

Contributions of the Study

7.1 Introduction

The focus of this chapter is to introduce and explain the main academic and theoretical contributions of the study. More specifically, this section discusses how the study contributes to the Institutional Theory and the Resource-Based view of the firm. A relevant implication for the international marketing literature is also debated at the end of the chapter.

7.2 Academic and Theoretical Contributions

This research makes theoretical contributions to improve the understanding of the development of capabilities of Chinese firms, including marketing. It does this by analysing the role of the home institutional environment (including both formal and informal institutional elements) in shaping these capabilities, first in the domestic market and, second, in the international scene outside China, mainly in the EU (Haasis & Liefner, 2019), following the internationalisation path of the firms. In this context, this study makes theoretical contributions in the

M. Altamira, *Chinese Firms in the Global Market*, Palgrave Macmillan Asian Business Series, https://doi.org/10.1007/978-3-031-59227-0_7

following two areas: (i) Institutional Theory and (ii) The Resource-Based view of the firm and capability building. Finally, the research brings implications for the international marketing literature.

7.2.1 Institutional Theory

Institutional Theory states that institutions, especially the political, social, cultural, and economic systems surrounding firms, have an impact and play a fundamental role in firms' behaviour and in the social environment in which those firms operate (Hoskisson et al., 2000; North, 1990) and as a consequence shape social and organisational behaviour (Scott, 1995). The institutional environment in China has been through radical transformation during the past decades and as a consequence firms' strategic options have been influenced by their industry environment as well as by the formal and informal institutional frameworks (Cardoza et al., 2014, 2015; Hoskisson et al., 2000; Peng, 2002; Wright et al., 2005). Domestic institutions in China, such as the legal and regulatory frameworks, ownership patterns, social norms, informal relations, tradition, or philosophy have proven to have an important effect on firms' decision-making process and as a result in the definition and development of their capabilities (Buckley et al., 2007, 2018; Cardoza et al., 2014, 2015; Cui & Jiang, 2012; Hong et al., 2015; Yi et al., 2017). In addition, different types of firms in China, especially related to ownership type, seem to be subject to different environmental and institutional influences (Lin, 2010). It is in this context where the findings of this research contribute to the understanding of how different Chinese institutions, formal and informal, influence the development of strategic decisions in different types of Chinese firms: SOEs, NCs (SO and Private), and OPFs (from strategic industries with support of the government and the rest of OPFs) in China and the EU, following the internationalisation path of the firms. As identified in the early parts of this work, few studies include both formal and informal institutional elements and also different types of firms (Haasis & Liefner, 2019). So this research contributes to the development of this emerging line of enquiry.

Three market institutions, coupled with a huge, dynamic, and fast-changing market, were identified by Chinese managers having a key influence in the development of strategic decisions: (a) discriminatory government support, (b) the intensive use of personal networks, and (c) a unique strategic mindset embedded in the Chinese culture and philosophy.

The Chinese government played a fundamental role in SOEs and NCs, as well as in OPFs operating in strategic industries as a result of an almost unrestricted support, basing their development on political relations. OPFs did not have access to this support and therefore based their development on both political and business relations. Political relations helped firms to align with government interests, to gain political legitimacy, and to avoid uncertainty. They also provided shortcuts to government-related resources (loans with preferential conditions, tax benefits, government support plans, trends, etc.) which in the medium term created the perception of low business risk that guided the managers' decisions. Managers in OPFs (especially those not operating in strategic industries) also found it relevant to develop their political relations, but only so as not to feel at a disadvantage. They implied a negative impression of this perceived unfair discrimination among the other types of firms. Business relationships were a highly valued asset for managers working in OPFs, but not that important for managers from firms linked to the government. These relations have been key in finding new market opportunities, in reducing uncertainty, and in getting protection against unfair competitors.

Once companies started to operate outside the domestic market, both the government support and the political and business relations were still found to be key elements influencing the internationalisation strategies designed and implemented by the managers in the sample. SOEs, NCs, as well as OPFs in strategic industries benefited from strong support and special conditions from the Chinese government during the first step of their internationalisation process within the government-led internationalisation policies. Similar to what happened in the domestic market, political and business relationships proved to be crucial in the EU. The reliance on political relations with home government officials along with the relations between Chinese and host government officials facilitated the deployment of the first steps of the firms in the EU. Business relationships with local partners and/or local teams in the host market were determinant for Private NCs and OPFs after they started operating outside China as they facilitated the process. In the first stages, they helped to reduce the uncertainty of landing in a new environment and also to access relevant resources (Fornes et al., 2021; Lin et al., 2016; Oliveira et al., 2017).

After the initial stages, political connections with Chinese government officials continued to be decisive for the development of SOEs and NCs (SO and private). This support seems to have reinforced the perception of low business risk that guided the managers' decisions although this time far away from Beijing and also in a completely different business environment. Further research is needed on the sustainability of this government-supported international expansion and on the long-term competitiveness of these companies; government support may be a good way to kick off the expansion, but it may also divert attention from risks, competitors, new trends in the market (domestic and international), and/or technology and productivity (Porter, 2008).

Narratives showed that the managers' mindset, developed within the Chinese culture and philosophy, influenced their strategic decisions both at individual and organisational levels. Managers from private firms adopted a competitor orientation and as a result focused on agility and the use of stratagems for their business strategies in the domestic market. Managers from SOEs and SO NCs also used dialectical thinking to follow guidelines from Beijing and operated with the feeling of belonging to a mighty government (as part of Tao). These behaviours were followed in the first stages of the international operation, although thanks to their agile and flexible mindset (mainly managers in private firms), they managed to move away from the focus on competitors and successfully adapted to marketing strategies led by consumers' needs.

All in all, this study links three formal and informal Chinese institutional elements: (i) the discriminatory support from the government, (ii) the strong reliance on personal relations, as well as (iii) the Chinese strategic mindset embedded in the Chinese culture and philosophy. This analysis intends to enrich the understanding of the influence of domestic institutions in the development of strategic options of different types of firms, more specifically in the definition and development of marketing capabilities, both in the domestic (first narrative) and international (second narrative) markets. The study also supports the relevance of Government Specific Advantages (GSA) (Ramamurti & Hillemann, 2018) as one of the most important factors enhancing both the national and the international competitiveness of Chinese firms. This is evident in the fact that the development of the different capabilities identified in this research is highly influenced by government decisions; the industry only makes a difference when it is part of the government-strategic plans.

7.2.2 The Resource-Based View of the Firm and Capability Building

According to the Resource-Based View of the firm (RBV) (Barney, 1991), a firm should accumulate unique resources or capabilities that are heterogenous, immobile, valuable, rare, and costly to imitate in order to achieve sustained competitive advantage. In addition, and probably more importantly, the firm should be organised to capture the resulting value (Barney, 1991; Ju et al., 2013; Wernerfelt, 1984). Several researchers have questioned the suitability of the RBV in Chinese firms, arguing that they lack strong Firm-Specific Advantages (FSA) that are the pillars of the unique tangible and intangible capabilities (Lattemann et al., 2017; Peng, 2012; Ramamurti & Hillemann, 2018) and that they have mainly basic and ordinary resources that make it difficult to create strong core competences (Peng et al., 2018). However, Chinese firms have demonstrated capabilities and assets defined by and embedded in their domestic business and institutional environment (He et al., 2019; Lattemann et al., 2017). In fact, narratives showed that an adaptive capability and a resource-bridging capability (Chen & Wu, 2011) were at the core of SOEs, SO and Private NCs, and OPFs in China. In addition, what is more relevant is that these capabilities, embedded in the Chinese institutional environment, were also the source of the competitive advantage of Chinese firms in the international context. As such, this study contributes to the understanding of how capabilities are defined in

Chinese companies in China and how the home institutional environment shapes these capabilities both at home and abroad, contributing to the analysis of firm-specific capability building and exploitation of country-specific assets, both at home and abroad.

Narratives showed that two elements of the domestic environment, a huge dynamic and fast-changing market, and the distinctive market institutions, shaped the capabilities developed by firms in China. In this sense, the adaptive capability and the resource-bridging capability are the relevant unique capabilities at the core of the firms in the sample. On the one hand, the adaptive capability, resulting from operating in a complex and dynamic environment with strong competition and poor support from the government, was identified in private firms (NCs and OPFs, but mainly OPFs because of the perceived negative discrimination). On the other hand, every type of firm developed its competitive advantage around a resource-bridging capability. While SOEs and NCs developed their resource-bridging capability within their political connections, private firms (including private NCs and all OPFs) based their resource-bridging capability on both political and business connections.

The study shows that the domestic environment has a great impact on the capabilities developed and applied by Chinese firms in the EU and that firms create sustainable competitive advantages through the same capabilities developed at home, although reinforced by domestic advantages. In the first stage, a resource-bridging capability developed at home helped every type of firm to successfully select the market and partners, as well as to enter the EU. While SOEs, SO and Private NCs, and OPFs from specific industries relied on their resource-bridging capability with both home and host governments' officials, private firms, including NCs and OPFs, based their first steps in Europe on a resource-bridging capability with business partners. After the first stage, a resource-bridging capability with home government officials was at the core of the success of SOEs and NCs (including private NCs), being their main source of competitive advantage.

In the case of private NCs and OPFs, managers integrated the knowledge acquired in the host market with flexibility and agility (elements defining the strategic mindset embedded in the Chinese culture) and were able to improve the adaptive capability developed at home with Country-Specific Advantages (CSA) (Oliveira et al., 2017). These CSA are an increasingly well-prepared and large labour force working long hours, shorter times to market, shorter product cycles, an increase in cost efficiency as well as a large customer and profit base at home able to support the lower than expected results obtained in the host market in the first stage of their internationalisation to the EU. At the same time, this questions the sustainability of firms with strong support from the government as they showed a lower adaptive capability as discussed in the narratives. In short, this study enriches the RBV of the firm by providing a deep analysis of the relevant capabilities of different types of Chinese firms which are also the source of competitive advantage for these firms in the EU.

Finally, the study presents a relevant implication for the international marketing literature. As introduced in the theoretical framework as well as in the discussion section above, the marketing literature states that a company that has adopted the marketing concept will place their customers at the top of the organisation's list of priorities and will focus on capturing and satisfying them in order to create a sustainable and profitable relationship (Darroch et al., 2004; Day, 1994). A firm implementing this marketing concept is said to be market-oriented or to have adopted market orientation as an asset or capability. In this context, marketing capabilities are defined as complex bundles of skills and accumulated knowledge, exercised through organisational processes that enable firms to coordinate activities and make use of their market-based knowledge and assets (Day, 1994).

Findings from the narratives confirmed that the capabilities and behaviour of Chinese firms in the domestic market, as expected, were heavily influenced by the business and institutional environment; in particular, the huge, dynamic, and fast-changing market, and the three distinctive market institutions listed throughout the text. These elements, unique characteristics of the Chinese environment, as discussed in the previous section, strongly influenced the orientation adopted by Chinese managers when defining and developing their strategic options, marketing capabilities in particular. This was evident in the adoption of a competitor-oriented mindset; Chinese managers were reactive to competitors' actions rather than active and forward-looking. This mindset is a consequence of the business and institutional environment and is based on the unique development of the Chinese business and economy since the late 70s. In the case of SOEs and SO NCs, the demand was protected and influenced by the government. In the case of private firms, especially OPFs, they faced a challenging run to the bottom with competitors due to the strong competition on prices as Chinese consumers seem to be price-sensitive. It is in this context that firms had been developing their tactical actions with a focus on competitors rather than on consumers as would have been expected by Western-developed marketing theories (Gundlach & Wilkie, 2009; Kotler & Amstrong, 2001). Chinese firms in the sample had developed, by chance or by design (the findings of the narratives seem to weigh towards by chance) and in a reactive way, two relevant capabilities: the adaptive capability, and the resource-bridging capability.

This suggests that Chinese firms in China did not adopt the marketing concept as defined by Western-developed theories. Instead, they implemented a different approach. In this context, it is not surprising that, due to the uniqueness of Chinese firms' marketing capabilities and how deeply they are embedded in the Chinese culture, managers at individual level and firms at organisational level still apply them when developing their internationalisation strategies. Moreover, firms, especially private ones, demonstrated that even considering a longer timeframe, they are still able to create competitive advantages based on their home-developed marketing capabilities reinforced with domestic advantages.

7.3 Conclusions

In sum, this study analysed how the domestic institutional environment shaped the decisions about marketing capabilities at home and abroad and how Chinese firms understood the need to adapt their marketing capabilities in the EU. Chinese firms possess different ownership advantages and capabilities to the ones present in most MNEs from developed countries and explained by received theories; these differences are rooted in the business and institutional environment and are combined with country-specific advantages. This contributes to the emerging literature on the rapid growth and success of Chinese multinationals in Western markets (Bruton & Lau, 2008; Hanemann et al., 2019; He et al., 2019; Kim et al., 2019; Mathews, 2006; Parmentola, 2017; Williamson et al., 2013; Yang & Stoltenberg, 2014; Yang et al., 2012; Yip & McKern, 2014). In addition, findings enrich the scholarly debate on the need to develop a theory of Chinese management or the need to develop a Chinese theory of management (Barney & Zhang, 2009; Bruton & Lau, 2008; Buckley, 2018; Child & Rodrigues, 2005; Haasis & Liefner, 2019). More specifically, the study highlighted the competitor orientation adopted by Chinese firms to successfully operate in the domestic market against the customer orientation linked to the marketing concept defined by traditional marketing theories. This implication for the international marketing literature represents a new opportunity to expand research on the need to develop a Chinese theory of marketing.

References

Barney, J. (1991). Firm resources and sustained competitive advantage. *Journal of Management, 17*(1), 99–120.

Barney, J., & Zhang, S. (2009). The future of Chinese management research: A theory of Chinese management versus a Chinese theory of management. *Management and Organization Review, 5*(1), 15–28.

Bruton, G., & Lau, C. (2008). Asian management research: Status today and future outlook. *Journal of Management Studies, 45*(3), 636–659.

Buckley, J. (2018). Internalisation theory and outward direct investment by emerging market multinationals. *Management International Review, 58*, 195–224. https://doi.org/10.1007/s11575-017-0320-4

Buckley, P., Clegg, J., Cross, A., Liu, X., Voss, H., & Zheng, P. (2007). The determinants of Chinese outward foreign direct investment. *Journal of International Business Studies, 38*(4), 499–518.

Buckley, P., Clegg, J., Voss, H., Cross, A., Liu, X., & Zheng, P. (2018). A retrospective and agenda for future research on Chinese outward foreign direct investment. *Journal of International Business Studies, 49*(1), 4–23.

Cardoza, G., Fornes, G., Li, P., Xu, N., & Xu, S. (2014). China goes global: Public policies' influence on small and medium-size enterprises' international expansion. *Asia Pacific Business Review*. https://doi.org/10.1080/13602381.2013.876183

Cardoza, G., Fornes, G., Li, P., Xu, N., & Xu, S. (2015). China goes global: Public policies' influence on small- and medium-sized enterprises' international expansion. *Asia Pacific Business Review, 21*(2), 188–210.

Chen, X., & Wu, J. (2011). Do different guanxi types affect capability building differently? A contingency view. *Industrial Marketing Management, 40*(4), 581–592.

Child, J., & Rodrigues, S. (2005). The internationalization of Chinese firms: A case for theoretical extension? *Management and Organization Review, 1*(3), 381–410.

Cui, L., & Jiang, F. (2012). State ownership effect on firms' FDI ownership decisions under institutional pressure: A study of Chinese outward-investing firms. *Journal of International Business Studies, 43*(3), 264–284.

Darroch, J., Miles, M. P., Jardine, A., & Cook, E. (2004). The 2004 AMA definition of marketing and its relationship to a market orientation: An extension of Cook, Rayburn, & Abercrombie (1992). *Journal of Marketing Theory and Practice, 12*(4), 29–38.

Day, G. (1994). The capabilities of market-driven organizations. *Journal of Marketing, 58*, 37–51. https://doi.org/10.1177/002224299405800404

Fornes, G., Cardoza, G., & Altamira, M. (2021). Do informal business and political relations help SMEs from emerging markets in their national and international expansion? Evidence from Brazil and China. *International Journal of Emerging Markets, 17*(8). https://doi.org/10.1108/IJOEM-01-2020-0058

Gundlach, G., & Wilkie, W. (2009). The American Marketing Association's new definition of marketing: Perspective and commentary on the 2007 revision. *Journal of Public Policy & Marketing, 28*(2), 259–264.

Haasis, T., & Liefner, I. (2019). Reviewing the research on the internationalization of Chinese firms: Thematic expansion, new impulses and potential future development. *International Journal of Emerging Markets, 14*(1), 24–50.

Hanemann, T., Huotari, M., & Kratz, A. (2019). *Chinese FDI in Europe: 2018 trends and impact of new screening policies*. https://rhg.com/wp-content/uploads/2019/03/RHG-MERICS-COFDI-Update-2019.pdf

He, S., Khan, Z., Lew, Y., & Fallon, G. (2019). Technological innovation as a source of Chinese multinationals' firm-specific advantages and internationalization. *International Journal of Emerging Markets, 14*(4). https://doi.org/10.1108/IJOEM-02-2017-0059

Hong, J., Wang, C., & Kafouros, M. (2015). The role of the state in explaining the internationalization of emerging market enterprises. *British Journal of Management, 26*, 45–62. https://doi.org/10.1111/1467-8551.12059

Hoskisson, R., Eden, L., Lau, C., & Wright, M. (2000). Strategy in emerging economies. *Academy of Management Journal, 43*(3), 249–267.

Ju, M., Fung, H., & Mano, H. (2013). Firm capabilities and performance: Institutional perspective on foreign and local firms in China. *The Chinese Economy, 46*(5), 86–104.

Kim, K., Lattemann, C., Park, I., & Zhang, W. (2019). New international business theories for China goes global? The importance of institutions, innovativeness and learning. *International Journal of Emerging Markets, 14*(1), 2–5. https://doi.org/10.1108/ijoem-01-2019-574

Kotler, P., & Amstrong, G. (2001). *Principles of marketing*. Prentice Hall.

Lattemann, C., Alon, I., Spigarelli, F., & Marinova, S. (2017). Dynamic embeddedness in Chinese firm internationalization. *Thunderbird International Business Review, 59*(4), 547–559.

Lin, S., Mercier-Suissa, C., & Salloum, C. (2016). The Chinese born globals of the Zhejiang Province: A study on the key factors for their rapid internationalization. *Journal of International Enterpreneurship, 14*(1), 75–95.

Lin, X. (2010). State versus private MNCs from China: Initial conceptualizations. *International Marketing Review, 27*(3), 366–380.

Mathews, J. (2006). Dragon multinationals: New players in 21st century globalization. *Asia Pacific Journal of Management, 23*(1), 5–27.

North, D. (1990). *Institutions, institutional change, and economic performance*. Cambridge University Press.

Oliveira, R., Menzies, J., Borgia, D., & Figueira, S. (2017). Outward foreign direct investment from emerging countries: Theoretical extension and evidence from China. *The International Trade Journal, 31*(5), 402–428.

Parmentola, A. (2017). Why Chinese companies go abroad? A theoretical model to explain the drivers of the internationalisation strategy of Chinese MNEs. *International Business Research, 10*(10), 82–93.

Peng, M. (2002). Towards an institution-based view of business strategy. *Asia Pacific Journal of Management, 19*, 251–267.

Peng, M. (2012). The global strategy of emerging multinationals from China. *Global Strategy Journal*. https://doi.org/10.1002/gsj.1030

Peng, M., Lebedev, S., Vlas, C., Wang, J., & Shay, J. (2018). The growth of the firm in (and out of) emerging economies. *Asia Pacific Journal of Management, 35*(4), 829–857.

Porter, M. (2008). *On competition* (Updated and Expanded ed.). Harvard Business School Publishing.

Ramamurti, R., & Hillemann, J. (2018). What is "Chinese" about Chinese multinationals? *Journal of International Business Studies, 49*(1), 34–48.

Scott, W. (1995). *Institutions and organizations*. Sage.

Wernerfelt, B. (1984). A resource-based view of the firm. *Strategic Management Journal, 5*(2), 171–180.

Williamson, P., Ramamurti, R., Fleury, A., & Leme Fleury, M. (2013). *The competitive advantage of emerging market multinationals*. Cambridge University Press.

Wright, M., Filatotchev, I., Hoskisson, R., & Peng, M. (2005). Strategy research in emerging economies: Challenging the conventional wisdom. *Journal of Management Studies, 42*(1), 1–33. http://search.ebscohost.com/login.aspx?direct=true&db=buh&AN=15645292&site=ehost-live

Yang, X., & Stoltenberg, C. (2014). A review of institutional influences on the rise of made-in-China multinationals. *International Journal of Emerging Markets, 9*(2). https://doi.org/10.1108/IJoEM-09-2012-0095

Yang, Y., Wang, Q., Zhu, H., & Zhu, H. (2012). What are the effective strategic orientations for new product success under different environments? An empirical study of Chinese businesses. *Journal of Product Innovation Management, 29*(2), 166–179.

Yi, J., Hong, J., Hsu, W., & Wang, C. (2017). The role of state ownership and institutions in the innovation performance of emerging market enterprises: Evidence from China. *Technovation, 62*(63), 4–13.

Yip, G., & McKern, B. (2014). Innovation in emerging markets—The case of China. *International Journal of Emerging Markets, 9*(1). https://doi.org/10.1108/IJoEM-11-2013-0182

8

Practical Implications in Today's Business Context and Concluding Remarks

8.1 Introduction

The present chapter discusses the practical implications of the study for practitioners, companies, and policymakers. It does this by linking the findings of the study to the current business environment and the future challenges of Chinese firms, as introduced in Chapter 2, with a focus on geopolitics. The section ends with an analysis of the limitations of the project, a proposal of areas for future research, and some concluding remarks.

8.2 Implications of the Study

The present study has several implications for practitioners, companies, and policymakers. First, this study provides useful insights to understand the development of the relevant capabilities by Chinese multinationals at home and abroad, which are embedded in the Chinese business and institutional environment. Findings are expected to help Western firms to deeply understand the rapid rise of Chinese multinationals overseas, especially in the EU while becoming more familiar with the Chinese

M. Altamira, *Chinese Firms in the Global Market*, Palgrave Macmillan Asian Business Series, https://doi.org/10.1007/978-3-031-59227-0_8

business and institutional environment and practices. This will also assist Western firms to adapt better their marketing strategies and minimise cross-cultural misunderstandings and/or conflict.

Second, the study focuses on why and how Chinese multinationals have been able to develop sustained competitive advantages in the EU. Western firms and managers will therefore gain a more in-depth understanding of Chinese firms' business strategies, objectives, and the capabilities they have developed in this market based on their home environment, filling the existing gap regarding knowledge about China, more specifically independent China expertise and capacity (Ghiretti et al., 2023). In this sense, the study will provide Western firms, managers, and governments with useful tools to identify and benefit from the advantages of cooperating with Chinese firms or developing joint projects. More importantly, it is expected that the study helps to develop a deeper and more critical understanding of Chinese government-led initiatives and the behaviour of companies following it, more specifically the BRI and companies benefiting from it. For example, the study can contribute to explain the assumptions behind projects proposed and even already developed by Chinese firms within the BRI, the Maritime Silk Road in particular. For example, COSCO's investment in the port of Piraeus (Greece) which serves as a major transhipping hub in the Mediterranean and the Black Sea or in the port of Rotterdam (where COSCO owns 35% of one terminal and CMG owns around 15% of another) providing China with a more direct access to European consumers (Banach & Gunter, 2023).

Third, the research includes the sample state-owned firms and National Champions. In this context, findings show that beyond some other relevant capabilities (adaptive capability in the case of Private NCs), the resource-bridging capability with Chinese government officials is key to secure a long-term presence in the EU. This contributes to the existing debate among Western firms and institutions about the strong support of the Chinese government for these firms and to what extent the government is responsible for their success. On the one hand, findings show that the Chinese government has a big influence on the development of the international strategies of these firms in the international market. On the other hand, it also shows, especially in the case of Private

NCs, that the development of other capabilities provides relevant insights on how these firms create advantages to compete in the international context with the backing of the Chinese government and its internationalisation policies. Indeed, the findings shed some light on the current business scenario of tensions between the EU and China described in Chapter 2; this study is developed at a moment of tremendous challenges between the two markets for the coming years.

In fact, this scenario would affect Chinese firms' future internationalisation path and the future collaboration between the two regions. It seems that the growing scrutiny and scepticism shown by the EU in recent years encouraging countries and companies to review and control investments in the so-called "sensitive sectors", operations traditionally developed by SOEs and NCs following Chinese government-strategic international plans, along with the "Dual Circulation" strategy (Yao, 2020), would influence the future behaviour of Chinese firms and therefore the development and application of the capabilities analysed in this study. But despite the doubts about the latest government policy and especially about whether China would be considering an increasingly inward-looking strategy while relying less on its international development and international partners (Chandler & McGregor, 2020), the country's international presence (especially in the context of the BRI) would still be key for the business and economic future of the country.

In this context, the country has been recently showing its determination in achieving strategic goals on the international scene while developing an adapted and tailored BRI. Since 2013, the policy has successfully helped the government to meet key strategic goals and interests such as more certainty in accessing raw materials, or an impressive market share growth of rail, energy and oil and gas SOEs especially in EMs making the country more influential and secure (Banach & Gunter, 2023). However, China has recognised the need to adapt to smaller and more financially sustainable projects, emphasising the relevance of alternative dimensions of connectivity now that hard infrastructures are already implemented, and that there is less demand for more traditional ones, as introduced by Xi Jinping during the 10th anniversary of the government-led policy at the end of November 2023 (The Economist Reporters, 2023).

In addition, and in an attempt to address criticisms, President Xi Jinping announced that priority will be given to digital (following the path of the Digital Silk Road), technological, and green investments; new strategic projects in which, not surprisingly, Chinese SOEs and NCs need new or more expanded markets, to deal with the overcapacity found in the domestic market. For example, it is expected that by the end of the year, China will produce twice as many photovoltaic panels than the global demand can absorb. Similarly, electric and new-energy vehicles are facing a slower demand growth, both domestically and internationally (Allison, 2023; Li & White, 2023). These two industries have been fuelled for many years by strong incentives from the government to become economic drivers, resulting in an overcapacity that has already been very difficult to face domestically (Leahy, 2023). As a result, it seems that internationalisation, especially exporting through the BRI, is widely regarded as the new direction and possibly the more suitable solution to overcapacity, while supporting national goals to stimulate global demand for green and digital projects. Industrial policies recently promoted in the West for domestic companies, especially in the US and in the EU, may be good opportunities for these sectors and companies willing to take advantage of the incentives by expanding internationally. Some Chinese companies have already been partnering with Western firms through Joint Ventures, for example, Renault Group and Geely, which partnered in early 2023 with the aim of becoming leaders in the next-generation of hybrid cars while providing highly efficient powertrain solutions to meet worldwide demand for the years to come (Renault Group, 2023). These partnerships might also represent good opportunities for Western companies to strengthen their presence in China in the future (Banach & Gunter, 2023).

However, the development of these strategies is expected to encounter some obstacles in the near future. In addition to the above-mentioned scrutiny by Western institutions, other barriers, such as President Joe Biden's restrictions on exports of chips, software, and other equipment to China needed to produce semiconductors and slow its progress in the development of major technologies (AI in particular; which is a key area for China within the Made in China 2025) (Fornes & Altamira, 2023), and the EU's newly launched anti-subsidy investigation into Chinese

EVs, represent real challenges to China's expansion, adding uncertainty over the viability of the BRI (Grieger, 2023). Furthermore, the EU has recently implemented the Global Gateway; a strategy that focuses on promoting and expanding Western markets across the globe. This initiative, which not surprisingly was announced only seven days after the 10th anniversary of the BRI, represents a major milestone for the EU, as it aims at promoting its investments and development cooperation on the global scene, especially in the MENA (Middle East North Africa) region, prioritising projects on green energies, digital transformation, and sustainability. While EU officials have avoided mentioning that the Global Gateway intends to compete against and replace BRI investments, it seems that the EU is willing to propose an alternative to it (European Commission, 2023; Rock & Hanelt, 2023).

In any case, there are still several uncertainties about the Global Gateway, despite the perceived positive potential outcomes for the region. Implementation and absorption capacities of both the EU and its partners are subject to several challenges such as demographic development, public opinion, and private investment (Rock & Hanelt, 2023). More importantly, attractiveness of the projects promoted by Europe for recipient countries with regards to China's, will still be a key issue to analyse in the near future, especially for the Global South. Tensions between regions were already evident during the anniversary of the BRI, showing a decline in the embracing of the initiative, especially by high-level European countries. Among participants in the event, mainly leaders from the Global South were present, making evident China's current influence and the direction of future plans. From a European perspective, China's relations with Russia, lockdowns during the pandemic, and the country's position towards Taiwan have resulted in a more pragmatic, lower-risk approach with regard to the region's engagement with China (Ghiretti et al., 2023).

In such a challenging geopolitical context, Chinese firms expanding overseas (especially SOEs and NCs) would need to rely less on the resource-bridging capability with the Chinese government and enhance the resource-bridging capability with host governments in the medium and long term (and not only in the first stage, as discussed in the present study) while they develop other capabilities, especially the adaptive capability. This might become crucial in the short term now that the EU Global Gateway seems to start its projects in the short term. There will be a need for China to realign its strategy in Europe and especially its relationship with authorities in order to reassess their collaboration or refine a new one, especially in emerging and strategic areas for both regions. The Chinese government, but more importantly Chinese firms (including private), would need to demonstrate to European partners and governments their ability to adapt to the market and their willingness to fill the current trust gap between the EU and China.

8.3 Limitations and Suggestions for Future Research

This study opens new and interesting opportunities for future research. First, the study focuses on Chinese firms internationalising into the EU. Today, the EU is China's main trade partner, but this presents potential limitations for the generalisability of the results regarding the development of capabilities of Chinese firms in Western environments. In this context, it would be interesting to analyse how Chinese firms adapt or develop the same capabilities in other Western markets, such as the United States. In addition, a further analysis of the same phenomenon but in other EMs would provide relevant insights on how Chinese firms develop or adapt their marketing strategies depending on the type of host environment. In addition, a further comparative analysis of Chinese and host institutional elements would be worth developing in order to study how host institutional elements influence marketing capabilities abroad and how Chinese multinationals adapt (or not) to this new environment.

Second, the analysis and findings in the study consider two stages: first steps in the domestic market and second steps in the EU, selecting firms with more than three years of experience that have survived and have been successful in the EU. However, there is evidence that some firms have come back to China due to the unexpected failure of their international strategy in the EU. These experiences did not come up in the narratives analysed and future research should consider them in order to complement, reinforce, and test the application of the capabilities leading to sustainable competitive advantage found in this study.

Third, the study suggests that state-owned firms mainly rely on their resource-bridging capabilities with the government to develop sustained competitive advantages in the long term (both at home and in the EU). In this context, it would be interesting to analyse whether these firms are able to develop further capabilities while being able to survive without the support of the government; several studies show that over-reliance on government support can weaken the development of further capabilities (Porter, 2008). This will require a deep analysis of SOEs' national and international development paths in the long term while having access to a larger number of firms. The recent decrease in the support from the Chinese government to some sectors or industries in the international context, representing an investment decline in sectors such as real estate or infrastructure (Hanemann et al., 2019), may provide opportunities in this direction.

Finally, IT and the RBV stress the performance outcomes of firms. However, the present study only focuses on the development and application of capabilities and sustainable competitive advantage, using the experience of the companies in the EU as a proxy for performance, this is, survival and maintenance of activities in the medium and long term, instead of marketing or financial performance. Narrative interviews showed that Chinese firms' international presence is sometimes supported by the firms' domestic strong position or by the backup of the government (especially in the case of SOEs and NCs). This would represent some opportunities for further research. On the one hand, findings could be enriched and expanded by analysing the relationship between the capabilities identified and the performance outcomes of firms in the sample. On the other hand, it would be interesting to further test and analyse the applicability of IT and the RBV in the context of the internationalisation of Chinese firms.

8.4 Concluding Remarks

The main goal of this study was to analyse and understand how the home institutional environment (formal and informal) influenced the definition and development of Chinese firms' marketing capabilities at home, and whether and how this domestic environment influenced the development of marketing capabilities of these firms in a different environment (in this case the EU), combining, thus, Institutional Theory and the Resource-Based View of the firm. Following a Narrative Enquiry strategy and narrative analysis of forty stories from managers from three different types of firms (SOE, SO NCs and Private NCs, and OPFs), the author analysed how different formal and informal elements from the Chinese business and institutional environment influenced the definition and development of marketing capabilities depending on the type of firm. In addition, stories shed light on how managers understood and defined marketing capabilities in China, helping to identify capabilities that were relevant to the specific home environment. Finally, the study helps to understand how Chinese firms adapt their home-developed capabilities, reinforced by country-specific advantages (domestic advantages) to create sustainable competitive advantages in the EU.

In this sense, the main finding of this research is the understanding of the definition, development, and application of two main marketing capabilities that are relevant to the Chinese context—the adaptive capability and the resource-bridging capability—following the analysis of a process and sequence of events related to the domestic development and further internationalisation expansion of Chinese companies in the EU. Findings also show how these capabilities are the source of competitive advantage of Chinese firms in the EU. Moreover, the study emphasises the three most relevant types of firms in China while considering the personal experiences of forty different managers working in these firms. As such, the research makes theoretical contributions in two main areas of research: (i) Institutional Theory and (ii) the Resource-Based View of the firm and capability building, while having relevant implications for the international marketing literature. The study also provides relevant insights for practitioners, companies, and policymakers.

References

Allison, G. (2023). China's dominance of solar poses difficult choices for the west. *Financial Times*. https://www.ft.com/content/fd8e7175-9423-4042-a6f7-c404afdfcda4

Banach, C., & Gunter, J. (2023). *How the BRI is shaping global trade and what to expect from the initiative in its second decade*. https://merics.org/en/tracker/how-bri-shaping-global-trade-and-what-expect-initiative-its-second-decade

Chandler, C., & McGregor, G. (2020). Xi Jinping's new economic strategy for China: 'Dual circulation' or doublespeak? *Fortune*.

European Commission. (2023). *Global gateway forum 2023*. https://commission.europa.eu/strategy-and-policy/priorities-2019-2024/stronger-europe-world/global-gateway_en

Fornes, G., & Altamira, M. (2023). *Digitalization, technology and global business: How technology is shaping value creation across borders*. Palgrave.

Ghiretti, F., Legarda, H., Stec, G., & Vasselier, A. (2023). *Profiling relations of European countries with China*. https://merics.org/en/profiling-relations-european-countries-china

Grieger, G. (2023). *EU anti-subsidy probe into electric vehicle imports from China*. https://www.europarl.europa.eu/RegData/etudes/ATAG/2023/754553/EPRS_ATA(2023)754553_EN.pdf

Hanemann, T., Huotari, M., & Kratz, A. (2019). *Chinese FDI in Europe: 2018 trends and impact of new screening policies*. https://rhg.com/wp-content/uploads/2019/03/RHG-MERICS-COFDI-Update-2019.pdf

Leahy, J. (2023). EU companies warn China on EV overcapacity. *Financial Times*. https://www.ft.com/content/4e1b2cdb-3a67-4567-be9b-062e6af69ee9

Li, G., & White, E. (2023). Chinese electric vehicle groups braced for wave of consolidation. *Financial Times*. https://www.ft.com/content/43da3223-2311-4b73-97d9-83d20baedc6a

Porter, M. (2008). *On competition* (Updated and Expanded ed.). Harvard Business School Publishing.

Renault Group. (2023). *Renault Group and Geely sign joint venture agreement to launch leading powertrain technology company* [Press release]. https://media.renaultgroup.com/renault-group-and-geely-sign-joint-venture-agreement-to-launch-leading-powertrain-technology-company/

Rock, K., & Hanelt, H. (2023). *Global gateway: The EU maps a different path than belt and road*. https://globaleurope.eu/europes-future/global-gateway-the-eu-maps-a-different-path-than-belt-and-road/

The Economist Reporters. (2023). How China's Belt and Road Initiative is changing. *The Economist*. https://www.economist.com/the-economist-explains/2023/10/17/how-chinas-belt-and-road-initiative-is-changing

Yao, K. (2020). *What we know about China's 'dual circulation' economic strategy*. https://www.reuters.com/article/china-economy-transformation-explainer-idUSKBN2600B5

Appendix A: Theoretical Framework of the Methodology

Introduction

This appendix introduces the theoretical framework of the methodology. It begins with a description and definition of the main research philosophies. It continues with an analysis of the different research designs, with a focus on Narrative Inquiry, and on the soundness of the research conclusions. The chapter continues with an identification of the different sample techniques, and finally, it describes the data collection tools that could be applied within a Narrative Inquiry strategy and main data analysis methods.

Research Philosophy and Epistemological Framework

Epistemology is the branch of philosophy related to the study of knowledge and justified belief (Steup, 2013). In this context, the researcher defines the epistemological framework involved in his/her project by answering the following questions: What constitutes knowledge? Where

M. Altamira, *Chinese Firms in the Global Market*, Palgrave Macmillan Asian Business Series, https://doi.org/10.1007/978-3-031-59227-0

Table A.1 Main research philosophies in the literature

	Positivism	Social constructivism
Basic beliefs	• The world is external and objective • The observer is independent • Science is value-free	• The world is socially constructed and subjective • The observer is part of what is observed • Science is driven by human interests
Researcher should	• Focus on facts • Look for causality and fundamental laws • Reduce phenomena to simplest elements • Formulate hypotheses and then test them	• Focus on meanings • Try to understand what is happening • Look at the totality of each situation • Develop ideas through induction from data
Preferred methods include	• Operationalising concepts so that they can be measured • Taking large samples	• Using multiple methods to establish different views of phenomena • Small samples investigated in depth or over time

is knowledge located? How is knowledge attained? How is it described or written? Finally, how is it studied? As such, the definition of the epistemological framework will help the researcher to understand his work and improve his/her research work (Cunningham & Fitzerald, 1996). The definition of epistemology is a relevant decision as it involves the definition of the paradigm which is the system of beliefs and practices that influence how the researcher selects both the questions he/she studies and the methods that he/she uses to study them (Morgan, 2007). In this context, Easterby-Smith et al. (2002) analysed the two main perspectives of philosophies in the literature: Positivism and Social Constructivism. Table 1 summarises the contrasting implications of both perspectives (Easterby-Smith et al., 2002, p. 27).

Knowledge development involves the use of theory that will be made explicit in the development of the findings and conclusions of the research (Saunders et al., 2003). This is related to the research approach and the reasoning taken by the researcher and is usually limited to (i) the deductive approach in which the "conclusions are derived logically from a set of premises" (p. 144), that is, when the researcher first defines the theory and hypothesis and then develops a research design to test these hypotheses and (ii) the inductive approach in which the "conclusions are judged to be supported by the observations made" (p. 144), that is, when the researcher develops a theory based on the analysis of data. In this context it seems possible to say that the deductive approach is closer to the Positivist philosophy while the inductive approach is closer to Social Constructivism. Saunders et al. (2003) defined a third approach to theory which is abduction that happens when the researcher starts by collecting the data and identifies themes to explain patterns "to generate a new or modify an existing theory which you (the researcher) subsequently test through additional data collection" (p. 145).

The deductive approach, in which the researcher is an observer and is not involved, is used "in the natural sciences, where laws present the basis of explanation, allow the anticipation of phenomena, predict the occurrence and therefore permit them to be controlled" (Saunders et al., 2003, p. 571). As such, the researcher looks to explain relationships between the concepts and variables; this is, after reading the literature, theory and hypotheses are developed and quantitative data is collected. In addition, in the deductive approach, a structured methodology is used to facilitate replication while ensuring reliability. Another characteristic is operationalisation, enabling facts to be measured and leading to reductionism. Finally, the last characteristic is generalisation by carefully selecting a sample of sufficient size.

The inductive approach, in which the researcher is part of what is being studied, is used when a theory is developed after analysing data and is often expressed in a conceptual framework (Saunders et al., 2003). Another characteristic is that the inductive approach helps to develop an understanding of the way in which humans interpret their social world. Induction facilitates the development of alternative explanations by allowing the construction of a less rigid methodology collecting mainly qualitative data. Finally, this approach is concerned about the context in which events take place so a smaller sample than in the deductive approach might be more appropriate.

Research Designs

Saunders et al. (2003) defined the research design as the "general plan of how the researcher will go about answering the research question(s)" (p. 163). The authors identified the main research strategies that guide the research and ensure coherence within the project: (i) Experiment, (ii) Survey, (iii) Archival research, (iv) Case study, (v) Ethnography, (vi) Action research, (vii) Grounded theory, and (viii) Narrative Inquiry. Each of the strategies is usually linked to and fits within one research philosophy as well as within quantitative, qualitative, or mixed methods methodologies. Then, the methodological choice and research strategies will define the selection of the appropriate time horizon. Finally, data collection techniques are selected accordingly.

Narrative Inquiry

As further explained and discussed in the following chapter about the application of the methodology, the present study will follow a Narrative Inquiry research strategy. This strategy refers to a qualitative research approach that evaluates a sequence of events and character identities which have a storied form (Boje, 2012; Kim, 2015; Riessman, 2008), representing a narrative. Narratives can be collected from different sources, such as observations, reports, or interviews in the form of texts, and are further analysed through narrative analysis that considers their content, form, and context while keeping them as whole and unfragmented as possible (Lieblich et al., 1998; Riessman, 2008). In narrative texts, events are represented in chronological order and present a whole structure of elements that relate to each other as in a story to examine the past and how it shaped the present; that is, narrative texts are about sequences and consequences where events are "selected, organised, connected, and evaluated as meaningful for a particular audience" (Riessman, 2005, p. 1). Storytellers help the researcher to develop an understanding of the meaning they give to themselves, their world, their own events, and their lived experiences (Boje, 2012; Kim, 2015; Lieblich et al., 1998; Riessman, 1993).

Furthermore, Narrative Inquiry involves interpretation, directly engaging in subjectivity that affects the researcher's choice of representation of stories (Lieblich et al., 1998). In Narrative Inquiry, analysis and interpretation are developed together as narrative data is analysed to develop an understanding of the meaning each participant gives to the story he/she is telling. As Riessman (1993) mentioned, "narratives are interpretive and in turn, they require interpretation" (p. 21). Although description is an essential first step, Narrative Inquiry helps the researcher to go from the surface to a deeper structure in the story told; from description to explanation and interpretation of the events told by the storyteller. Narrative researchers try to interpret the meaning the storytellers give to their story by extensively analysing plotlines, thematic structures, and social and cultural contexts (Kim, 2015).

Abbott (1990) identified three areas that the researcher can find in narratives under analysis: (i) the existence and classification of sequential patterns, (ii) antecedents to those patterns, and (iii) consequences to those patterns. In this sense, narratives are helpful to the development of explanations where these sequential patterns are critical elements while at the same time, stories explain the relationship between the different events in the process. Also, Pentland (1999) showed the different features of narratives that define the stories and help interpretation. These are (i) sequence in time, (ii) actors, (iii) the narrative voice reflecting a point of view, (iv) an evaluative frame of references like meaning and cultural value, as well as (v) further indicators of content and context relevant to the research and for the interpretation of the events. That is, not just sequence is relevant in narratives, but other elements should be considered for a complete interpretation.

Soundness of Research Conclusions

The research design will also influence the soundness of the research conclusions which will be based on its reliability and validity, central to "judgements about the quality of the research" (Saunders et al., 2003, p. 203). Reliability refers to replication and to what extent the same findings could be achieved by replicating the research design, while validity refers to the "appropriateness of the measures used, accuracy of the analysis of the results and generalisability of the findings" (Saunders et al., 2003, p. 203).

Potential threats to reliability are:

1. Participant error: any element that can influence the performance of the participant in the research.
2. Participant bias: any element inducing false response.
3. Researcher error: any element that can influence the interpretation of the researcher.
4. Researcher bias: any element that induces bias in the recording of the responses.

On the other hand, validity can be divided into (i) internal validity and (ii) external validity or to what extent generalisability of the conclusions can be applied in different contexts. Internal validity is a causal relationship between two variables that can be demonstrated. Threats to internal validity are:

1. History: any event that happened before the research that could affect it.
2. Testing: the influence of previous testing on participants' views or actions.
3. Instrumentation: the influence of a change in a research instrument between different stages of the research project affecting the comparability of results.
4. Mortality: when participants withdraw their participation in the research.
5. Maturation: when a change in participants outside of the influence of the study affects their participation.
6. Ambiguity about causal direction: the difficulty of stating the causal relationship between two variables.

However, these two dimensions, reliability, and validity, may not be valid to assess the soundness of research findings in qualitative studies where the researcher tends to be part of what is being observed, leading to subjectivity and interpretations, and where reality is socially constructed. In this sense, Lincoln and Guba (1985) formulated alternative quality criteria to be applied in qualitative research: (i) "dependability", instead of reliability, (ii) "credibility" instead of "internal validity", (iii) "transferability" for "external validity", and (iv) "authenticity criteria" as an alternative to "validity". Furthermore, Lieblich et al. (1998) argued that the criteria of reliability and validity as defined above are difficult to apply in Narrative Inquiry as they contradict its nature, which states that narrative materials can be "read, understood, and analysed in extremely diverse ways and that reaching alternative narrative accounts is a manifestation of the wealth of such material and the range of sensitivities of different readers" (Lieblich et al., 1998, p. 171). In this context, the authors defined four criteria that are qualitative in nature and are helpful to the evaluation of narrative studies:

1. Width: this refers to the quality of the interview and the proposed interpretations and analysis. This includes reporting quotations or alternative explanations for the reader's judgment of the evidence.
2. Coherence: this refers to the way different parts of the analysis create a meaningful picture and it can be evaluated internally (how different parts fit together) or externally (how the analysis fits within existing theories or previous research).
3. Insightfulness: this refers to the originality in the presentation of the study and analysis and whether this contributes to a greater comprehension regarding the reader's own life.
4. Parsimony: this refers to the ability of providing an interpretation and analysis based on a small number of concepts and aesthetic appeal.

Selecting a Sample

Sample techniques enable the researcher to reduce the amount of data needed to collect by considering only data from a subgroup of the population rather than the whole number of elements or cases. These techniques are usually employed when it is difficult or even impossible to have access to the complete population or when there are time and budget restrictions (Saunders et al., 2003).

Sampling techniques can be divided into probability sampling and non-probability sampling. The difference between them is that while in probability sampling the chance of each element being selected from the population is known and is the same for all elements (therefore, it is used for statistical estimations), in non-probability sampling the chance is not known and the researcher cannot generalise on statistical grounds.

Figure A.1 presents the different sample techniques defined by Saunders et al. (2003, p. 276).

The selection among the two main sample techniques will depend on the characteristics of the study, the time, and the budget available, among others. Also, a combination of the two might be possible.

Data Collection

Research interviews are a powerful method to collect primary data through a purposeful conversation between the researcher or interviewer and the research participant or interviewee. Interviews can adopt an objective approach in which the interviews are developed to obtain answers to questions that are mainly factual, or a subjective approach, in which the interview data is co-produced by the views and interpretations of the participant as well as by the interpretation made by the interviewer during the analysis of the data collected (Saunders et al., 2003).

Interviews can be divided into structured, semi-structured, and unstructured interviews. On the one hand, structured interviews follow a standardised set of questions and are close to a positivistic approach, useful for quantitative research (Easterby-Smith et al., 2002). On the other hand, semi-structured interviews contain different themes and questions and can differ from interview to interview. Finally, unstructured interviews do not have a defined structure, a clear order, or a specific question, and the interviewer and interviewee can talk freely about the issues under study. These two types of interviews are useful for qualitative research. While semi-structured interviews are more

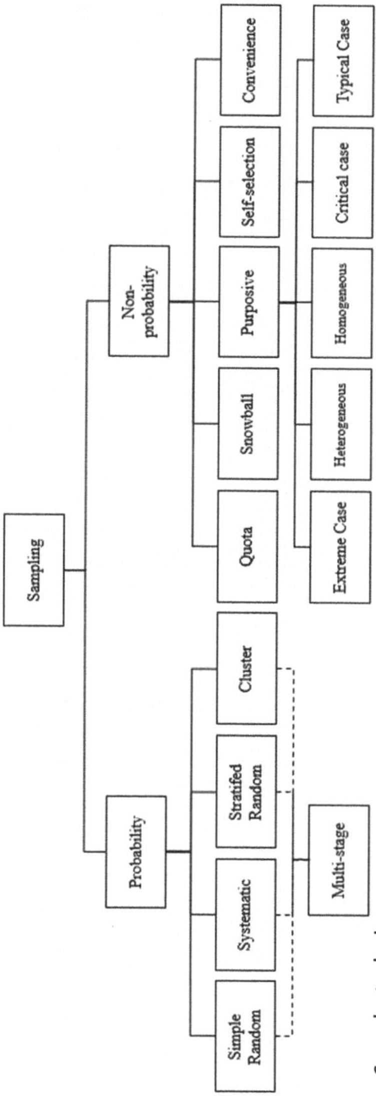

Fig. A.1 Sample techniques

frequently used for explanatory purposes, unstructured interviews are used for exploratory studies.

The main reason to conduct qualitative interviews is to understand how participants construct their meaning and the significance of their situations from the "complex personal framework of beliefs and values which they have developed over their lives in order to help explain and predict events in their own world" (Easterby-Smith et al., 2002, p. 73). In the context of Narrative Inquiry, narratives can be collected from different sources, such as observations or reports, but also through narrative interviews in the form of texts, further analysed through narrative analysis which considers their content, form, and context (Lieblich et al., 1998; Riessman, 2008), a data collection tool considered as the most appropriate for the research. Further details about narrative interviews in the context of the present study are developed in the following chapter. Narrative interviews are a suitable tool for qualitative studies aiming at engaging and stimulating the participant to investigate representations of his reality (Jovchelovitch & Bauer, 2000). This type of interview is characterised by being an in-depth unstructured or semi-structured tool which emerges from life experiences while examining the situational context (Pentland, 1999). Although the influence of the researcher should be minimal following the idea of reconstructing social events from the point of view of the participant, collaboration between both parts is key as the story emerges from their interaction, exchange of information, and dialogue.

Data Analysis

The Nature of the Research

The nature of this research is exploratory following an inductive approach. This can be seen in the fact that the study is based on a conceptual framework derived from the analysis of the theoretical framework of the research and develops research questions to answer them and identify relationships among the data. In this approach, theory emerges from the process of data collection, analysis, and interpretation (Saunders et al., 2003). In this context, narrative interviews would represent a story that describes a process leading to explanations and further interpretations, where the researcher needs to identify the generative structures that enable or constrain these explanations and interpretations. Narratives contain indicators for an underlying process theory; that is, narrative interviews help connect cause and effect, being the core of good theory (Pentland, 1999).

Narrative Analysis

Saunders et al. (2003) described the narrative analysis as a "collection of analytical approaches to analyse different aspects of narrative that can be combined depending of the research questions, the purpose of the research and the nature of the data" (p. 600). In this context, the authors identified two approaches:

1. Thematic narrative analysis. In this approach, the focus is on the content rather than on the structure, on what the narrative is about, rather than how it is constructed and can be applied to a single narrative or to a set of related narratives. It is relevant to pay attention to the chronological events as well as to the context of the narrative. In the case of multiple narratives, they should be related by a common event or focus of analysis. The initial focus can be the in-depth analysis of each of the narratives individually, to identify themes to then compare them considering the contextual differences across narratives. However, the analysis can also start by identifying themes across narratives deductively based on a prior theoretical framework to develop an explanation that evaluates the application of prior theory. In any case, to identify themes while keeping the narrative intact, any method of coding, such as colour coding, could be adapted.
2. Structural narrative analysis. In this approach, the focus is on how the narrative is constructed rather than on what it is about, examining the use of language to understand how it affects the audience. When using this approach, an understanding of socio-linguistic and cognitive theories must be developed. Labov and Waletzky (1967)

defined a key method for this kind of analysis based on the presence of six elements: (i) an abstract, (ii) an orientation, (iii) a complicating action, (iv) an evaluation, (v) a resolution, and (vi) a coda, providing a framework for evaluating narratives and how they are sequenced and structured. Structural analysis might be useful when the researcher collects accounts of interactions between individuals or across those in different groups.

These two approaches have in common that the data's narrative form is preserved and further analysed as a whole unit or as a narrative sequence where categories and themes are still able to be used, but always within a narrative. "In narrative analysis, it is important to preserve data within their narrated context to maintain the sequential and structural elements of each case" (Saunders et al., 2003, p. 600).

Lieblich et al. (1998) defined four models of reading, interpreting, and analysing narratives based on two independent dimensions: (a) holistic vs categorial and (b) content vs form:

- Holistic-content. This model focuses on the story as a whole and on the content told by the storyteller. When different parts are analysed, the meaning of the content is considered within the whole context of the story.
- Holistic-form. This mode looks at the structure of complete stories; the way the whole story is told.
- Categorical-content. In this approach, the analysis focuses on different and relevant parts or units of the story to understand the content.
- Categorical-form. This model focuses on the analysis of the language and style of defined parts or units of the narrative.

Polkinghorne (1995) proposes two types of analysis distinguishing between analysis of narratives and narrative analysis (Kim, 2015). On the one hand, the analysis of narratives, which is based on a paradigmatic mode of analysis, assumes that humans organise their life experiences around a specific area or topic as a sequence of ordered events and attend to "general features, and common categories and characteristics" (Kim, 2015, p. 196). Within this type of analysis, the author explains that two types of paradigmatic modes of analysis are possible: (i) concepts, categories, and common themes are derived from precious theory and (ii) concepts, categories, and themes are identified inductively after the analysis of data. In both cases, in this type of analysis, the researcher reads and interprets the interviews while identifying common themes and categories across the storytellers to develop findings.

On the other hand, the narrative mode of analysis is based on narrative cognition or a narrative mode of thinking "that attends to the particular and special characteristics of human action that take place in a particular setting" (Kim, 2015, p. 197). In this case, stories are produced as an outcome of the analysis of actions and events. Stories are created by storying and restoring and by integrating these actions and events into a plot that will be further analysed by the researcher to show the reader why and how things happened and why participants acted that way. This mode of analysis helps to understand the feelings, values, and motivations of the storyteller. While the paradigmatic mode of analysis is more rigid and focuses on categories, generalities, and patterns that can or cannot be deducted from theory, the narrative mode of analysis is more flexible, allowing the researcher to develop multiple interpretations. The selection of the model will depend on the objectives of the research as well as on the proposed conceptual framework, research questions, the data collection method, and units of analysis.

Conclusion

The aim of this chapter was to show an overview of the methodological framework employed in this study, with a special focus on Narrative Inquiry. The following chapter will focus on how these concepts are applied to the specific situation under analysis.

Bibliography

Abbott, A. (1990). A primer on sequence methods. *Organization Science, 1*(4), 375–392.

Adams, P., Freitas, I. M. B., & Fontana, R. (2019). Strategic orientation, innovation performance and the moderating influence of marketing management. *Journal of Business Research, 97*, 129–140.

Allison, G. (2023). China's dominance of solar poses difficult choices for the west. *Financial Times*. https://www.ft.com/content/fd8e7175-9423-4042-a6f7-c404afdfcda4

Alon, I., Anderson, J., Ziaul Haque, M., & Ho, A. (2018). A review of the internationalization of Chinese enterprises. *Asia Pacific Journal of Management*. https://doi.org/10.1007/s10490-018-9597-5

Alqahtani, N., & Uslay, C. (2020). Entrepreneurial marketing and firm performance: Synthesis and conceptual development. *Journal of Business Research, 113*, 62–71.

Altamira, M., Fornes, G., & Mendez, A. (2022). Chinese institutions and international expansion within the BRI: Firm capabilities of Chinese companies in the European Union. *Asia Pacific Business Review*. https://doi.org/10.1080/13602381.2022.2093520

M. Altamira, *Chinese Firms in the Global Market*, Palgrave Macmillan Asian Business Series, https://doi.org/10.1007/978-3-031-59227-0

Amendolagine, V., Amighini, A., & Rabelloti, R. (2017). Chinese multinationals in Europe. In *Understanding China Today*. Springer International Publishing.

Angulo-Ruiz, F., Pergelova, A., & Wei, W. (2019). How does home government influence the internationalization of emerging market firms? The mediating role of strategic intents to internationalize. *International Journal of Emerging Markets, 14*(1). https://doi.org/10.1108/IJoEM-08-2017-0274

Asian Development Bank. (2021). *The 14th five-year plan of the People's Republic of China: Fostering high-quality development*. https://www.adb.org/publications/14th-five-year-plan-high-quality-development-prc

Banach, C., & Gunter, J. (2023). *How the BRI is shaping global trade and what to expect from the initiative in its second decade*. https://merics.org/en/tracker/how-bri-shaping-global-trade-and-what-expect-initiative-its-second-decade

Barney, J. (1991). Firm resources and sustained competitive advantage. *Journal of Management, 17*(1), 99–120.

Barney, J., & Zhang, S. (2009). The future of Chinese management research: A theory of Chinese management versus a Chinese theory of management. *Management and Organization Review, 5*(1), 15–28.

Barrales-Molina, V., Martínez-López, F. J., & Gázquez-Abad, J. (2013). Dynamic marketing capabilities: Toward an integrative framework. *International Journal of Management Reviews*. https://doi.org/10.1111/ijmr.12026

Bellabona, P., & Spigarelli, F. (2007). Moving from open door to go global: China goes on the world stage. *International Journal of Chinese Culture and Management, 1*(1), 93–107. https://doi.org/10.1504/IJCCM.2007.016170

Birkinshaw, J., Brannen, M., & Tung, R. (2011). From a distance and generalizable to upclose and grounded: Reclaiming a place for qualitative methods in international business research. *Journal of International Business Studies, 42*, 573–581. https://doi.org/10.1057/jibs.2011.19

Boisot, M., & Meyer, M. (2008). Which way through the open door? Reflections on the internationalization of Chinese firms. *Management and Organization Review, 4*(3), 349–365.

Boje, D. M. (1994). Organizational storytelling: Struggles of pre-modern, modern and postmodern organizational learning discourses. *Management Learning, 25*(3), 433–461.

Boje, D. M. (2001). *Narrative methods for organizational and communication research*. Sage.

Boje, D. M. (2012). Narrative analysis. In A. J. D. Mills, G. Durepos, & E. Wiebe (Eds.), *Encyclopedia of case study research* (pp. 591–591). Sage.

Boyce, M. E. (1996). Organizational story and storytelling: A critical review. *Journal of Organizational Change Management, 9*(5), 5–26.

Bruton, G., & Lau, C. (2008). Asian management research: Status today and future outlook. *Journal of Management Studies, 45*(3), 636–659.

Buckley, J. (2018). Internalisation theory and outward direct investment by emerging market multinationals. *Management International Review, 58*, 195–224. https://doi.org/10.1007/s11575-017-0320-4

Buckley, P., Clegg, J., Cross, A., Liu, X., Voss, H., & Zheng, P. (2007). The determinants of Chinese outward foreign direct investment. *Journal of International Business Studies, 38*(4), 499–518.

Buckley, P., Clegg, J., Voss, H., Cross, A., Liu, X., & Zheng, P. (2018). A retrospective and agenda for future research on Chinese outward foreign direct investment. *Journal of International Business Studies, 49*(1), 4–23.

Cardoza, G., & Fornes, G. (2011). National and international expansion of Chinese SMEs: A different story? In X. Fu (Ed.), *China's role in global economic recovery*. Routledge.

Cardoza, G., & Fornes, G. (2013). The international expansion of China's small and medium-sized business: Status today and future outlook. *Journal of Chinese Entrepreneurship, 5*(3), 252–273.

Cardoza, G., Fornes, G., Farber, V., Duarte, R., & Gutierrez, J. (2016). Barriers and public policies affecting the international expansion of Latin American SMEs: Evidence from Brazil, Colombia, and Peru. *Journal of Business Research, 69*(6), 2030–2039. https://doi.org/10.1016/j.jbusres.2015.10.148

Cardoza, G., Fornes, G., Li, P., Xu, N., & Xu, S. (2014). China goes global: Public policies' influence on small and medium-size enterprises' international expansion. *Asia Pacific Business Review*. https://doi.org/10.1080/13602381.2013.876183

Cardoza, G., Fornes, G., Li, P., Xu, N., & Xu, S. (2015). China goes global: Public policies' influence on small- and medium-sized enterprises' international expansion. *Asia Pacific Business Review, 21*(2), 188–210.

Cardoza, G., Fornes, G., & Xu, N. (2011). *Institutional determinants of Chinese SMEs' internationalization: The case of Jiangsu Province*. Paper presented at the Chinese Economic Association, Dublin.

Cash, J., & Zhang, E. (2023, July 13). *China's exports fall most in three years as global economy falters*. https://www.reuters.com/markets/asia/chinas-june-exports-fall-124-imports-drop-68-2023-07-13/

CEIC. (2020). https://www.ceicdata.com/datapage/en/country/china

Cerdeiro, D., & Jain-Chandra, S. (2023). *China's economy is rebounding, but reforms are still needed*. https://www.imf.org/en/News/Articles/2023/02/02/cf-chinas-economy-is-rebounding-but-reforms-are-still-needed

Chandler, C., & McGregor, G. (2020). Xi Jinping's new economic strategy for China: 'Dual circulation' or doublespeak? *Fortune*.

Chen, C., Chen, X., & Huang, S. (2013). Chinese guanxi: An integrative review and new directions for future research. *Management and Organization Review, 9*(1), 167–207.

Chen, X., & Wu, J. (2011). Do different guanxi types affect capability building differently? A contingency view. *Industrial Marketing Management, 40*(4), 581–592.

Chen, Z. (2023). *Review of economic impact of COVID-19 on China's economy: Positive and negative*. Paper presented at the Proceedings of the 6th International Conference on Economic Management and Green Development, Singapore.

Chenyan, Z., Wei, Z., Junjie, H., & Mario, K. (2022). The role of government policies in explaining the internationalization of Chinese firms. *Journal of Business Research, 141*, 552–563. https://doi.org/10.1016/j.jbusres.2021.11.056

Child, J., & Marinova, S. (2014). The role of contextual combinations in the globalization of Chinese firms. *Management and Organization Review, 10*(3), 347–371.

Child, J., & Rodrigues, S. (2005). The internationalization of Chinese firms: A case for theoretical extension? *Management and Organization Review, 1*(3), 381–410.

Chow, L. (2023). *Overview of China outbound investment of 2022*. https://www.ey.com/en_cn/china-overseas-investment-network/overview-of-china-outbound-investment-of-2022#:~:text=China%20overall%20outward%20direct%20investment,to%20US%2421.0%20billion1

Creswell, J. W. (2009). *Research design: Qualitative and quantitative approaches*. Sage.

Cui, L., & Jiang, F. (2012). State ownership effect on firms' FDI ownership decisions under institutional pressure: A study of Chinese outward-investing firms. *Journal of International Business Studies, 43*(3), 264–284.

Cunningham, J. W., & Fitzerald, J. (1996). Epistemology and reading. *Reading Research Quarterly, 31*(1), 36–60.

D'Oria, L., Crook, T., Ketchen Jr., D., Sirmon, D., & Wright, M. (2021). The evolution of resource-based inquiry: A review and meta-analytic integration of the strategic resources–actions–performance pathway. *Journal of Management, 47*(6), 1383–1429.

Darroch, J., Miles, M. P., Jardine, A., & Cook, E. (2004). The 2004 AMA definition of marketing and its relationship to a market orientation: An extension of Cook, Rayburn, & Abercrombie (1992). *Journal of Marketing Theory and Practice, 12*(4), 29–38.

Davis, L., & North, D. (1971). *Institutional change and American economic growth.* Cambridge University Press.

Day, G. (1994). The capabilities of market-driven organizations. *Journal of Marketing, 58,* 37–51. https://doi.org/10.1177/002224299405800404

Day, G. (2011). Closing the marketing capabilities gap. *Journal of Marketing, 75,* 183–195.

Day, G. (2013). Closing the marketing capability gap. *Journal of Marketing, 75*(4), 183–195.

Deng, P. (2009). Why do Chinese firms tend to acquire strategic assets in international expansion? *Journal of World Business, 44*(1), 74–84.

Deng, P. (2012). The internationalization of Chinese firms: A critical review and future research. *International Journal of Management Reviews, 14*(4). https://doi.org/10.1111/j.1468-2370.2011.00323.x

Deng, P., Yang, X., Wang, L., & Doyle, B. (2017). Chinese investments in advanced economies: Opportunities and challenges. *Thunderbird International Business Review, 59*(4). https://doi.org/10.1002/tie.21903

DeSarbo, W., Di Benedetto, C., Jedidi, K., & Song, M. (2006). Identifying sources of heterogeneity for empirically deriving strategic types: A constrained finite-mixture structural equation methodology. *Management Science, 52*(6), 909–924.

Dollar, D., Huang, Y., & Yao, Y. (2021). *China's long-term success will depend primarily on addressing its internal challenges* [Press release]. https://www.imf.org/external/pubs/ft/fandd/2021/06/the-future-of-china-dollar-huang-yao.htm

Dong, C., Bingxin Li, C., & Tse, D. K. (2013). Do business and political ties differ in cultivating marketing channels for foreign and local firms in China? *Journal of International Marketing, 21*(1), 39–56.

Du, J., & Zhang, Y. (2018). Does One belt one road initiative promote Chinese overseas direct investment? *China Economic Review, 47*(C), 189–205.

Easterby-Smith, M., Thorpe, R., & Lowe, A. (2002). *Management research: An introduction* (2nd ed.). Sage.

Eisenhardt, K. (1989). Building theories from case study research. *Academy of Management Review, 14*(4), 532–550.

Eisenhardt, K., & Graebner, M. (2007). Theory building from cases: Opportunities and challenges. *Academy of Management Journal, 50*(1), 25–32.

Elango, B., & Pattnaik, C. (2007). Building capabilities for international operations through networks: A study of Indian firms. *Journal of International Business Studies, 38*(4), 541–555.

Estrin, S., & Prevezer, M. (2011). The role of informal institutions in corporate governance: Brazil, Russia, India, and China compared. *Asia Pacific Journal of Management, 28*(1), 41–67.

European Commission. (2019). *EU-China trade*. https://ec.europa.eu/trade/policy/countries-and-regions/countries/china/

European Commission. (2020). *Countries and regions*. China. https://ec.europa.eu/trade/policy/countries-and-regions/countries/china/

European Commission. (2023). *Global gateway forum 2023*. https://commission.europa.eu/strategy-and-policy/priorities-2019-2024/stronger-europe-world/global-gateway_en

European Parliament. (2020). *Legal analysis of international trade law and digital trade*. Policy Department for External Relations.

European Union Chamber of Commerce in China. (2020). *The road less travelled: European involvement in China's Belt and Road Initiative*. https://reconasia.csis.org/road-less-travelled/

Fainshmidt, S., Witt, M. A., Aguilera, R. V., & Verbeke, A. (2020). The contributions of qualitative comparative analysis (QCA) to international business research. In (Vol. 51, pp. 455–466). Springer.

Fang, C., Garnaut, R., & Song, L. (2018). 40 years of China's reform and development: How reform captured China's demographic dividend. In S. S. A. Press (Ed.), *China's 40 years of reform and development* (pp. 1978–2018). Anu Press.

Fang, E., & Zou, S. (2009). Antecedents and consequences of marketing dynamic capabilities in international joint ventures. *Journal of International Business Studies, 40*(5), 742–761.

Financial Times Reporters. (2022, October 22). How the US chip export controls have turned the screws on China. *Financial Times*.

Fornes, G., & Altamira, M. (2023). *Digitalization, technology and global business: How technology is shaping value creation across borders*. Palgrave.

Fornes, G., & Cardoza, G. (2018). Internationalization of Chinese SMEs: The perception of disadvantages of foreignness. *Emerging Markets Finance & Trade*, 1–20. https://doi.org/10.1080/1540496X.2018.1518218

Fornes, G., Cardoza, G., & Altamira, M. (2016). *Informal structures and practices in the national and international expansion of SMEs from emerging markets: Evidence from Brazil and China.* Paper presented at the Academy of Management annual conference, Anaheim.

Fornes, G., Cardoza, G., & Altamira, M. (2021). Do informal business and political relations help SMEs from emerging markets in their national and international expansion? Evidence from Brazil and China. *International Journal of Emerging Markets, 17*(8). https://doi.org/10.1108/IJOEM-01-2020-0058

Fornes, G., Lopez, B., Bierens de Haan, M., & Blanch, J. (2018). Best practice example of CSR and S&E engagement in emerging economies: Analysis of a case study based in China. *Journal of Asian Business Studies, 13*(4). https://doi.org/10.1108/JABS-08-2017-0120

Fornes, G., & Mendez, A. (2018). *The China-Latin America axis: Emerging markets and their role in an increasingly globalised world* (2nd ed.). Palgrave Macmillan.

Ge, G. L., & Ding, D. Z. (2005). Market orientation, competitive strategy and firm performance: An empirical study of Chinese firms. *Journal of Global Marketing, 18*(3–4), 115–142.

Gertsen, M., & Soderberg, A. (2011). Intercultural collaboration stories: On narrative inquiry and analysis as tools for research in international business. *Journal of International Business Studies, 42*, 787–804.

Ghiretti, F., Legarda, H., Stec, G., & Vasselier, A. (2023). *Profiling relations of European countries with China.* https://merics.org/en/profiling-relations-european-countries-china

Gong, X. (2023). *The Belt and Road Initiative is still China's "Gala" but without as much luster* [Press release]. https://carnegieendowment.org/2023/03/03/belt-and-road-initiative-is-still-china-s-gala-but-without-as-much-luster-pub-89207

Grieger, G. (2023). *EU anti-subsidy probe into electric vehicle imports from China.* https://www.europarl.europa.eu/RegData/etudes/ATAG/2023/754553/EPRS_ATA(2023)754553_EN.pdf

Guenzi, P., & Troilo, G. (2006). Developing marketing capabilities for customer value creation through Marketing-Sales integration. *Industrial Marketing Management, 35*(8), 974–988.

Gundlach, G., & Wilkie, W. (2009). The American Marketing Association's new definition of marketing: Perspective and commentary on the 2007 revision. *Journal of Public Policy & Marketing, 28*(2), 259–264.

Haasis, T., & Liefner, I. (2019). Reviewing the research on the internationalization of Chinese firms: Thematic expansion, new impulses and potential future development. *International Journal of Emerging Markets, 14*(1), 24–50.

Hale, T., & Langley, W. (2023, September 30). Weak China manufacturing data adds to pressure on economy. *Financial Times*. https://www.ft.com/content/386580c9-88f2-4368-84ff-fbe2d962e062

Hanemann, T., Huotari, M., & Kratz, A. (2019). *Chinese FDI in Europe: 2018 trends and impact of new screening policies*. https://rhg.com/wp-content/uploads/2019/03/RHG-MERICS-COFDI-Update-2019.pdf

He, S., Khan, Z., Lew, Y., & Fallon, G. (2019). Technological innovation as a source of Chinese multinationals' firm-specific advantages and internationalization. *International Journal of Emerging Markets, 14*(4). https://doi.org/10.1108/IJOEM-02-2017-0059

He, X., K., B., & Filatotchev, I. (2012). Resource-based and institutional perspectives on export channel selection and export performance. *Journal of Management*. https://doi.org/10.1177/0149206312445926

He, X., & Wei, Y. (2011). Linking market orientation to international market selection and international performance. *International Business Review, 20*(5), 535–546.

Hemphill, T., & White III, G. (2013). *China's national champions: The evolution of a national industrial policy—Or a new era of economic protectionism?* Wiley Online Library.

Hernandez, E., & Guillen, M. (2018). What's theoretically novel about emerging market multinationals? *Journal of International Business Studies, 49*(1), 24–33.

Ho-Him, C. (2023, April 23). Shifting production from China is impossible, says shipping boss. *Financial Times*. https://www.ft.com/content/ed7357fa-1da5-485c-ae59-ed21ab1e6e9d

Hofman, B. (2018). *Reflections on forty years of China's reforms*. Fudan University's Fanhai School of International Finance.

Hofstede, G. (1981). Culture and organisations. *International Studies of Managament and Organization, 10*(4), 15–41.

Hong, J., Wang, C., & Kafouros, M. (2015). The role of the state in explaining the internationalization of emerging market enterprises. *British Journal of Management, 26*, 45–62. https://doi.org/10.1111/1467-8551.12059

Hoskisson, R., Eden, L., Lau, C., & Wright, M. (2000). Strategy in emerging economies. *Academy of Management Journal, 43*(3), 249–267.

Hsu, S. (2017). Foreign firms wary of 'Made in China 2025,' but it may be China's best chance at innovation. *Forbes*.

Huang, Y. (2016). Understanding China's Belt & Road Initiative: Motivation, framework and assessment. *China Economic Review, 40*(C), 314–321.

Huenemann, R. (2017). *Economic reforms, 1978–present*. https://www.oxfordbibliographies.com/view/document/obo-9780199920082/obo-9780199920082-0008.xml

Hult, G., Ketchen, D., & Slater, S. (2005). Market orientation and performance: An integration of disparate approaches. *Strategic Management Journal, 26*(12), 1173–1181.

IMF. (2011). *World Economic Outlook database*. http://www.imf.org/external/pubs/ft/weo/2010/02/weodata/index.aspx

International Monetary Fund. (2023). *People's Republic of China 2022 Article IV Consultation—Press release; staff report; and statement by the executive director for the People's Republic of China* [Press release].

Johanson, J., & Vahlne, J. (1977). The internationalization process of the firm—A model of knowledge development and increasing foreign market commitments. *Journal of International Business Studies, 8*(1), 23–32.

Jovchelovitch, S., & Bauer, M. W. (2000). Narrative interviewing. In M. W. Bauer & Gaskell, G. (Eds.), *Qualitative researching with text, image and sound: A practical handbook* (pp. 57–74). Sage.

Ju, M., Fung, H., & Mano, H. (2013). Firm capabilities and performance: Institutional perspective on foreign and local firms in China. *The Chinese Economy, 46*(5), 86–104.

Kamboj, S., & Rhaman, Z. (2015). Marketing capabilities and firm performance: Literature review and future research agenda. *International Journal of Productivity and Performance Management International Review, 64*(8), 1041–1067.

Katsikeas, C., Samiee, S., & Theodosiou, M. (2006). Strategy fit and performance consequences of international marketing standardization. *Strategic Management Journal, 27*(9), 867–890.

Kaufmann, L., & Roesch, J.-F. (2012). Constraints to building and deploying marketing capabilities by emerging market firms in advanced markets. *Journal of International Marketing, 20*(4), 1–24.

Kawase, K. (2022, August 2). Made in China 2025 plan thrives with subsidies for tech and EV makers. *Financial Times*. https://www.ft.com/content/f7df0f64-25b5-4526-82fa-ca1b554b541b

Khanna, T., & Palepu, K. (1997). Why focused strategies may be wrong for emerging markets. *Harvard Business Review, 4*(75), 3–10.

Khanna, T., & Palepu, K. (2010). *Winning in emerging markets: A road map for strategy and execution.* Harvard Business School Publishing Corporation.

Kim, J. (2015). Narrative data analysis and interpretation. In *Understanding narrative inquiry: The crafting and analysis of stories as research.* Sage.

Kim, K., Lattemann, C., Park, I., & Zhang, W. (2019). New international business theories for China goes global? The importance of institutions, innovativeness and learning. *International Journal of Emerging Markets, 14*(1), 2–5. https://doi.org/10.1108/ijoem-01-2019-574

Kotler, P., & Amstrong, G. (2001). *Principles of marketing*. Prentice Hall.

Kotler, P., & Keller, K. (2011). *Marketing management* (14th ed.). Pearson.

Kratz, A., Zenglein, M., Sebastian, G., & Witzke, M. (2023). *Chinese FDI in Europe: 2022 update*. https://rhg.com/research/chinese-fdi-in-europe-2022-update/

Labov, W., & Waletzky, J. (1967). Narrative analysis: Oral versions of personal experience. *Journal of Narrative and Life History, 7*, 3–38. https://doi.org/10.1075/jnlh.7.1-4

Lattemann, C., & Alon, I. (2015). The rise of Chinese multinationals: A strategic threat or an economic opportunity? *Georgetown Journal of International Affairs, 16*(1), 168–175.

Lattemann, C., Alon, I., Spigarelli, F., & Marinova, S. (2017). Dynamic embeddedness in Chinese firm internationalization. *Thunderbird International Business Review, 59*(4), 547–559.

Leahy, J. (2023). EU companies warn China on EV overcapacity. *Financial Times*. https://www.ft.com/content/4e1b2cdb-3a67-4567-be9b-062e6af69ee9

Li, G., & White, E. (2023). Chinese electric vehicle groups braced for wave of consolidation. *Financial Times*. https://www.ft.com/content/43da3223-2311-4b73-97d9-83d20baedc6a

Li, S., & Li, S. (2000). The road to capitalism: Competition and institutional change in China. *Journal of Comparative Economics, 28*(2), 269–292.

Lieblich, A., Tuval-Mashiach, R., & Zilber, T. (1998). *Narrative research: Reading, analysis and interpretation* (Vol. 47). Sage.

Lin, S., Mercier-Suissa, C., & Salloum, C. (2016). The Chinese born globals of the Zhejiang Province: A study on the key factors for their rapid internationalization. *Journal of International Enterpreneurship, 14*(1), 75–95.

Lin, X. (2010). State versus private MNCs from China: Initial conceptualizations. *International Marketing Review, 27*(3), 366–380.

Lincoln, Y., & Guba, E. (1985). *Naturalistic enquiry*. Sage

Ling, C., & Naughton, B. (2016). An institutionalized policy-making mechanism: China's return totechno-industrial policy. *Research Policy, 45*(10), 2138–2152.

Liu, H. (2015). *The Chinese strategic mind*. Edward Elgar Publishing.

Liu, J., & Su, J. (2013). *How does market orientation affect product innovation in China's manufacturing industry: The contingent value of dynamic capabilities*. Paper presented at the International Conference on Education Technology and Management Science.

Liu, Y., Oberg, C., Yedidia Tarba, S., & Xing, Y. (2018). Brand management in mergers and acquisitions: Emerging market multinationals venturing into advanced economies. *International Marketing Review, 35*(5), 710–732.

Luo, Y., & Child, J. (2015). A composition-based view of firm growth. *Management and Organization Review, 11*(3), 379–411.

Ma, H., Wu, X., Yan, L., Huang, H., Wu, H., Xiong, J., & Zhang, J. (2018). Strategic plan of "Made in China 2025" and its implementation. In *Analysing the impacts of industry 4.0 in modern business environments*. IGI Global.

Mathews, J. (2006). Dragon multinationals: New players in 21st century globalization. *Asia Pacific Journal of Management, 23*(1), 5–27.

Mellahi, K., Demirbag, M., Tamer Cavusgil, S., & Danis, W. (2010). Marketing strategies of MNCs for emerging markets: Internationalisation and market entry mode. *International Marketing Review, 27*(2), 267–271.

Meyer, K., Estrin, S., Kumar Bhaumik, S., & Peng, M. (2009). Institutions, resources, and entry strategies in emerging economies. *Strategic Management Journal, 30*(1), 61–80.

Meyer, K., & Peng, M. (2016). Theoretical foundations of emerging economy business research. *Journal of International Business Studies, 47*, 3–22. https://doi.org/10.1057/jibs.2015.34

Meyer, K. E. (2004). Perspectives on multinational enterprises in emerging economies. *Journal of International Business Studies, 35*(4), 259–276.

Morgan, D. L. (2007). Paradigms lost and pragmatism regained: Methodological implications of combining qualitative and quantitative methods. *Journal of Mixed Methods Research, 1*(1), 48–76.

Morgan, N. (2012). Marketing and business performance. *Journal of the Academy of Marketing Science, 40*(1), 102–119.

Morgan, N., Douglas, W., & Mason, C. (2009a). Market orientation, marketing capabilities and firm performance. *Strategic Management Journal, 30*, 909–920. https://doi.org/10.1002/smj.764

Morgan, N., Feng, H., & Whitler, K. (2018). Marketing capabilities in international marketing. *Journal of International Marketing, 26*(1), 61–95.

Morgan, N., Slotegraaf, R., & Vorhies, D. (2009b). Linking marketing capabilities with profit growth. *Internartional Journal of Research in Marketing, 26*, 284–296.

Morse, J. M., Barret, M., Mayan, M., Olson, K., & Spiers, J. (2002). Verification strategies for establishing reliability and validity in qualitative research. *Evidence Based Nursing, 1*(2), 13–22.

Mutlu, C., Zhan, W., Peng, M., & Lin, Z. (2015). Competing in (and out of) transition economies. *Asia Pacific Journal of Management, 32*(3), 571–596.

Narula, R. (2012). Do we need different frameworks to explain infant MNEs from developing countries? *Global Strategy Journal, 2*(3). https://doi.org/10.1111/j.2042-5805.2012.01035.x

Nee, V., & Opper, S. (2012). *Capitalism from below: Markets and institutional change in China*. Harvard University Press.

Noble, C., Rajiv, K., & Kumar, A. (2002). Market orientation and alternative strategic orientations: A longitudinal assessment of performance implications. *Journal of Marketing, 66*(4), 25–39.

North, D. (1990). *Institutions, institutional change, and economic performance*. Cambridge University Press.

OECD. (2018a). China's Belt and Road Initiative in the global trade, investment and finance landscape. In *OECD Business and Finance Outlook 2018*. OECD Publishing.

OECD. (2018b). *Ownership and governance of state-owned enterprises: A compendium of national practices*. https://www.oecd.org/corporate/ca/Ownership-and-Governance-of-State-Owned-Enterprises-A-Compendium-of-National-Practices.pdf

Oliveira, R., Menzies, J., Borgia, D., & Figueira, S. (2017). Outward foreign direct investment from emerging countries: Theoretical extension and evidence from China. *The International Trade Journal, 31*(5), 402–428.

Otto, A. S., Szymanski, D. M., & Varadarajan, R. (2020). Customer satisfaction and firm performance: Insights from over a quarter century of empirical research. *Journal of the Academy of Marketing Science, 48*, 543–564.

Park, S., & Luo, Y. (2001). Guanxi and organizational dynamics: Organizational networking in Chinese firms. *Strategic Management Journal, 22*(5), 455–477.

Parmentola, A. (2017). Why Chinese companies go abroad? A theoretical model to explain the drivers of the internationalisation strategy of Chinese MNEs. *International Business Research, 10*(10), 82–93.

Pasa, M., & Shugan, S. (1996). The value of marketing expertise. *Management Science, 42*(3), 370–388.

Paul, J., & Benito, G. (2018). A review of research on outward foreign direct investment from emerging countries, including China: What do we know, how do we know and where should we be heading? *Asia Pacific Business Review, 24*(1), 90–115.

Peng, M. (2002). Towards an institution-based view of business strategy. *Asia Pacific Journal of Management, 19*, 251–267.

Peng, M. (2012). The global strategy of emerging multinationals from China. *Global Strategy Journal*. https://doi.org/10.1002/gsj.1030

Peng, M., Lebedev, S., Vlas, C., Wang, J., & Shay, J. (2018). The growth of the firm in (and out of) emerging economies. *Asia Pacific Journal of Management, 35*(4), 829–857.

Peng, M., Lee, S., & Wang, D. (2005). What determines the scope of the firm over time? A focus on institutional relatedness. *Academy of Management Review, 30*(3), 622–633.

Peng, M., & Luo, Y. (2000). Managerial ties and firm performance in a transition economy: The nature of a micro-macro link. *Academy of Management Journal, 43*(3), 486–501.

Peng, M., Wang, D., & Jiang, Y. (2008). An institution-based view of international business strategy: A focus on emerging economies. *Journal of International Business Studies, 39*, 920–936.

Pentland, B. T. (1999). Building process theory with narrative: From description to explanation. *Academy of Management Review, 24*(4), 711–724.

Peterson Institute for International Economics. (2023). China's state vs. private company tracker: Which sector dominates? *PIIE*. https://www.piie.com/research/piie-charts/chinas-state-vs-private-company-tracker-which-sector-dominates

Polkinghorne, D. (1988). *Narrative knowing and the human sciences*. State University of New York Press.

Polkinghorne, D. (1995). Narrative configuration in qualitative analysis. *International Journal of Qualitative Studies in Education, 8*(1), 5–23.

Porter, M. (2008). *On competition* (Updated and Expanded ed.). Harvard Business School Publishing.

PRC, T. S. C. (2017). *Made in China 2025*. http://english.gov.cn/2016special/madeinchina2025/

Ramamurti, R. (2012). What is really different about emerging market multinationals? *Global Strategy Journal, 2*(1), 41–47.

Ramamurti, R., & Hillemann, J. (2018). What is "Chinese" about Chinese multinationals? *Journal of International Business Studies, 49*(1), 34–48.

Rauch, J., & Trindale, V. (2002). Ethnic Chinese networks in international trade. *The Review of Economics and Statistics, 84*(1), 116–130.

Renault Group. (2023). *Renault Group and Geely sign joint venture agreement to launch leading powertrain technology company* [Press release]. https://media.renaultgroup.com/renault-group-and-geely-sign-joint-venture-agreement-to-launch-leading-powertrain-technology-company/

Rhodes, C., & Brown, D. (2005). Narrative, organizations and research. *International Journal of Management Reviews, 7*(3), 167–188.

Riessman, C. K. (1993). *Narrative analysis*. Sage.

Riessman, C. K. (2005). Narrative analysis. *Narrative, memory & everyday life* (pp. 1–7). University of Huddersfield.

Riessman, C. K. (2008). *Narrative methods for the human sciences*. Sage.

Robson, C. (2002). *Real world research a resource for social scientists and practitioner-researchers* (2nd ed.). Blackwell.

Rock, K., & Hanelt, H. (2023). *Global gateway: The EU maps a different path than belt and road*. https://globaleurope.eu/europes-future/global-gateway-the-eu-maps-a-different-path-than-belt-and-road/

Rottig, D. (2016). Institutions and emerging markets: Effects and implications for multinational corporations. *International Journal of Emerging Markets, 11*(1), 2–17.

Rugman, A., & Li, J. (2007). Will China's multinationals succeed globally or regionally? *European Management Journal, 25*(5), 333–343.

Saunders, M., Lewis, P., & Thornhill, A. (2003). *Research methods for business students*. FT Prentice Hall.

Scott, W. (1995). *Institutions and organizations*. Sage.

Shou, Z., Chen, J., Zhu, W., & Yang, L. (2012). Firm capability and performance in China: The moderating role of guanxi and institutional forces in domestic and foreign contexts. *Journal of Business Research, 67*(2), 77–82.

Silverman, D. (2015). *Interpreting qualitative data*. Sage.

Singh, A. (2002). Understanding China's 'Go-West' campaign. *China Report, 38*(1), 121–127.

Slater, S., & Narver, J. (1993). Product-market strategy and performance: An analysis of the Miles and Snow strategy types. *European Journal of Marketing, 27*(2), 33–51.

Spar, D., & Oi, J. (2006). China: Building "capitalism with socialist characteristics". *Harvard Business School*.

Steup, M. (2013). *Epistemology*. http://plato.stanford.edu/archives/win2013/entries/epistemology/

Sun, F. (2017). Relationship versus transaction marketing in China: An institutional approach. *Business and Management Studies, 3*(2), 47–60.

Surdu, I., Mellahi, K., & Glaister, K. (2018). Emerging market multinationals' international equity-based entry mode strategies: Review of theoretical foundations and future directions. *International Marketing Review, 35*(2), 342–359. https://doi.org/10.1108/IMR-10-2015-0228

Tajeddini, K., & Ratten, V. (2020). The moderating effect of brand orientation on inter-firm market orientation and performance. *Journal of Strategic Marketing, 28*(3), 194–224.

Teece, D., Pisano, G., & Shuen, A. (1997). Dynamic capabilities and strategic management. *Strategic Management Journal, 19*(7), 509–533.

The Economist Reporters. (2023). How China's Belt and Road Initiative is changing. *The Economist*. https://www.economist.com/the-economist-explains/2023/10/17/how-chinas-belt-and-road-initiative-is-changing

The Editorial Board. (2023, July 17). China's sluggish economic recovery. *Financial Times*. https://www.ft.com/content/d7528b7f-d879-4b47-a45b-cbb58545e7be

Tracey, P., & Phillips, N. (2011). Entrepreneurship in emerging markets: Strategies for new venture creation in uncertain institutional contexts. *Management International Review, 51*(1), 23–39.

Tripsas, M. (1997). Unraveling the process of creative destruction: Complementary assets and incumbent survival in the typesetter industry. *Strategic Management Journal, 18*(Summer Special Issue), 119–142.

UNCTAD. (2019). *World investment report*. United Nations Conference on Trade and Development.

Vorhies, D., Morgan, R., & Autry, C. W. (2009). Product-market strategy and the marketing capabilities of the firm: Impact on market effectiveness and cash flow performance. *Strategic Management Journal, 30*(12), 1310–1334.

Wang, B., & Gao, K. (2019). Forty years development of China's outward foreign direct investment: Retrospect and the challenges ahead. *China & World Economy, 27*(3), 1–24. https://doi.org/10.1111/cwe.12278

Wang, C., Hong, J., Kafouros, M., & Baoteng, A. (2012). What drives outward FDI of Chinese firms? Testing the explanatory power of three theoretical frameworks. *International Business Review, 21*, 425–438.

Wei, J., Cong, S., Wang, C., & Pan, Q. (2020). The critical role of the institution-led market in the technological catch-up of emerging market enterprises: Evidence from Chinese enterprises. *R&D Management, 50*(4), 478–493.

Weinland, D. (2022, November 18). The tech war between America and China is just getting started. *The Economist*.

Wernerfelt, B. (1984). A resource-based view of the firm. *Strategic Management Journal, 5*(2), 171–180.

Williamson, P., Ramamurti, R., Fleury, A., & Leme Fleury, M. (2013). *The competitive advantage of emerging market multinationals*. Cambridge University Press.

World Bank. (2020). *World Bank data*. https://data.worldbank.org/country/china

World Bank. (2023). *China's GDP (current thousands US$) per capita evolution 1978–2022*. https://data.worldbank.org/indicator/NY.GDP.PCAP.CD?locations=CN

Wright, M., Filatotchev, I., Hoskisson, R., & Peng, M. (2005). Strategy research in emerging economies: Challenging the conventional wisdom. *Journal of Management Studies, 42*(1), 1–33. http://search.ebscohost.com/login.aspx?direct=true&db=buh&AN=15645292&site=ehost-live

Wu, J. (2013a). Diverse institutional environments and product innovation of emerging market firms. *Management International Review, 53*(1), 39–59.

Wu, J. (2013b). Marketing capabilities, institutional development, and the performance of emerging market firms: A multinational study. *International Journal of Research in Marketing, 30*(1), 36–45.

Yan, H., He, X., & Cheng, B. (2017). Managerial ties, market orientation, and export performance: Chinese firms experience. *Management and Organization Review, 13*(3), 611–638.

Yang, X., & Stoltenberg, C. (2014). A review of institutional influences on the rise of made-in-China multinationals. *International Journal of Emerging Markets, 9*(2). https://doi.org/10.1108/IJoEM-09-2012-0095

Yang, Y., Wang, Q., Zhu, H., & Wu, G. (2012a). What are the effective strategic orientations for new product success under different environments? An empirical study of Chinese businesses. *Journal of Product Innovation Management, 29*(2), 166–179.

Yang, Y., Wang, Q., Zhu, H., & Zhu, H. (2012b). What are the effective strategic orientations for new product success under different environments? An empirical study of Chinese businesses. *Journal of Product Innovation Management, 29*(2), 166–179.

Yao, K. (2020). *What we know about China's 'dual circulation' economic strategy*. https://www.reuters.com/article/china-economy-transformation-explainer-idUSKBN2600B5

Yau, O. (1988). Chinese cultural values: Their dimensions and marketing implications. *European Journal of Maketing, 22*(5), 44–56.

Yau, O., Chan, T. S., & Lau, K. F. (2009). Influence of Chinese cultural values on consumer behavior. *Journal of International Consumer Marketing, 11*(1), 97–116.

Yi, J., Hong, J., Hsu, W., & Wang, C. (2017). The role of state ownership and institutions in the innovation performance of emerging market enterprises: Evidence from China. *Technovation, 62*(63), 4–13.

Yip, G., & McKern, B. (2014). Innovation in emerging markets—The case of China. *International Journal of Emerging Markets, 9*(1). https://doi.org/10.1108/IJoEM-11-2013-0182

Zhang, M., Qian, G., Wheeler, J. V., & Kwon, J. (2015). Institutional effect on born global firms in China: The role of Sun Tzu's The Art of War strategies. *Journal of Asia Business Studies, 10*(1), 1–19.

Zheng Zhou, K. (2006). Innovation, imitation, and new product performance: The case of China. *Industrial Marketing Management, 35*(3), 394–402.

Zipser, D., Seong, J., & Woetzel, J. (2021). *Five consumer trends shaping the next decade of growth in China*. https://www.mckinsey.com/cn/our-insights/our-insights/five-consumer-trends-shaping-the-next-decade-of-growth-in-china

Zou, L., Shen, J. H., Zhang, J., & Lee, C.-C. (2022). What is the rationale behind China's infrastructure investment under the Belt and Road Initiative. *Journal of Economic Surveys, 36*(3), 605–633. https://doi.org/10.1111/joes.12427

Index

M. Altamira, *Chinese Firms in the Global Market*, Palgrave Macmillan Asian Business Series, https://doi.org/10.1007/978-3-031-59227-0

SPRINGER NATURE

GPSR Compliance

The European Union's (EU) General Product Safety Regulation (GPSR) is a set of rules that requires consumer products to be safe and our obligations to ensure this.

If you have any concerns about our products, you can contact us on ProductSafety@springernature.com

In case Publisher is established outside the EU, the EU authorized representative is:

Springer Nature Customer Service Center GmbH
Europaplatz 3
69115 Heidelberg, Germany

The manufacturer's authorised representative in the EU is Springer Nature Customer Service Centre GmbH, Europaplatz 3, 69115 Heidelberg, Germany. If you have any concerns regarding our products, please contact ProductSafety@springernature.com

Printed and bound by CPI Group (UK) Ltd, Croydon, CR0 4YY
01/10/2026
02225924-0003